Year 1A
A Guide to Teaching for Mastery

Series Editor: Tony Staneff

Contents

Introduction

Foreword by the series editor and author, Tony Staneff

For far too long in the UK, maths has been feared by learners – and by many teachers, too. As a result, most learners consistently underachieve. More crucially, negative beliefs about ability, aptitude and the nature of maths are entrenched in children's thinking from an early age.

Yet, as someone who has loved maths all my life, I've always believed that every child has the capacity to succeed in maths. I've also had the great pleasure of leading teams and departments who share that belief and passion. Teaching for mastery, as practised in China and other South-East Asian jurisdictions since the 1980s, has confirmed my conviction that maths really is for everyone and not just those who have a special talent. In recent years my team and I at Trinity Academy, Halifax, have had the privilege of researching with and working with some of the finest mastery practitioners from the UK and beyond, whose impact on learners' confidence, achievement and attitude is an inspiration.

The mastery approach recognises the value of developing the power to think rather than just do. It also recognises the value of making a coherent journey in which whole-class groups tackle concepts in very small steps, one by one. You can not build securely on loose foundations – and it is just the same with maths: by creating a solid foundation of deep understanding, our children's skills and confidence will be strong and secure. What's more, the mindset of learner and teacher alike is fundamental: everyone can do maths… EVERYONE CAN!

I am proud to have been part of the extensive team responsible for turning the best of the world's practice, research, insights, and shared experiences into *Power Maths*, a unique teaching and learning resource developed especially for UK classrooms. *Power Maths* embodies our vision to help and support primary maths teachers to transform every child's mathematical and personal development. 'Everyone can!' has become our mantra and our passion, and we hope it will be yours, too.

Now, explore and enjoy all the resources you need to teach for mastery, and please get back to us with your *Power Maths* experiences and stories!

What is *Power Maths*?

Created especially for UK primary schools, and aligned with the new National Curriculum, *Power Maths* is a whole-class, textbook-based mastery resource that empowers every child to understand and succeed. *Power Maths* rejects the notion that some people simply 'can't do' maths. Instead, it develops growth mindsets and encourages hard work, practice and a willingness to see mistakes as learning tools.

Best practice consistently shows that mastery of small, cumulative steps builds a solid foundation of deep mathematical understanding. *Power Maths* combines interactive teaching tools, high-quality textbooks and continuing professional development (CPD) to help you equip children with a deep and long lasting understanding. Based on extensive evidence, and developed in partnership with practising teachers, *Power Maths* ensures that it meets the needs of children in the UK.

Power Maths and Mastery

Power Maths makes mastery practical and achievable by providing the structures, pathways, content, tools and support you need to make it happen in your classroom.

To develop mastery in maths children must be enabled to acquire a deep understanding of maths concepts, structures and procedures, step by step. Complex mathematical concepts are built on simpler conceptual components and when children understand every step in the learning sequence, maths becomes transparent and makes logical sense. Interactive lessons establish deep understanding in small steps, as well as effortless fluency in key facts such as tables and number bonds. The whole class works on the same content and no child is left behind.

Power Maths

- Builds every concept in small, progressive steps
- Is built with interactive, whole-class teaching in mind
- Provides the tools you need to develop growth mindsets
- Helps you check understanding and ensure that every child is keeping up
- Establishes core elements such as intelligent practice and reflection

The *Power Maths* approach

Everyone can!

Founded on the conviction that every child can achieve, *Power Maths* enables children to build number fluency, confidence and understanding, step by step.

Child-centred learning

Children master concepts one step at a time in lessons that embrace a concrete-pictorial-abstract (C-P-A) approach, avoid overload, build on prior learning and help them see patterns and connections. Same-day intervention ensures sustained progress.

Continuing professional development

Embedded teacher support and development offer every teacher the opportunity to continually improve their subject knowledge and manage whole-class teaching for mastery.

Whole-class teaching

An interactive, whole-class teaching model encourages thinking and precise mathematical language and allows children to deepen their understanding as far as they can.

Introduction to the author team

Power Maths arises from the work of maths mastery experts who are committed to proving that, given the right mastery mindset and approach, **everyone can do maths**. Based on robust research and best practice from around the world, *Power Maths* was developed in partnership with a group of UK teachers to make sure that it not only meets our children's wide-ranging needs but also aligns with the National Curriculum in England.

Tony Staneff, Series Editor and Author

Vice Principal at Trinity Academy, Halifax, Tony also leads a team of mastery experts who help schools across the UK to develop teaching for mastery via nationally-recognised CPD courses, problem-solving and reasoning resources, schemes of work, assessment materials and other tools.

➕ A team of experienced authors, including:

- ⚡ **Josh Lury** – a specialist maths teacher, author and maths consultant with a passion for innovative and effective maths education

- ⚡ **Jenny Lewis, Stephen Monaghan, Beth Smith and Kelsey Brown** – skilled maths teachers and mastery experts

- ⚡ **Cherri Moseley** – a maths author, former teacher and professional development provider

- ⚡ **Paul Wrangles** – a maths author and former teacher, Paul's goal is to "ignite creative thought in teachers and pupils by providing creative teaching resources".

➕ Professor Jian Liu, Series Consultant and Author, and his team of mastery expert authors:

- ⚡ **Hou Huiying, Huang Lihua, Wang Mingming, Yin Lili, Zhang Dan, Zhang Hong and Zhou Da**

Used by over 20 million children, Professor Liu's textbook programme is one of the most popular in China. He and his author team are highly experienced in intelligent practice and in embedding key maths concepts using a C-P-A approach.

➕ A group of 15 teachers and maths co-ordinators

We have consulted our teacher group throughout the development of *Power Maths* to ensure we are meeting their real needs in the classroom.

Your *Power Maths* resources

To help you teach for mastery, *Power Maths* comprises a variety of high-quality resources.

Pupil Textbooks

'Discover', 'Share' and 'Think together' sections promote discussion and introduce mathematical ideas logically, so that children understand more easily.

Using a Concrete-Pictorial-Abstract approach, clear mathematical models help children to make connections and grasp concepts.

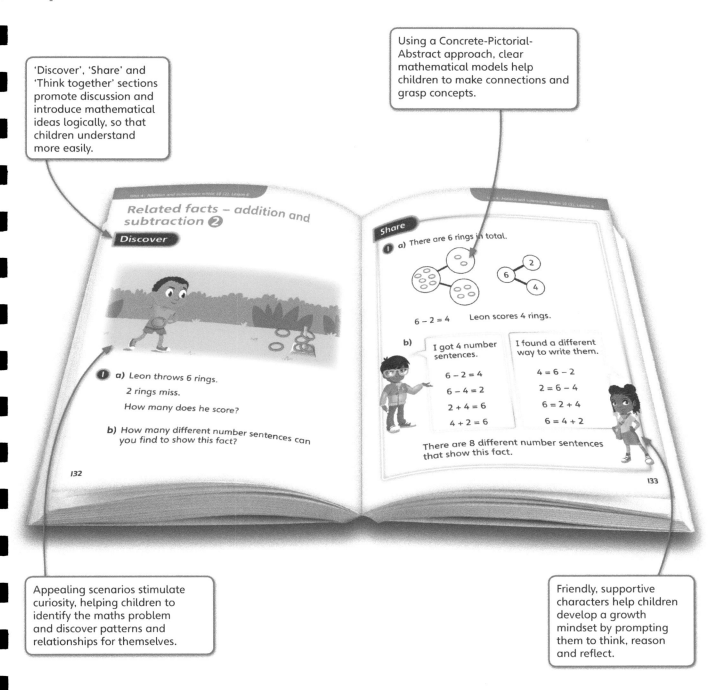

Appealing scenarios stimulate curiosity, helping children to identify the maths problem and discover patterns and relationships for themselves.

Friendly, supportive characters help children develop a growth mindset by prompting them to think, reason and reflect.

The coherent *Power Maths* lesson structure carries through into the vibrant, high-quality textbooks. Setting out the core learning objectives for each class, the lesson structure follows a carefully mapped journey through the curriculum and supports children on their journey to deeper understanding.

Pupil Practice Books

The Practice Books offer just the right amount of intelligent practice for children to complete independently in the final section of each lesson.

The practice questions are for everyone – each question varies one small element to move children on in their thinking. Look at the different parts in question 1!

Calculations are connected so that children think about the underlying concept. In question 3, children have to write out the calculation to find the answer. Concepts are presented differently again in question 4 to challenge children.

Practice questions are finely tuned to move children forward in their thinking and to reveal misconceptions.

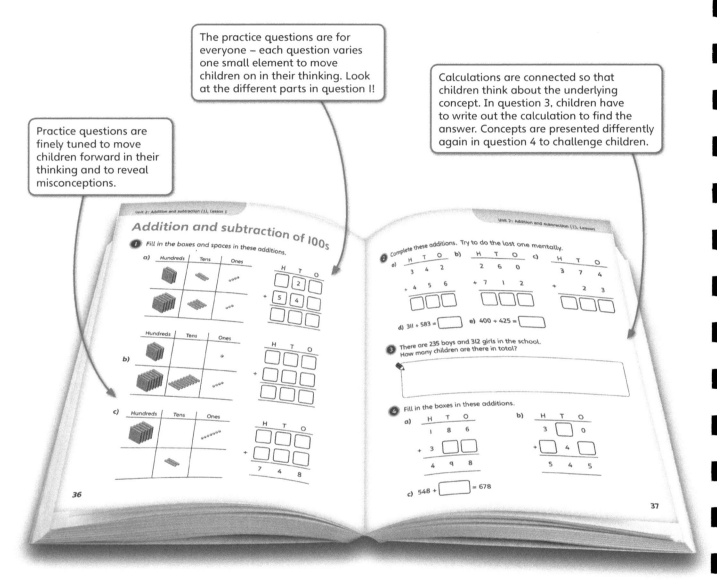

Challenge questions allow children to delve deeper into a concept.

Reflect questions reveal the depth of each child's understanding before they move on.

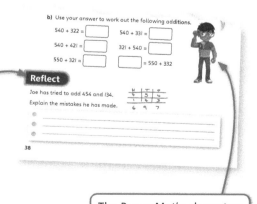

The *Power Maths* characters support and encourage children to think and work in different ways.

Online subscriptions

The online subscription will give you access to additional resources.

eTextbooks

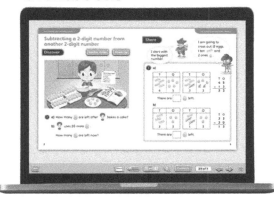

Digital versions of *Power Maths* Textbooks allow class groups to share and discuss questions, solutions and strategies. They allow you to project key structures and representations at the front of the class, to ensure all children are focusing on the same concept.

Teaching tools

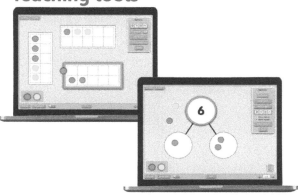

Here you will find interactive versions of key *Power Maths* structures and representations.

Power Ups

Use this series of daily activities to promote and check number fluency.

Online versions of Teacher Guide pages

PDF pages give support at both unit and lesson levels. You will also find help with key strategies and templates for tracking progress.

Unit videos

Watch the professional development videos at the start of each unit to help you teach with confidence. The videos explore common misconceptions in the unit, and include intervention suggestions as well as suggestions on what to look out for when assessing mastery in your students.

End of unit Strengthen and Deepen materials

Each Strengthen activity at the end of every unit addresses a key misconception and can be used to support children who need it. The Deepen activities are designed to be low ceiling/high threshold and will challenge those children who can understand more deeply. These resources will help you ensure that every child understands and will help you keep the class moving forward together. These printable activities provide an optional resource bank for use after the assessment stage.

Underpinning all of these resources, *Power Maths* is infused throughout with continual professional development, supporting you at every step.

The *Power Maths* teaching model

At the heart of *Power Maths* is a clearly structured teaching and learning process that helps you make certain that every child masters each maths concept securely and deeply. For each year group, the curriculum is broken down into core concepts, taught in units. A unit divides into smaller learning steps – lessons. Step by step, strong foundations of cumulative knowledge and understanding are built.

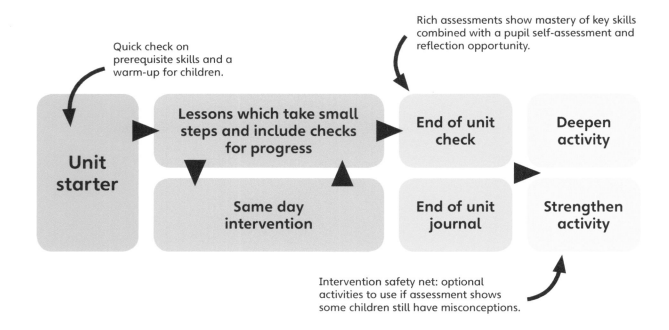

Quick check on prerequisite skills and a warm-up for children.

Rich assessments show mastery of key skills combined with a pupil self-assessment and reflection opportunity.

Unit starter → Lessons which take small steps and include checks for progress → Same day intervention → End of unit check → End of unit journal → Deepen activity → Strengthen activity

Intervention safety net: optional activities to use if assessment shows some children still have misconceptions.

Unit starter

Each unit begins with a unit starter, which introduces the learning context along with key mathematical vocabulary and structures and representations.

- The Pupil Textbooks include a check on readiness and a warm-up task for children to complete.

- Your Teacher Guide gives support right from the start on important structures and representations, mathematical language, common misconceptions and intervention strategies.

- Unit-specific videos develop your subject knowledge and insights so you feel confident and fully equipped to teach each new unit. These are available via the online subscription.

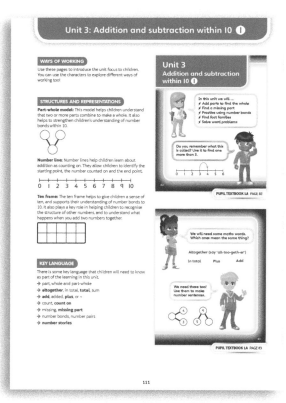

Lesson

Once a unit has been introduced, it is time to start teaching the series of lessons.

- Each lesson is scaffolded with Pupil Textbook and Practice Book activities and always begins with a Power Up activity (available via online subscription).
- *Power Maths* identifies lesson by lesson what concepts are to be taught.
- Your Teacher Guide offers lots of support for you to get the most from every child in every lesson. As well as highlighting key points, tricky areas and how to handle them, you will also find question prompts to check on understanding and clarification on why particular activities and questions are used.

Same-day intervention

Same-day interventions are vital in order to keep the class progressing together. Therefore, *Power Maths* provides plenty of support throughout the journey.

- Intervention is focused on keeping up now, not catching up later, so interventions should happen as soon as they are needed.
- Practice section questions are designed to bring misconceptions to the surface, allowing you to identify these easily as you circulate during independent practice time.
- Child-friendly assessment questions in the Teacher Guide help you identify easily which children need to strengthen their understanding.

End of unit check and journal

At the end of a unit, summative assessment tasks reveal essential information on each child's understanding. An End of unit check in the Pupil Textbook lets you see which children have mastered the key concepts, which children have not and where their misconceptions lie. The Practice Books also include an end of unit journal in which children can reflect on what they have learned. Each unit also offers Strengthen and Deepen activities, available via the online subscription.

> The Teacher Guide offers different ways of managing the end of unit assessments as well as giving support with handling misconceptions.

> The End of unit check presents four multiple-choice questions. Children think about their answer, decide on a solution and explain their choice.

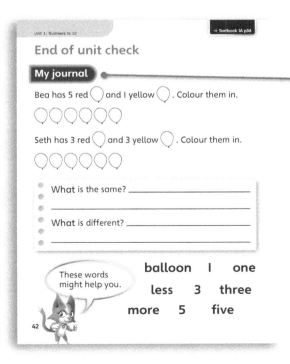

> The End of unit journal is an opportunity for children to test out their learning and reflect on how they feel about it. Tackling the 'journal' problem reveals whether a child understands the concept deeply enough to move on to the next unit.

The *Power Maths* lesson sequence

At the heart of *Power Maths* is a unique lesson sequence designed to empower children to understand core concepts and grow in confidence. Embracing the National Centre for Excellence in the Teaching of Mathematics' (NCETM's) definition of mastery, the sequence guides and shapes every *Power Maths* lesson you teach.

Flexibility is built into the *Power Maths* programme so there is no one-to-one mapping of lessons and concepts and you can pace your teaching according to your class. While some children will need to spend longer on a particular concept (through interventions or additional lessons), others will reach deeper levels of understanding. However, it is important that the class moves forward together through the termly schedules.

Power Up ⏱ 5 minutes

Each lesson begins with a Power Up activity (available via the online subscription) which supports fluency in key number fact.

The whole-class approach depends on fluency, so the Power Up is a powerful and essential activity.

TOP TIP
If the class is struggling with the task, revisit it later and check understanding.

Power Ups reinforce the two key things that are essential for success: times-tables and number bonds.

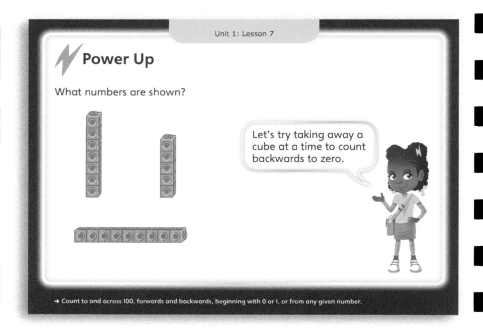

Unit 1: Lesson 7

⚡ Power Up

What numbers are shown?

Let's try taking away a cube at a time to count backwards to zero.

→ Count to and across 100, forwards and backwards, beginning with 0 or 1, or from any given number.

Discover ⏱ 10 minutes

A practical, real-life problem arouses curiosity. Children find the maths through story telling.

TOP TIP
Discover works best when run at tables, in pairs with concrete objects.

Question ❶ a) tackles the key concept and question ❶ b) digs a little deeper. Children have time to explore, play and discuss possible strategies.

Unit 1: Numbers to 10, Lesson 1

Sorting objects

Discover

❶ a) Sort the ◯ and 🎲 into two groups.

b) Sort the fruit. What groups did you make?

8

Share ⏱ 10 minutes

Teacher-led, this interactive section follows the Discover activity and highlights the variety of methods that can be used to solve a single problem.

TOP TIP
Bring children to the front or onto the carpet to discuss their methods. Pairs sharing a textbook is a great format for this!

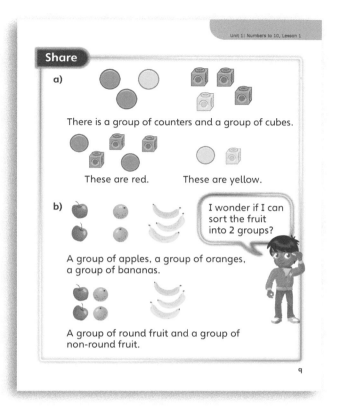

Your Teacher Guide gives target questions for children. The online toolkit provides interactive structures and representations to link concrete and pictorial to abstract concepts.

Bring children to the front to share and celebrate their solutions and strategies.

Think together

⏱ 10 minutes

Children work in groups on the carpet or at tables, using their textbooks or eBooks.

TOP TIP
Make sure children have mini whiteboards or pads to write on if they are not at their tables.

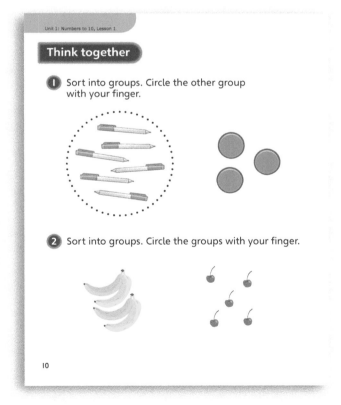

Using the Teacher Guide, model question ❶ for your class.

Question ❷ is less structured. Children will need to think together in their groups, then discuss their methods and solutions as a class.

Question ❸ – the openness of the Challenge question helps to check depth of understanding.

Practice ⏱ 15 minutes

Using their Practice Books, children work independently while you circulate and check on progress.

Questions follow small steps of progression to deepen learning.

TOP TIP
Some children could work separately with a teacher or assistant.

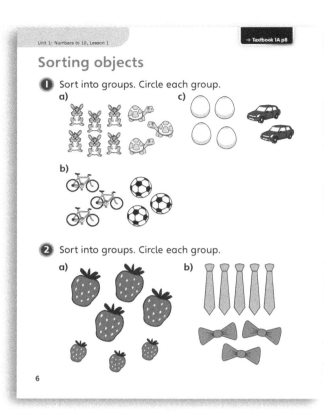

Are some children struggling? If so, work with them as a group, using mathematical structures and representations to support understanding as necessary.

There are no set routines: for real understanding, children need to think about the problem in different ways.

Reflect ⏱ 5 minutes

'Spot the mistake' questions are great for checking misconceptions.

The Reflect section is your opportunity to check how deeply children understand the target concept.

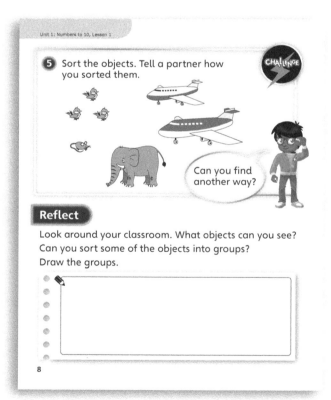

The Practice Books use various approaches to check that children have fully understood each concept.

Looking like they understand is not enough! It is essential that children can show they have grasped the concept.

Using the *Power Maths* Teacher Guide

Think of your Teacher Guides as *Power Maths* handbooks that will guide, support and inspire your day-to-day teaching. Clear and concise, and illustrated with helpful examples, your Teacher Guides will help you make the best possible use of every individual lesson. They also provide wrap-around professional development, enhancing your own subject knowledge and helping you to grow in confidence about moving your children forward together.

There is a Teacher Guide per year group for every term with unit and lesson level guidance and support.

Tips and advice on key elements such as C-P-A approaches, misconceptions, language, modelling growth mindsets and same day intervention.

Annotations for every Pupil Textbook and Practice Book page, providing prompts for key questions to ask to expose understanding and explanations as to why key questions have been chosen.

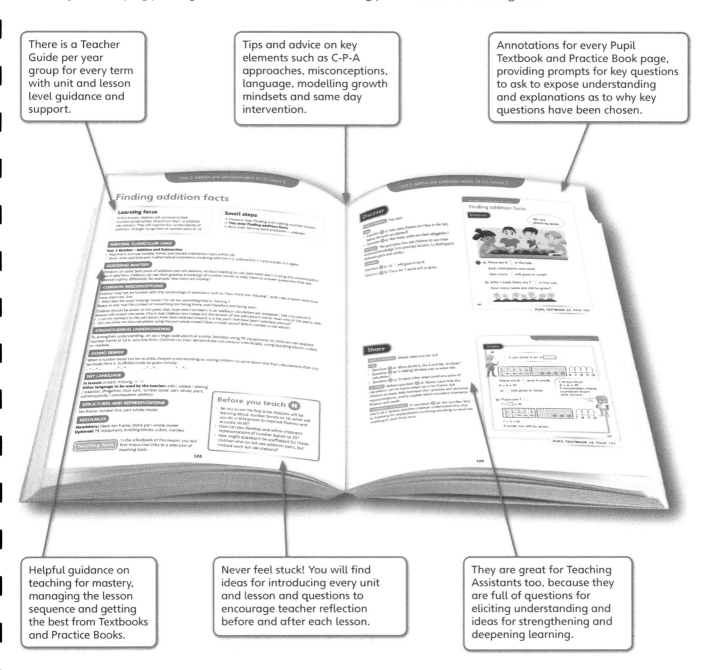

Helpful guidance on teaching for mastery, managing the lesson sequence and getting the best from Textbooks and Practice Books.

Never feel stuck! You will find ideas for introducing every unit and lesson and questions to encourage teacher reflection before and after each lesson.

They are great for Teaching Assistants too, because they are full of questions for eliciting understanding and ideas for strengthening and deepening learning.

At the end of each unit, your Teacher Guide helps you identify who has fully grasped the concept, who has not and how to move every child forward. This is covered later in the Assessment strategies section.

Power Maths Year 1, yearly overview

Textbook	Strand	Unit	Number of Lessons	
Textbook A / Practice Pupil Book A (Term 1)	Number – number and place value	1	Numbers to 10	12
	Number – number and place value	2	Part-whole within 10	5
	Number – addition and subtraction	3	Addition and subtraction within 10 (1)	6
	Number – addition and subtraction	4	Addition and subtraction within 10 (2)	12
	Geometry – properties of shape	5	2D and 3D shapes	5
	Number – number and place value	6	Numbers to 20	7
Textbook B / Practice Pupil Book B (Term 2)	Number – addition and subtraction	7	Addition within 20	6
	Number – addition and subtraction	8	Subtraction within 20	8
	Number – number and place value	9	Numbers to 50	11
	Measurement	10	Introducing length and height	5
	Measurement	11	Introducing weight and volume	7
Textbook C / Practice Pupil Book C (Term 3)	Number – multiplication and division	12	Multiplication	6
	Number – multiplication and division	13	Division	5
	Number – fractions	14	Halves and quarters	5
	Geometry – position and direction	15	Position and direction	3
	Number – number and place value	16	Numbers to 100	9
	Measurement	17	Time	7
	Measurement	18	Money	3

Power Maths Year I, Textbook IA (Term I) overview

Strand 1	Strand 2	Unit		Lesson number	Lesson title	NC Objective 1	NC Objective 2	NC Objective 3
Number - number and place value		Unit 1	Numbers to 10	1	Sorting objects	Identify and represent numbers using concrete objects and pictorial representations including the number line, and use the language of: equal to, more than, less than (fewer), most, least		
Number - number and place value		Unit 1	Numbers to 10	2	Counting objects to 10	Count to and across 100, forwards and backwards, beginning with 0 or 1, or from any given number	Identify and represent numbers using concrete objects and pictorial representations including the number line, and use the language of: equal to, more than, less than (fewer), most, least	
Number - number and place value		Unit 1	Numbers to 10	3	Counting and writing numbers to 10	Count to and across 100, forwards and backwards, beginning with 0 or 1, or from any given number	Count, read and write numbers to 100 in numerals; count in multiples of twos, fives and tens	Read and write numbers from 1 to 20 in numerals and words
Number - number and place value		Unit 1	Numbers to 10	4	Counting backwards from 10 to 0	Count to and across 100, forwards and backwards, beginning with 0 or 1, or from any given number		
Number - number and place value		Unit 1	Numbers to 10	5	Counting one more	Given a number, identify one more and one less	Identify and represent numbers using concrete objects and pictorial representations including the number line, and use the language of: equal to, more than, less than (fewer), most, least	Count to and across 100, forwards and backwards, beginning with 0 or 1, or from any given number
Number - number and place value		Unit 1	Numbers to 10	6	Counting one less	Given a number, identify one more and one less	Identify and represent numbers using concrete objects and pictorial representations including the number line, and use the language of: equal to, more than, less than (fewer), most, least	Count to and across 100, forwards and backwards, beginning with 0 or 1, or from any given number
Number - number and place value		Unit 1	Numbers to 10	7	Comparing groups	Identify and represent numbers using concrete objects and pictorial representations including the number line, and use the language of: equal to, more than, less than (fewer), most, least		
Number - number and place value		Unit 1	Numbers to 10	8	Comparing numbers of objects	Identify and represent numbers using concrete objects and pictorial representations including the number line, and use the language of: equal to, more than, less than (fewer), most, least		
Number - number and place value		Unit 1	Numbers to 10	9	Comparing numbers	Identify and represent numbers using concrete objects and pictorial representations including the number line, and use the language of: equal to, more than, less than (fewer), most, least		
Number - number and place value		Unit 1	Numbers to 10	10	Ordering objects and numbers	Identify and represent numbers using concrete objects and pictorial representations including the number line, and use the language of: equal to, more than, less than (fewer), most, least		
Number - number and place value		Unit 1	Numbers to 10	11	First, second, third…	Identify and represent numbers using concrete objects and pictorial representations including the number line, and use the language of: equal to, more than, less than (fewer), most, least		
Number - number and place value		Unit 1	Numbers to 10	12	The number line	Identify and represent numbers using concrete objects and pictorial representations including the number line, and use the language of: equal to, more than, less than (fewer), most, least		
Number - addition and subtraction		Unit 2	Part-whole within 10	1	The part-whole model (1)	Represent and use number bonds and related subtraction facts within 20		
Number - addition and subtraction		Unit 2	Part-whole within 10	2	The part-whole model (2)	Read, write and interpret mathematical statements involving addition (+), subtraction (−) and equals (=) signs	Represent and use number bonds and related subtraction facts within 20	

Strand 1	Strand 2	Unit		Lesson number	Lesson title	NC Objective 1	NC Objective 2	NC Objective 3
Number - addition and subtraction		Unit 2	Part-whole within 10	3	Related facts – number bonds	Read, write and interpret mathematical statements involving addition (+), subtraction (–) and equals (=) signs	Represent and use number bonds and related subtraction facts within 20	
Number - addition and subtraction		Unit 2	Part-whole within 10	4	Finding number bonds	Represent and use number bonds and related subtraction facts within 20		
Number - addition and subtraction		Unit 2	Part-whole within 10	5	Comparing number bonds	Represent and use number bonds and related subtraction facts within 20		
Number - addition and subtraction		Unit 3	Addition and subtraction within 10 (1)	1	Finding the whole – adding together	Represent and use number bonds and related subtraction facts within 20		
Number - addition and subtraction		Unit 3	Addition and subtraction within 10 (1)	2	Finding the whole – adding more	Represent and use number bonds and related subtraction facts within 20		
Number - addition and subtraction		Unit 3	Addition and subtraction within 10 (1)	3	Finding a part	Represent and use number bonds and related subtraction facts within 20		
Number - addition and subtraction		Unit 3	Addition and subtraction within 10 (1)	4	Finding and making number bonds	Represent and use number bonds and related subtraction facts within 20		
Number - addition and subtraction		Unit 3	Addition and subtraction within 10 (1)	5	Finding addition facts	Represent and use number bonds and related subtraction facts within 20	Read, write and interpret mathematical statements involving addition (+), subtraction (–) and equals (=) signs	
Number - addition and subtraction		Unit 3	Addition and subtraction within 10 (1)	6	Solving word problems – addition	Solve one-step problems that involve addition and subtraction, using concrete objects and pictorial representations, and missing number problems such as 7 = _ – 9.	Represent and use number bonds and related subtraction facts within 20	
Number - addition and subtraction		Unit 4	Addition and subtraction within 10 (2)	1	Subtraction – how many are left? (1)	Represent and use number bonds and related subtraction facts within 20	Solve one-step problems that involve addition and subtraction, using concrete objects and pictorial representations, and missing number problems such as 7 = _ – 9.	
Number - addition and subtraction		Unit 4	Addition and subtraction within 10 (2)	2	Subtraction – how many are left? (2)	Represent and use number bonds and related subtraction facts within 20	Solve one-step problems that involve addition and subtraction, using concrete objects and pictorial representations, and missing number problems such as 7 = _ – 9.	
Number - addition and subtraction		Unit 4	Addition and subtraction within 10 (2)	3	Subtraction – breaking apart (1)	Represent and use number bonds and related subtraction facts within 20		
Number - addition and subtraction		Unit 4	Addition and subtraction within 10 (2)	4	Subtraction – breaking apart (2)	Represent and use number bonds and related subtraction facts within 20		
Number - addition and subtraction		Unit 4	Addition and subtraction within 10 (2)	5	Related facts – addition and subtraction (1)	Represent and use number bonds and related subtraction facts within 20		
Number - addition and subtraction		Unit 4	Addition and subtraction within 10 (2)	6	Related facts – addition and subtraction (2)	Represent and use number bonds and related subtraction facts within 20		
Number - addition and subtraction		Unit 4	Addition and subtraction within 10 (2)	7	Subtraction – counting back	Solve one-step problems that involve addition and subtraction, using concrete objects and pictorial representations, and missing number problems such as 7 = _ – 9.	Read, write and interpret mathematical statements involving addition (+), subtraction (–) and equals (=) signs	Add and subtract one-digit and two-digit numbers to 20, including zero
Number - addition and subtraction		Unit 4	Addition and subtraction within 10 (2)	8	Subtraction – finding the difference	Solve one-step problems that involve addition and subtraction, using concrete objects and pictorial representations, and missing number problems such as 7 = _ – 9.	Read, write and interpret mathematical statements involving addition (+), subtraction (–) and equals (=) signs	Add and subtract one-digit and two-digit numbers to 20, including zero
Number - addition and subtraction		Unit 4	Addition and subtraction within 10 (2)	9	Solving word problems – subtraction	Solve one-step problems that involve addition and subtraction, using concrete objects and pictorial representations, and missing number problems such as 7 = _ – 9.	Read, write and interpret mathematical statements involving addition (+), subtraction (–) and equals (=) signs	Add and subtract one-digit and two-digit numbers to 20, including zero
Number - addition and subtraction		Unit 4	Addition and subtraction within 10 (2)	10	Comparing additions and subtractions (1)	Read, write and interpret mathematical statements involving addition (+), subtraction (–) and equals (=) signs	One-step problems that involve addition and subtraction, using concrete objects and pictorial representations, and missing number problems such as 7 = _ – 9.	

Strand 1	Strand 2	Unit		Lesson number	Lesson title	NC Objective 1	NC Objective 2	NC Objective 3
Number - addition and subtraction		Unit 4	Addition and subtraction within 10 (2)	11	Comparing additions and subtractions (2)	Read, write and interpret mathematical statements involving addition (+), subtraction (–) and equals (=) signs	Solve one-step problems that involve addition and subtraction, using concrete objects and pictorial representations, and missing number problems such as 7 = _ – 9.	
Number - addition and subtraction		Unit 4	Addition and subtraction within 10 (2)	12	Solving word problems – addition and subtraction	Solve one-step problems that involve addition and subtraction, using concrete objects and pictorial representations, and missing number problems such as 7 = _ – 9.	Read, write and interpret mathematical statements involving addition (+), subtraction (–) and equals (=) signs	Add and subtract one-digit and two-digit numbers to 20, including zero
Geometry - properties of shape		Unit 5	2D and 3D shapes	1	Naming 3D shapes (1)	Recognise and name common 2-D and 3-D shapes, including: 3-D shapes [for example, cuboids (including cubes), pyramids and spheres]		
Geometry - properties of shape		Unit 5	2D and 3D shapes	2	Naming 3D shapes (2)	Recognise and name common 2-D and 3-D shapes, including: 3-D shapes [for example, cuboids (including cubes), pyramids and spheres]		
Geometry - properties of shape		Unit 5	2D and 3D shapes	3	Naming 2D shapes (1)	Recognise and name common 2-D and 3-D shapes, including: 2-D shapes [for example, rectangles (including squares), circles and triangles]		
Geometry - properties of shape		Unit 5	2D and 3D shapes	4	Naming 2D shapes (2)	Recognise and name common 2-D and 3-D shapes, including: 2-D shapes [for example, rectangles (including squares), circles and triangles]		
Geometry - properties of shape	Number - number and place value	Unit 5	2D and 3D shapes	5	Making patterns with shapes	Recognise and name common 2-D and 3-D shapes, including: 2-D shapes [for example, rectangles (including squares), circles and triangles]; 3-D shapes [for example, cuboids (including cubes), pyramids and spheres].	Recognise and create repeating patterns with objects and with shapes.	
Number - number and place value		Unit 6	Numbers to 20	1	Counting and writing numbers to 20	Count to and across 100, forwards and backwards, beginning with 0 or 1, or from any given number	Identify and represent numbers using concrete objects and pictorial representations including the number line, and use the language of: equal to, more than, less than (fewer), most, least	
Number - number and place value		Unit 6	Numbers to 20	2	Tens and ones (1)	Identify and represent numbers using objects and pictorial representations including the number line, and use the language of: equal to, more than, less than (fewer), most, least	Recognise the place value of each digit in a two-digit number (tens, ones) (year 2)	
Number - number and place value		Unit 6	Numbers to 20	3	Tens and ones (2)	Identify and represent numbers using objects and pictorial representations including the number line, and use the language of: equal to, more than, less than (fewer), most, least	Recognise the place value of each digit in a two-digit number (tens, ones) (year 2)	
Number - number and place value		Unit 6	Numbers to 20	4	Counting one more, one less	Identify and represent numbers using objects and pictorial representations including the number line, and use the language of: equal to, more than, less than (fewer), most, least	Given a number, identify one more and one less	
Number - number and place value		Unit 6	Numbers to 20	5	Comparing numbers of objects	Identify and represent numbers using objects and pictorial representations including the number line, and use the language of: equal to, more than, less than (fewer), most, least		
Number - number and place value		Unit 6	Numbers to 20	6	Comparing numbers	Identify and represent numbers using objects and pictorial representations including the number line, and use the language of: equal to, more than, less than (fewer), most, least	Compare and order numbers from 0 up to 100; use <, > and = signs (year 2)	
Number - number and place value		Unit 6	Numbers to 20	7	Ordering objects and numbers	Identify and represent numbers using objects and pictorial representations including the number line, and use the language of: equal to, more than, less than (fewer), most, least	Compare and order numbers from 0 up to 100; use <, > and = signs (year 2)	

Mindset: an introduction

Global research and best practice deliver the same message: learning is greatly affected by what learners perceive they can or cannot do. What is more, it is also shaped by what their parents, carers and teachers perceive they can do. Mindset – the thinking that determines our beliefs and behaviours – therefore has a fundamental impact on teaching and learning.

Everyone can!

Power Maths and mastery methods focus on the distinction between 'fixed' and 'growth' mindsets (Dweck, 2007).[1] Those with a fixed mindset believe that their basic qualities (for example, intelligence, talent and ability to learn) are pre-wired or fixed: 'If you have a talent for maths, you will succeed at it. If not, too bad!' By contrast, those with a growth mindset believe that hard work, effort and commitment drive success and that 'smart' is not something you are or are not, but something you become. In short, everyone can do maths!

Key mindset strategies

A growth mindset needs to be actively nurtured and developed. *Power Maths* offers some key strategies for fostering healthy growth mindsets in your classroom.

It is okay to get it wrong

Mistakes are valuable opportunities to re-think and understand more deeply. Learning is richer when children and teachers alike focus on spotting and sharing mistakes as well as solutions.

Praise hard work

Praise is a great motivator, and by focusing on praising effort and learning rather than success, children will be more willing to try harder, take risks and persist for longer.

Mind your language!

The language we use around learners has a profound effect on their mindsets. Make a habit of using growth phrases, such as, 'Everyone can!', 'Mistakes can help you *learn*' and 'Just try for a little longer'. The king of them all is one little word, 'yet'... I can't solve this...yet!' Encourage parents and carers to use the right language too.

Build in opportunities for success

The step-by-small-step approach enables children to enjoy the experience of success. In addition, avoid ability grouping and encourage every child to answer questions and explain or demonstrate their methods to others.

[1]Dweck, C (2007) The New Psychology of Success, Ballantine Books: New York

The *Power Maths* characters

The *Power Maths* characters model the traits of growth mindset learners and encourage resilience by prompting and questioning children as they work. Appearing frequently in the Textbooks and Practice books, they are your allies in teaching and discussion, helping to model methods, alternatives and misconceptions, and to pose questions. They encourage and support your children, too: they are all hardworking, enthusiastic and unafraid of making and talking about mistakes.

Meet the team!

Creative Flo is open-minded and sometimes indecisive. She likes to think differently and come up with a variety of methods or ideas.

Determined Dexter is resolute, resilient and systematic. He concentrates hard, always tries his best and he'll never give up – even though he doesn't always choose the most efficient methods!

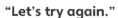

"Let's try again."

"Mistakes are cool!"

"Have I found all of the solutions?"

"Let's try it this way…"

"Can we do it differently?"

"I've got another way of doing this!"

"I'm going to try this!"

"I know how to do that!"

"Want to share my ideas?"

Curious Ash is eager, interested and inquisitive, and he loves solving puzzles and problems. Ash asks lots of questions but sometimes gets distracted.

"What if we tried this…?"

"I wonder…"

"Is there a pattern here?"

Sparks the Cat

Miaow!

Brave Astrid is confident, willing to take risks and unafraid of failure. She's never scared to jump straight into a problem or question, and although she often makes simple mistakes she's happy to talk them through with others.

Mathematical language

Traditionally, we in the UK have tended to try simplifying mathematical language to make it easier for young children to understand. By contrast, evidence and experience show that by diluting the correct language, we actually mask concepts and meanings for children. We then wonder why they are confused by new and different terminology later down the line! *Power Maths* is not afraid of 'hard' words and avoids placing any barriers between children and their understanding of mathematical concepts. As a result, we need to be planned, precise and thorough in building every child's understanding of the language of maths. Throughout the Teacher Guides you will find support and guidance on how to deliver this, as well as individual explanations throughout the Pupil Textbooks.

Use the following key strategies to build children's mathematical vocabulary, understanding and confidence.

Precise and consistent

Everyone in the classroom should use the correct mathematical terms in full, every time. For example, refer to 'equal parts', not 'parts'. Used consistently, precise maths language will be a familiar and non-threatening part of children's everyday experience.

Full sentences

Teachers and children alike need to use full sentences to explain or respond. When children use complete sentences, it both reveals their understanding and embeds their knowledge.

Stem sentences

These important sentences help children express mathematical concepts accurately, and are used throughout the *Power Maths* books. Encourage children to repeat them frequently, whether working independently or with others. Examples of stem sentences are:

"4 is a part, 5 is a part, 9 is the whole."

"There are …. groups. There are …. in each group."

Key vocabulary

The unit starters highlight essential vocabulary for every lesson. In the Pupil books, characters flag new terminology and the Teacher Guide lists important mathematical language for every unit and lesson. New terms are never introduced without a clear explanation.

Symbolic language

Symbols are used early on so that children quickly become familiar with them and their meaning. Often, the *Power Maths* characters will highlight the connection between language and particular symbols.

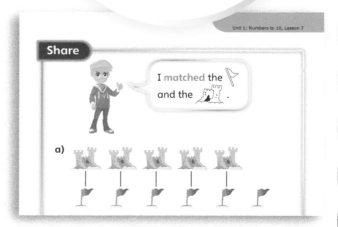

The role of talk and discussion

When children learn to talk purposefully together about maths, barriers of fear and anxiety are broken down and they grow in confidence, skills and understanding. Building a healthy culture of 'maths talk' empowers their learning from day one.

Explanation and discussion are integral to the *Power Maths* structure, so by simply following the books your lessons will stimulate structured talk. The following key 'maths talk' strategies will help you strengthen that culture and ensure that every child is included.

Sentences, not words

Encourage children to use full sentences when reasoning, explaining or discussing maths. This helps both speaker and listeners to clarify their own understanding. It also reveals whether or not the speaker truly understands, enabling you to address misconceptions as they arise.

Working together

Working with others in pairs, groups or as a whole class is a great way to support maths talk and discussion. Use different group structures to add variety and challenge. For example, children could take timed turns for talking, work independently alongside a 'discussion buddy', or perhaps play different *Power Maths* character roles within their group.

Think first – then talk

Provide clear opportunities within each lesson for children to think and reflect, so that their talk is purposeful, relevant and focused.

Give every child a voice

Where the 'hands up' model allows only the more confident child to shine, *Power Maths* involves everyone. Make sure that no child dominates and that even the shyest child is encouraged to contribute – and praised when they do.

Assessment strategies

Teaching for mastery demands that you are confident about what each child knows and where their misconceptions lie: therefore, practical and effective assessment is vitally important.

Formative assessment within lessons

The **Think together** section will often reveal any confusions or insecurities: try ironing these out by doing the first Think together question as a class. For children who continue to struggle, you or your teaching assistant should provide support and enable them to move on.

Performance in **Practice** can be very revealing: check Practice Books and listen out both during and after practice to identify misconceptions.

The **Reflect** section is designed to check on the all-important depth of understanding. Be sure to review how the children performed in this final stage before you teach the next lesson.

End of unit check – Textbook

Each unit concludes with a summative check to help you assess quickly and clearly each child's understanding, fluency, reasoning and problem solving skills. Your Teacher Guide will suggest ideal ways of organising a given activity and offer advice and commentary on what children's responses mean. For example, 'What misconception does this reveal?'; 'How can you reinforce this particular concept?'

For Year 1 and Year 2 children, assess in small, teacher-led groups, giving each child time to think and respond while also consolidating correct mathematical language. Assessment with young children should always be an enjoyable activity, so avoid one-to-one individual assessments, which they may find threatening or scary. If you prefer, the end of unit check can be carried out as a whole-class group using whiteboards and Practice Books.

End of unit check – Practice Book

The Practice Book contains further opportunities for assessment, and can be completed by children independently whilst you are carrying out diagnostic assessment with small groups. Your Teacher Guide will advise you on what to do if children struggle to articulate an explanation – or perhaps encourage you to write down something they have explained well. It will also offer insights into children's answers and their implications for next learning steps. It is split into three main sections, outlined below.

My journal and Think

My journal is designed to allow children to show their depth of understanding of the unit. It can also serve as a way of checking that children have grasped key mathematical vocabulary. The question children should answer is first presented in the Textbook in the Think section. This provides an opportunity for you to discuss the question first as a class to ensure children have understood their task. Children should have some time to think about how they want to answer the question, and you could ask them to talk to a partner about their ideas. Then children should write their answer in their Practice Book, using the word bank provided to help them with vocabulary.

Power check

The Power check allows pupils to self-assess their level of confidence on the topic by colouring in different smiley faces. You may want to introduce the faces as follows:

I am starting to understand. I need more practice

I don't yet know how to do this

I know how to do this, but I will keep practising

Power play or Power puzzle

Each unit ends with either a Power play or a Power puzzle. This is an activity, puzzle or game that allows children to use their new knowledge in a fun, informal way.

How to ask diagnostic questions

The diagnostic questions provided in children's Practice Books are carefully structured to identify both understanding and misconceptions (if children answer in a particular way, you will know why). The simple procedure below may be helpful:

Ask the question, offering the selection of answers provided.

▼

Children take time to think about their response.

▼

Each child selects an answer and shares their reasoning with the group.

▼

Give minimal and neutral feedback (for example, 'That's interesting', or 'Okay').

▼

Ask, 'Why did you choose that answer?', then offer an opportunity to change their mind by providing one correct and one incorrect answer.

▼

Note which children responded and reasoned correctly first time and everyone's final choices.

▼

Reflect that together, we can get the right answer.

▼

Record outcomes on the assessment grid (on the next page).

Power Maths Unit Assessment Grid

Year ___   Unit ___ _____

Record only as much information as you judge appropriate for your assessment of each child's mastery of the unit and any steps needed for intervention.

Name	Q1	Q2	Q3	Q4	Q5	My journal	Power check	Power play/puzzle	Mastery	Intervention/ Strengthen

Keeping the class together

Traditionally, children who learn quickly have been accelerated through the curriculum. As a consequence, their learning may be superficial and will lack the many benefits of enabling children to learn with and from each other.

By contrast, *Power Maths'* mastery approach values real understanding and richer, deeper learning above speed. It sees all children learning the same concept in small, cumulative steps, each finding and mastering challenge at their own level. Remember that when you teach for mastery, EVERYONE can do maths! Those who grasp a concept easily have time to explore and understand that concept at a deeper level. The whole class therefore moves through the curriculum at broadly the same pace via individual learning journeys.

For some teachers, the idea that a whole class can move forward together is revolutionary and challenging. However, the evidence of global good practice clearly shows that this approach drives engagement, confidence, motivation and success for all learners, and not just the high flyers. The strategies below will help you keep your class together on their maths journey.

Mix it up

Do not stick to set groups at each table. Every child should be working on the same concept, and mixing up the groupings widens children's opportunities for exploring, discussing and sharing their understanding with others.

Recycling questions

Reuse the Textbook and Practice Book questions with concrete materials to allow children to explore concepts and relationships and deepen their understanding. This strategy is especially useful for reinforcing learning in same-day interventions.

Strengthen at every opportunity

The next lesson in a *Power Maths* sequence always revises and builds on the previous step to help embed learning. These activities provide golden opportunities for individual children to strengthen their learning with the support of teaching assistants.

Prepare to be surprised!

Children may grasp a concept quickly or more slowly. The 'fast graspers' won't always be the same individuals, nor does the speed at which a child understands a concept predict their success in maths. Are they struggling or just working more slowly?

Depth and breadth

Just as prescribed in the National Curriculum, the goal of *Power Maths* is never to accelerate through a topic but rather to gain a clear, deep and broad understanding.

"Pupils who grasp concepts rapidly should be challenged through being offered rich and sophisticated problems before any acceleration through new content. Those who are not sufficiently fluent with earlier material should consolidate their understanding, including through additional practice, before moving on."

National Curriculum: Mathematics programmes of study: KS1 & 2, 2013

The lesson sequence offers many opportunities for you to deepen and broaden children's learning, some of which are suggested below.

Discover

As well as using the questions in the Teacher Guide, check that children are really delving into why something is true. It is not enough to simply recite facts, such as '6 + 3 = 9'. They need to be able to see why, explain it, and to demonstrate the solution in several ways.

Share

Make sure that every child is given chances to offer answers and expand their knowledge and not just those with the greatest confidence.

Think together

Encourage children to think about how they solved the problem and explain it to their partner. Be sure to make concrete materials available on group tables throughout the lesson to support and reinforce learning.

Practice

Avoid any temptation to select questions according to your assessment of ability: practice questions are presented in a logical sequence and it is important that each child works through every question.

Reflect

Open-ended questions allow children to deepen their understanding as far as they can by finding new ways of finding answers. For example, *Give me another way of working out how high the wall is... And another way?*

Online materials

For each unit you will find additional strengthening activities to support those children who need it and to deepen the understanding of those who need the additional challenge.

Same-day intervention

Since maths competence depends on mastering concepts one by one in a logical progression, it is important that no gaps in understanding are ever left unfilled. Same-day interventions – either within or after a lesson – are a crucial safety net for any child who has not fully made the small step covered that day. In other words, intervention is always about keeping up, not catching up, so that every child has the skills and understanding they need to tackle the next lesson. That means presenting the same problems used in the lesson, with a variety of concrete materials to help children model their solutions.

We offer two intervention strategies below, but you should feel free to choose others if they work better for your class.

Within-lesson intervention

The **Think together** activity will reveal those who are struggling, so when it is time for **Practice**, bring these children together to work with you on the first practice questions. Observe these children carefully, ask questions, encourage them to use concrete models and check that they reach and can demonstrate their understanding.

After-lesson intervention

You might like to use Think together before an assembly, giving you or teaching assistants time to recap and expand with slow graspers during assembly time. Teaching assistants could also work with strugglers at other convenient points in the school day.

The role of practice

Practice plays a pivotal role in the *Power Maths* approach. It takes place in class groups, smaller groups, pairs, and independently, so that children always have the opportunities for thinking as well as the models and support they need to practise meaningfully and with understanding.

Intelligent practice

In *Power Maths*, practice never equates to the simple repetition of a process. Instead we embrace the concept of intelligent practice, in which all children become fluent in maths through varied, frequent and thoughtful practice that deepens and embeds conceptual understanding in a logical, planned sequence. To see the difference, take a look at the following examples.

Traditional practice

- Repetition can be rote – no need for a child to think hard about what they are doing

- Praise may be misplaced

- Does this prove understanding?

Intelligent practice

- Varied methods – concrete, pictorial and abstract

- Equation expressed in different ways, requiring thought and understanding

- Constructive feedback

All practice questions are designed to move children on and reveal misconceptions.

Simple, logical steps build onto earlier learning.

C-P-A runs throughout – different ways of modelling and understanding the same concept.

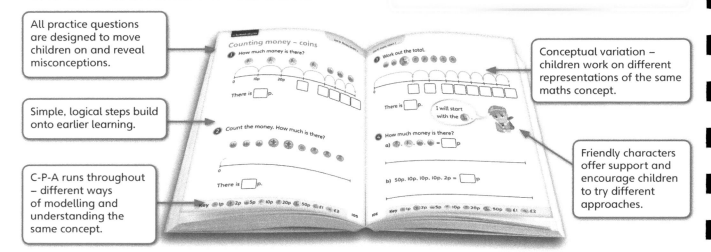

Conceptual variation – children work on different representations of the same maths concept.

Friendly characters offer support and encourage children to try different approaches.

A carefully designed progression

The Pupil Practice Books provide just the right amount of intelligent practice for children to complete independently in the final sections of each lesson. It is really important that all children are exposed to the practice questions, and that children are not directed to complete different sections. That is because each question is different and has been designed to challenge children to think about the maths they are doing. The questions become more challenging so children grasping concepts more quickly will start to slow down as they progress. Meanwhile, you have the chance to circulate and spot any misconceptions before they become barriers to further learning.

Homework and the role of carers

While *Power Maths* does not prescribe any particular homework structure, we acknowledge the potential value of practice at home. For example, practising fluency in key facts, such as number bonds and times tables, is an ideal homework task for Key Stage 1 children, and carers could work through uncompleted Practice Book questions with children at either primary stage.

However, it is important to recognise that many parents and carers may themselves lack confidence in maths, and few, if any, will be familiar with mastery methods. A Parents' and Carers' Evening that helps them understand the basics of mindsets, mastery and mathematical language is a great way to ensure that children benefit from their homework. It could be a fun opportunity for children to teach their families that everyone can do maths!

Structures and representations

Unlike most other subjects, maths comprises a wide array of abstract concepts – and that is why children and adults so often find it difficult. By taking a concrete-pictorial-abstract (C-P-A) approach, *Power Maths* allows children to tackle concepts in a tangible and more comfortable way.

Non-linear stages

Concrete

Replacing the traditional approach of a teacher working through a problem in front of the class, the concrete stage introduces real objects that children can use to 'do' the maths – any familiar object that a child can manipulate and move to help bring the maths to life. It is important to appreciate, however, that children must always understand the link between models and the objects they represent. For example, children need to first understand that three cakes could be represented by three pretend cakes, and then by three counters or bricks. Frequent practice helps consolidate this essential insight. Although they can be used at any time, good concrete models are an essential first step in understanding.

Pictorial

This stage uses pictorial representations of objects to let children 'see' what particular maths problems look like. It helps them make connections between the concrete and pictorial representations and the abstract maths concept. Children can also create or view a pictorial representation together, enabling discussion and comparisons. The *Power Maths* teaching tools are fantastic for this learning stage, and bar modelling is invaluable for problem solving throughout the primary curriculum.

Abstract

Our ultimate goal is for children to understand abstract mathematical concepts, symbols and notation and of course, some children will reach this stage far more quickly than others. To work with abstract concepts, a child must be comfortable with the meaning of and relationships between concrete, pictorial and abstract models and representations. The C-P-A approach is not linear, and children may need different types of models at different times. However, when a child demonstrates with concrete models and pictorial representations that they have grasped a concept, we can be confident that they are ready to explore or model it with abstract symbols such as numbers and notation.

Use at any time and with any age to support understanding

Variation helps visualisation

Children find it much easier to visualise and grasp concepts if they see them presented in a number of ways, so be prepared to offer and encourage many different representations.

For example, the number six could be represented in various ways:

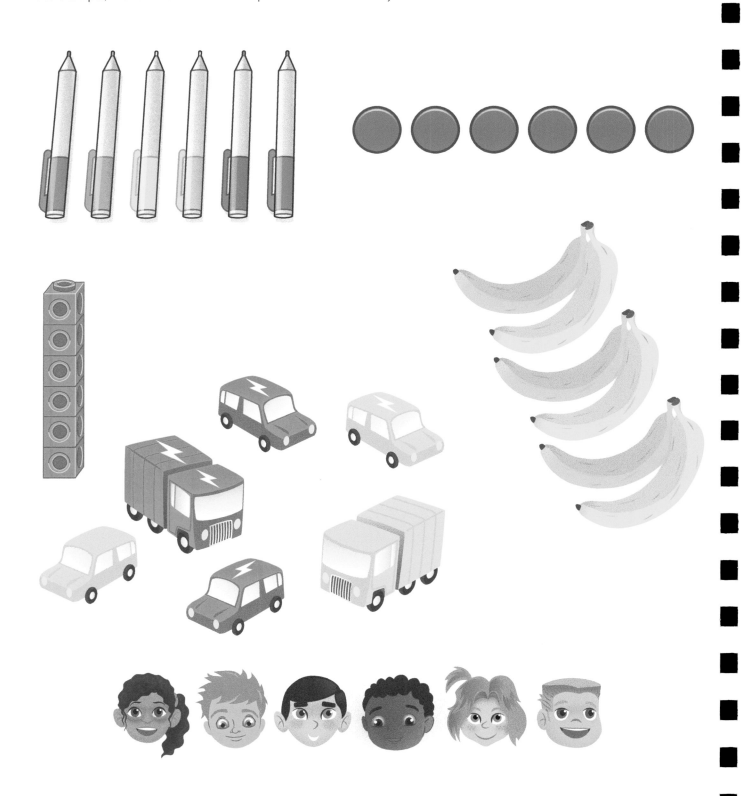

Getting started with *Power Maths*

As you prepare to put *Power Maths* into action, you might find the tips and advice below helpful.

STEP 1: Train up!

A practical, up-front full day professional development course will give you and your team a brilliant head-start as you begin your *Power Maths* journey. You will learn more about the ethos, how it works and why.

STEP 2: Check out the progression

Take a look at the yearly and termly overviews. Next take a look at the unit overview for the unit you are about to teach in your Teacher Guide, remembering that you can match your lessons and pacing to match your class.

STEP 3: Explore the context

Take a little time to look at the context for this unit: what are the implications for the unit ahead? (Think about key language, common misunderstandings and intervention strategies, for example.) If you have the online subscription, don't forget to watch the corresponding unit video.

STEP 4: Prepare for your first lesson

Familiarise yourself with the objectives, essential questions to ask and the resources you will need. The Teacher Guide offers tips, ideas and guidance on individual lessons to help you anticipate children's misconceptions and challenge those who are ready to think more deeply.

STEP 5: Teach and reflect

Deliver your lesson — and enjoy!

Afterwards, reflect on how it went… Did you cover all five stages? Does the lesson need more time? How could you improve it?

Unit I
Numbers to I0

Don't forget to watch the unit 1 video!

Mastery Expert tip! "When teaching this unit, I used the contexts given in the pictures to make the maths as practical as possible. The children were far more confident about explaining their ideas when we were role-playing the concepts or building them with resources."

WHY THIS UNIT IS IMPORTANT

This unit focuses on children's ability to recognise, represent and manipulate numbers to 10. Children begin by practising and developing their ability to sort and group objects using different criteria, then move on to counting groups of objects up to 10. Children will learn to recognise and count different representations of numbers to 10 and use a ten frame to help structure the counting and reasoning.

As children become more confident with counting they will be introduced to the appropriate vocabulary of counting: the word 'digit' and the written names of each number. They will move on to counting backwards and recognising 'one more' as a number increasing and 'one less' as a number decreasing.

Children will use all these skills to compare and order numbers to 10, using concrete and pictoral representations to support their reasoning. Finally, they will learn about ordinal numbers and be introduced to the number line as a representation of counting one more or one less.

WHERE THIS UNIT FITS

→ **Unit 1: Numbers to 10**

→ Unit 2: Part-whole within 10

In this unit, children begin by sorting and grouping objects up to 10. They then count to 10 and focus on 'one more' and 'one less' before learning how to use a number line to count forwards and backwards.

Before they start this unit, it is expected that children:
- can describe similarities and differences between objects
- can sort objects into groups based on simple criteria

ASSESSING MASTERY

Children who have mastered this unit will be able to confidently count forwards and backwards to and from 10. They will be able to recognise one more and one less than a number up to 10 and will be able to represent this using concrete, pictorial and abstract representations; they will use this understanding to correctly compare and order numbers. They will be able to use ordinal numbers to describe the order of things or events.

COMMON MISCONCEPTIONS	STRENGTHENING UNDERSTANDING	GOING DEEPER
Children may find counting backwards trickier and mistakenly counting forwards instead.	Role-play situations where counting down is necessary, such as a rocket launch or blowing out birthday candles, following the count on a number line or number track. Sing songs like 'Ten Green Bottles'.	Ask children to investigate how many times they need 'one more' or 'one less' to get from one number to another. Ask: *What representations could you use to show this?*
Children may struggle to remember the ordinal number names.	Watch or hold races, and discuss with children how to describe the order in which the contestants finished. Ask: *Who was first? How do you know? What do we call the person who came next?*	Challenge children to commentate on a race, describing their chosen contestant's position throughout the race fluently and flexibly.

Unit I: Numbers to 10

Use these pages to introduce the unit focus to children. You can use the characters to explore different ways of working too!

STRUCTURES AND REPRESENTATIONS

Ten frame: This model will help children visualise 10. It will also help strengthen children's fluency with numbers up to 10, demonstrating how they can be arranged in different ways but still be worth the same amount.

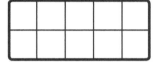

Number track: This model will help children organise their representations of numbers from 1 upwards. It can help children with comparing and ordering numbers.

Number line: This model helps children visualise the order of numbers. It can help them demonstrate concepts such as 'one more' and 'one less' in a more efficient way than using concrete resources.

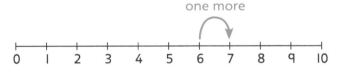

KEY LANGUAGE

There is some key language that children will need to know as a part of the learning in this unit.
- sort, groups, pattern
- digits, number
- count on, count back, one more, one more than, one less, one less than
- matched, equal to, =
- fewer, less than, <, least, fewest
- more, greater than, >, most, greatest
- number line, number track, ten frame

PUPIL TEXTBOOK 1A PAGE 6

PUPIL TEXTBOOK 1A PAGE 7

Sorting objects

Learning focus

In this lesson, children will develop their understanding of grouping objects. They will be able to recognise and explain different ways of sorting objects and that a single group of objects can be sorted in multiple ways.

Small steps

→ **This step: Sorting objects**
→ Next step: Counting objects to 10

NATIONAL CURRICULUM LINKS

Year 1 Number – Number and Place Value

Identify and represent numbers using concrete objects and pictorial representations including the number line, and use the language of: equal to, more than, less than (fewer), most, least.

ASSESSING MASTERY

Children can group objects based on their similarities and differences. Children can recognise that the same group of objects can be grouped in different ways by changing the grouping criteria.

COMMON MISCONCEPTIONS

Children may only want to group objects by one criterion with which they are most comfortable, such as colour. To elicit more criteria, ask: *What else is the same about the objects? What else is different about the objects?*

STRENGTHENING UNDERSTANDING

Ask children to group carefully chosen real-life objects, based on different criteria that you provide. Ask: *Can you group all the blue cubes? Can you group all the circles?*

GOING DEEPER

Challenge children to find as many different ways of grouping the same objects as possible. Ask children to justify their criteria each time and explain why they have chosen those criteria. Children could draw their groupings and write labels for each grouping.

KEY LANGUAGE

In lesson: sort, groups

Other language to be used by the teacher: same, different

STRUCTURES AND REPRESENTATIONS

Counters, multilink cubes

RESOURCES

Mandatory: counters, multilink cubes, a selection of groupable real-life objects such as toy cars, pens and pencils

Optional: other groupable 2D and 3D shapes

Teaching Tools In the eTextbook of this lesson, you will find interactive links to a selection of teaching tools.

Before you teach

- Are all children able to confidently explain similarities and differences between two or more objects?
- How could you add challenge to the process of grouping objects? For example, could all objects be the same in some way so that children have to use more than one criterion?

Discover

WAYS OF WORKING Pair work

ASK

- Question **1** a): *Does the colour of the multilink cubes and the counters matter? Why? Why not?*
- Question **1** b): *Why have you sorted the fruit in different ways? Are some ways more useful than others? Why or why not?*

IN FOCUS Question **1** a) introduces all of the lesson's key language, supporting children in understanding that different objects can be grouped together.

Question **1** b) allows children to begin designing their own criteria. This question allows paired and class discussion about how and why children have sorted the fruit differently.

ANSWERS

Question **1** a): There is a group of cubes and a group of counters. There is also a group of red objects and a group of yellow objects.

Question **1** b): The fruit can be sorted in two different ways. The first way is that it can be sorted into three groups: a group of two apples, a group of two oranges and a group of three bananas. The second way is that it could also be sorted into two groups: a group of four round fruit and a group of three non-round fruit.

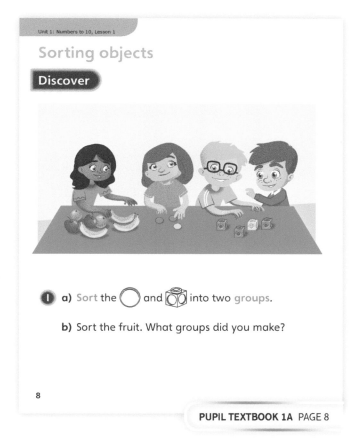

Sorting objects

Discover

1 a) Sort the ◯ and ⬜ into two groups.

b) Sort the fruit. What groups did you make?

8

PUPIL TEXTBOOK 1A PAGE 8

Share

WAYS OF WORKING Whole class teacher led

ASK

- *Do you think that the way in which Ash has sorted the fruit works? Can you explain why?*
- *Can you sort the fruit in a different way?*
- *How have you made your groups clear?*

IN FOCUS Question **1** a) demonstrates how a single group of objects can be sorted in more than one way. Use this opportunity to approach the potential misconception that objects can only be sorted using one criterion. Discuss how and why the groups change depending on the way in which the objects are sorted.

Ash's question can be used as scaffolding for a discussion about how you could sort the fruit differently. Can children explain how he has sorted the fruit?

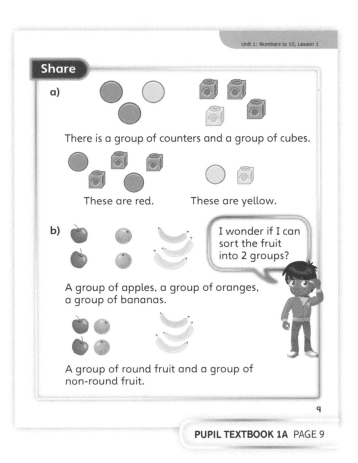

Share

a) There is a group of counters and a group of cubes.

These are red.　　These are yellow.

b) A group of apples, a group of oranges, a group of bananas.

I wonder if I can sort the fruit into 2 groups?

A group of round fruit and a group of non-round fruit.

9

PUPIL TEXTBOOK 1A PAGE 9

Think together

WAYS OF WORKING Whole class teacher led (I do, We do, You do)

ASK

• *What can you see?*
• *How are the objects the same or different?*
• *How will you know how to group the objects?*
• *How will you show the groups you have made?*

IN FOCUS Question ❶ and question ❷ allow children to begin sorting objects by themselves, asking them to group objects by circling the pictorial representations of the objects with their finger.

Question ❸ gives children the opportunity to group similar objects in different ways based on their own criteria. This question provides opportunities to discuss different children's criteria, looking for their reasoning and their ability to justify their choices. It is important that children recognise that the objects can be sorted in a number of different ways.

STRENGTHEN Give children a selection of real-life objects to sort. You could give children the criteria to use when sorting these objects or children could come up with their own criteria.

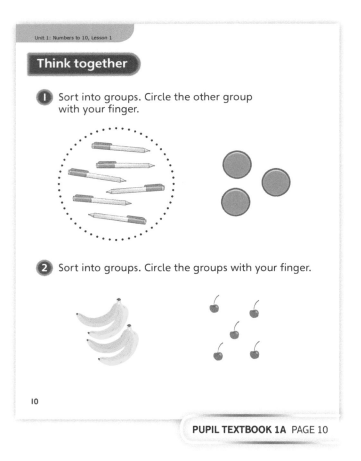

Think together

❶ Sort into groups. Circle the other group with your finger.

❷ Sort into groups. Circle the groups with your finger.

10

PUPIL TEXTBOOK 1A PAGE 10

DEEPEN Refer to Ash's question about if there is another way. This will prompt children to consider alternative criteria for their groupings. Ask children to sort the objects into three different groups.

ASSESSMENT CHECKPOINT Question ❸ assesses if children are able to confidently choose criteria by which to group objects and then group those objects successfully. It will also assess if children recognise how a set of objects can be grouped in more than one way.

ANSWERS

Question ❶: A group of pens and a group of counters.

Question ❷: A group of bananas and a group of cherries.

Question ❸: A group of cars and a group of trucks, or a group of vehicles with a white flash and a group of vehicles without a white flash, or a group of red vehicles and a group of yellow vehicles.

❸ Sort in two different ways.

CHALLENGE

Is there another way?

→ Practice book 1A p6

11

PUPIL TEXTBOOK 1A PAGE 11

Practice

WAYS OF WORKING Independent thinking

IN FOCUS Question ❶, question ❷ and question ❸ further support and develop children's ability to independently find, sort and group objects based on their own criteria.

STRENGTHEN Ask children to sort a selection of real-life objects. Depending on children's needs, you could give them criteria to use when sorting the objects or ask them to come up with their own criteria.

DEEPEN Question ❹ can be used to deepen understanding by asking children to not only identify the object that does not belong, but also to sort the objects that they think do belong into groups.

Question ❺ supports children in finding different ways of sorting a group of objects. Listen for children's explanations of how they have sorted and grouped the objects. Do they recognise that there were other ways of sorting? Can they tell you how many other ways they could see? Can they sort the objects using three criteria?

ASSESSMENT CHECKPOINT Questions ❶, ❷ and ❸ should help you to assess if children are able to independently sort and group objects according to their own criteria.

ANSWERS Answers for the **Practice** part of the lesson appear in the separate **Practice and Reflect answer guide**.

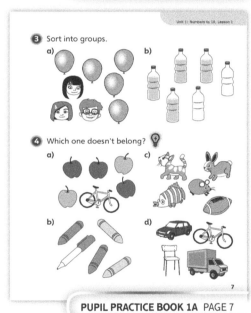

PUPIL PRACTICE BOOK 1A PAGE 6

PUPIL PRACTICE BOOK 1A PAGE 7

Reflect

WAYS OF WORKING Pair work

IN FOCUS This **Reflect** activity gives children the opportunity to put into practice all the skills that they have developed in this lesson. Encourage children to discuss their reasoning and justify their choices with their partner.

ASSESSMENT CHECKPOINT This **Reflect** activity should help you assess if children can choose objects that are in some way similar to one another. Assess if children can group their objects based on their chosen criteria.

ANSWERS Answers for the **Reflect** part of the lesson appear in the separate **Practice and Reflect answer guide**.

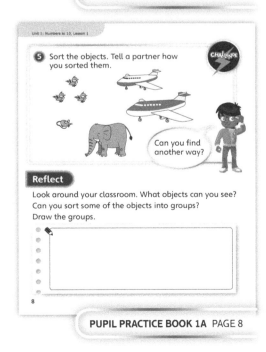

PUPIL PRACTICE BOOK 1A PAGE 8

After the lesson ⏸

- Are children more confident in recognising that objects can be sorted and grouped in many different ways?
- How has the lesson enabled children to explain their criteria for sorting the objects and justify their ideas?
- Could children's learning in this lesson be supported and developed through another area of the curriculum?

Counting objects to 10

Learning focus

In this lesson, children will start to count to 10. They will link the skill of counting concrete materials to the abstract numerals.

Small steps

→ Previous step: Sorting objects
→ **This step: Counting objects to 10**
→ Next step: Counting and writing numbers to 10

NATIONAL CURRICULUM LINKS

Year 1 Number – Number and Place Value
- Count to and across 100, forwards and backwards, beginning with 0 or 1, or from any given number.
- Identify and represent numbers using concrete objects and pictorial representations including the number line, and use the language of: equal to, more than, less than (fewer), most, least.

ASSESSING MASTERY

Children can correctly count a group of objects up to and including 10. Children can relate the abstract numeral to a group of concrete objects and can recognise that adding one more increases the count by one.

COMMON MISCONCEPTIONS

When using the ten frame, children may not recognise that it is not important which counters are coloured or filled in for a certain amount to be successfully counted.

Children may count too many or too few. Counting the same object more than once is common.

STRENGTHENING UNDERSTANDING

Ask children to place a group of objects along a number track or ten frame. As each object is placed on the number track or ten frame, children should count up and point to the corresponding number. This could be repeated with number tracks organised in different ways, such as a single row of 10, two rows of 5, five rows of 2 and so on.

GOING DEEPER

When children are confident counting up to 10, ask them to count down to 1 from a given number between 2 and 10.

KEY LANGUAGE

In lesson: 1, 2, 3, 4, 5, 6, 7, 8, 9, 10, how many, count

STRUCTURES AND REPRESENTATIONS

Ten frame, counters, multilink cubes, bead strings

RESOURCES

Mandatory: Ten frames, multilink cubes, bead strings

Optional: Number tracks, six-sided dice, number cards showing the numeral and a ten frame displaying the same number, a display board showing other representations of numbers 0–10, a selection of objects from the classroom for counting, such as straws, plastic bricks, cotton reels and glue sticks, a ten frame with the numbers labelled on it

Teaching Tools In the eTextbook of this lesson, you will find interactive links to a selection of teaching tools.

Before you teach ⏸

- What resources will you provide for children who find counting from a picture more difficult?
- How will you provide scaffolding to build up children's ability to relate amounts of concrete materials and abstract numbers to one another?

Discover

WAYS OF WORKING Pair work

ASK

- *How many cotton reels do you need?*
- *How could you check that you have the correct amount of each object?*
- *Can you show this in a different way?*
- *Can you show the same number using counters?*
- *Can you show the same number using a ten frame?*

IN FOCUS Question ❶ introduces the concept of 'How many … do you need?'. Children will begin to use the lesson's key language relating to the amounts of objects shown in the picture.

ANSWERS

Question ❶ a): I need 3 ⚡ .

Question ❶ b): I need 7 🧱 .

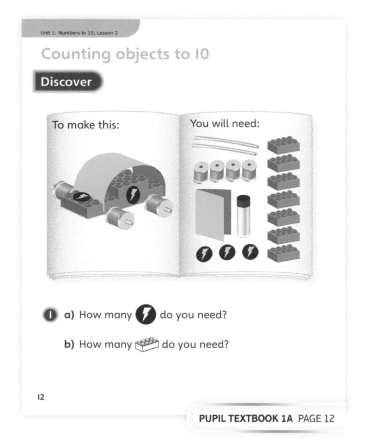

Counting objects to 10

Discover

To make this:

You will need:

❶ a) How many ⚡ do you need?

b) How many 🧱 do you need?

12

PUPIL TEXTBOOK 1A PAGE 12

Share

WAYS OF WORKING Whole class teacher led

ASK

- *How did you use the ten frame to help you?*
- *Could you have used the ten frame in a different way?*
- *What other resources could you use to help you count?*
- *Does it matter which squares you fill in on the ten frame? Explain your reasons.*

IN FOCUS Questions ❶ a) and ❶ b) reinforce the concept of one-to-one correspondence. Both questions give an opportunity to challenge the misconception that filling in the ten frame in a different way changes the amount counted. For example, in question ❶ a), ask: *If you had put a counter in every other square, would you still have 3 or would you now have 5?*

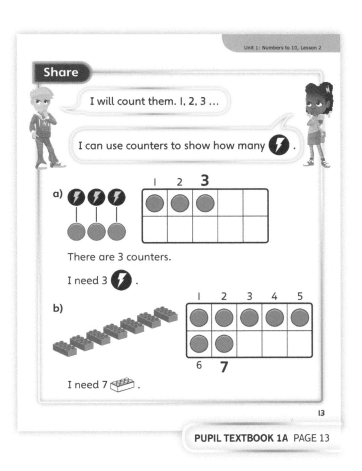

Share

I will count them. 1, 2, 3 …

I can use counters to show how many ⚡ .

a)

There are 3 counters.

I need 3 ⚡ .

b)

I need 7 🧱 .

13

PUPIL TEXTBOOK 1A PAGE 13

Think together

WAYS OF WORKING Whole class teacher led (I do, We do, You do)

ASK

- *What do you need to count?*
- *How will you use the ten frame to help you count?*
- *How will you use the counters to help you count?*
- Question **2**: *Can you explain how you know how many straws you need?*

IN FOCUS Questions **1** and **2** provide scaffolding for children to use their understanding of one-to-one correspondence to count the objects and represent them with counters.

Questions **3** a) and **3** b) allow children to demonstrate their understanding of one-to-one correspondence more independently, because there are no dotted outlines of counters in the ten frames.

STRENGTHEN Provide a ten frame labelled with the numbers. Children can then count a set of real-life objects by placing either the objects or counters on the ten frame and can read the number from the ten frame.

To support their conservation of number, present children with a variety of ten frames that show the same numbers in different ways. Can children sort the ten frames into groups of the same number?

DEEPEN Use Astrid's comment about using counters to discuss other ways in which the problem could be represented. Can children use the ten frame in a different way? Can they use different resources to represent the same problem?

ASSESSMENT CHECKPOINT Questions **3** a) and **3** b) should help you assess children's one-to-one correspondence and if they are able to relate the groups of concrete objects to the abstract numbers.

ANSWERS

Question **1**: There is 1 counter. I need 1 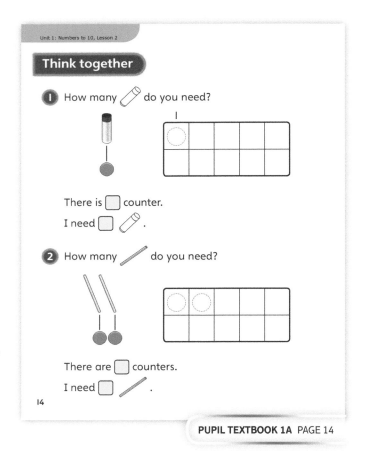.

Question **2**: There are 2 counters. I need 2 .

Question **3** a): I need 1 .

Question **3** b): I need 4 .

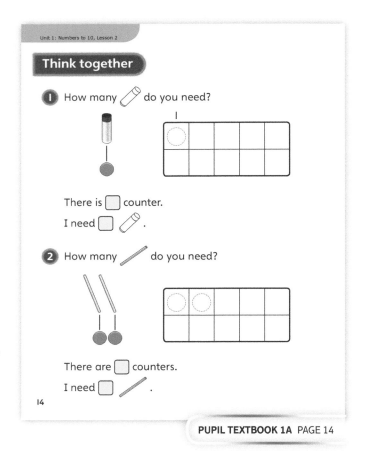

PUPIL TEXTBOOK 1A PAGE 14

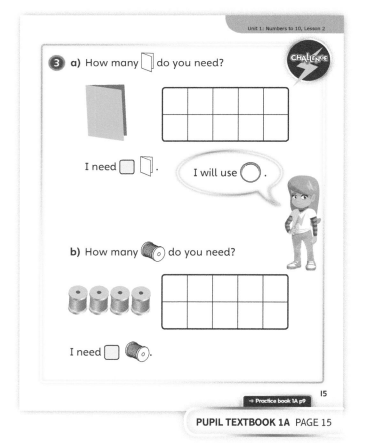

PUPIL TEXTBOOK 1A PAGE 15

Practice

WAYS OF WORKING Independent thinking

IN FOCUS Question ① supports children's one-to-one correspondence while providing scaffolding for their understanding of the link between the concrete amount of real-world objects and the abstract number.

Question ② builds on question ① by asking children to count the objects, then select and colour the correct number of counters and choose the correct numeral independently.

Question ③ requires children to begin with the abstract number and relate this to a concrete amount.

STRENGTHEN If children need support relating abstract numbers to concrete amounts, it may help to have number cards showing the numeral and a ten frame displaying the same number or a display board showing other representations of the numbers.

DEEPEN Question ④ requires children to demonstrate their mastery of the concepts from this lesson and the previous lesson as they need to count the objects within a groups subset. Use Astrid's comment to encourage deeper thinking by asking: *Why does Astrid think there are three? Is she correct? Can you show what you think?*

ASSESSMENT CHECKPOINT When children answer question ③, check they are able to read and understand the numbers. This question will demonstrate if children are aware of what the numbers 7 and 5 mean and look like in real life. It could be extended to cover other numbers if necessary.

Question ⑤ allows children to show their mastery of what makes the number 10 using multiple representations of the number.

ANSWERS Answers for the **Practice** part of the lesson appear in the separate **Practice and Reflect answer guide**.

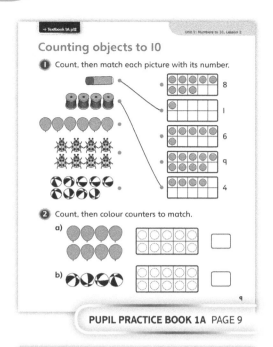

PUPIL PRACTICE BOOK 1A PAGE 9

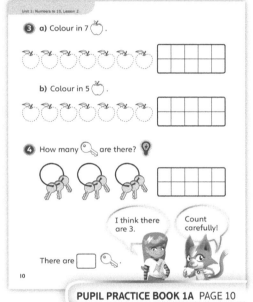

PUPIL PRACTICE BOOK 1A PAGE 10

Reflect

WAYS OF WORKING Independent thinking

IN FOCUS This **Reflect** activity allows children to reflect on the numbers they have learned about and pick one they would like to examine further. To expose any misconceptions, you could give children a second number to focus on after they have worked on their own choice of number.

ASSESSMENT CHECKPOINT Assess if children are using the correct number to represent an amount. Have they used the ten frame to represent the number? What other ways are they able to represent it?

ANSWERS Answers for the **Reflect** part of the lesson appear in the separate **Practice and Reflect answer guide**.

After the lesson ⏸

- Are all children able to represent numbers to 10 in a concrete and an abstract manner?
- Are you confident that all children know what each number looks like as a concrete amount of objects?
- How will you use the representations introduced in this lesson to support children in the future?

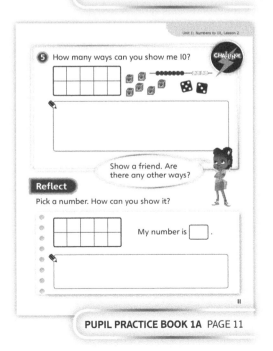

PUPIL PRACTICE BOOK 1A PAGE 11

Counting and writing numbers to 10

Learning focus

In this lesson, children will be able to relate the amount of objects to the correct number in digits and the correct number in words.

Small steps

→ Previous step: Counting objects to 10
→ **This step: Counting and writing numbers to 10**
→ Next step: Counting backwards from 10 to 0

NATIONAL CURRICULUM LINKS

Year 1 Number – Number and Place Value
- Count to and across 100, forwards and backwards, beginning with 0 or 1, or from any given number.
- Count, read and write numbers to 100 in numerals; count in multiples of twos, fives and tens.
- Read and write numbers from 1 to 20 in numerals and words.

ASSESSING MASTERY

Children can count objects accurately and link the amount to the correct digit and word. Children can recognise that countable objects may be represented in many different ways, not just as regularly ordered rows of single objects.

COMMON MISCONCEPTIONS

When using the ten frame, children may not recognise that it is not important which counters are coloured or filled in for a certain amount to be successfully counted.

Children may count too many or too few. Counting the same object more than once is common.

Children may relate the size of the objects to the amount of the objects. For example, when comparing two elephants to two mice, they may suggest there are more elephants because they are larger in size.

STRENGTHENING UNDERSTANDING

Give children number cards, each of which should show a digit, the corresponding number in words and the corresponding number in pictures. These will support understanding throughout this lesson.

Children could role play going to the shops with a shopping list and buying the correct number of items. This reinforces understanding of the link between an abstract number and a concrete amount.

GOING DEEPER

Ask children to show how many different ways they can represent a given number. Ask: *How many ways can you arrange the milk cartons to make 7?*

KEY LANGUAGE

In lesson: one, two, three, four, five, six, seven, eight, nine, ten, **number track**, **digits**

Other language to be used by the teacher: number track, different, same

STRUCTURES AND REPRESENTATIONS

Ten frames, counters, multilink cubes, number tracks

RESOURCES

Mandatory: Ten frames, counters, multilink cubes, number cards, number tracks

Optional: A selection of countable real-life objects from the classroom, bead strings

Teaching Tools In the eTextbook of this lesson, you will find interactive links to a selection of teaching tools.

Before you teach ⏸

- Do children confidently recognise and understand each number up to 10?

Discover

WAYS OF WORKING Pair work

ASK

- *Before you count the objects, can you predict which group contains more objects?*
- *How many boxes of cereal are there?*
- *Are there more cans than boxes? How do you know?*

IN FOCUS Questions ❶ a) and ❶ b) consolidate children's learning from Lesson 2 by asking them to count the number of objects and record the number in two different ways. They begin to challenge the potential misconception that the fact that the cereal boxes make a bigger pile does not mean that there are more boxes than cans.

ANSWERS

Question ❶ a): There are 10 🥫.

Question ❶ b): The number is 10. The word is ten.

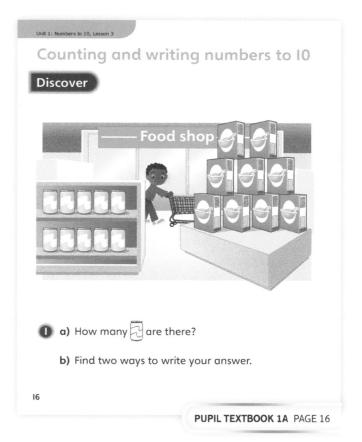

PUPIL TEXTBOOK 1A PAGE 16

Share

WAYS OF WORKING Whole class teacher led

ASK

- *How did you show 10?*
- *Why did you show it in that way?*
- *Did anyone else show it in a different way?*
- *Can you explain how the two representations are the same and how they are different?*
- *Can you think of another way to show 10?*
- *How could you show the number of cereal boxes?*

IN FOCUS Questions ❶ a) and ❶ b) introduce children to the written word representation of the numbers 1–10. They also provide children with different visual arrangements of the numbers 1–10, beginning to show the comparative size of each number.

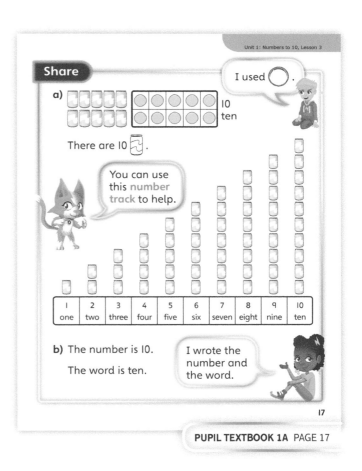

PUPIL TEXTBOOK 1A PAGE 17

Think together

Whole class teacher led (I do, We do, You do)

ASK
- *What do you need to count?*
- *How could you check your answer?*
- *How can you show your answer?*
- *Which arrangement is easiest to count? Explain your ideas.*
- *Could you show the numbers in a different way?*
- *How many different ways could you show the numbers?*

IN FOCUS Question ❸ introduces the lesson's key language: 'digit'. It also provides the opportunity to assess children's one-to-one correspondence and their ability to recognise that the size of an object does not influence how many of that object there are. This question could be introduced by asking children to predict which arrangement has more objects, with children justifying their ideas.

STRENGTHEN Provide children with the real-life objects or concrete materials to represent them. Ask children to arrange the objects or materials as they are shown in the pictures. Then arrange them either on a ten frame or a number track. What do children notice? Focus particularly on objects that have a considerable size difference.

DEEPEN Ask children if the bottles in question ❸ can be arranged so that their arrangement looks bigger than the boxes. Ask: *Does this change how many bottles there are? Are there any patterns in how the objects have been arranged? If you added another row above or below, what would that row look like?*

ASSESSMENT CHECKPOINT Question ❸ should help you to assess if children are counting accurately and confidently, particularly when objects have been arranged differently or are of different sizes.

ANSWERS

Question ❶: There are 7 🟤.

Question ❷: There are three 🍌.

Question ❸: There are 9 🟤. There are nine 🟤.

There are 9 🟤. There are nine 🟤.

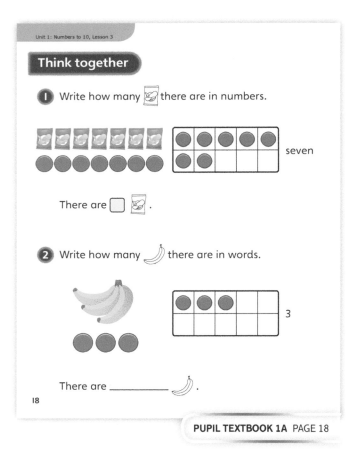

PUPIL TEXTBOOK 1A PAGE 18

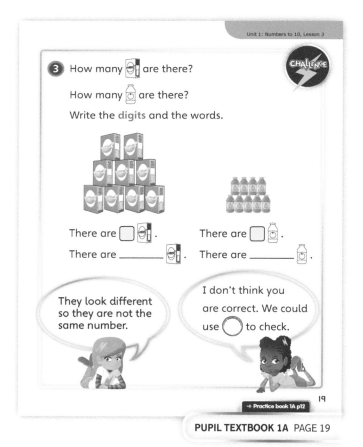

PUPIL TEXTBOOK 1A PAGE 19

Practice

WAYS OF WORKING Independent thinking

IN FOCUS Question **4** introduces children to 0. They may be tempted to colour something in because this has been the process for all other questions so far. Use this question as an opportunity to explore what 0 looks like and how much it represents.

Question **5** uses an unfamiliar arrangement of multilink cubes which makes it more challenging to recognise the number of cubes.

STRENGTHEN Provide number cards that display a digit, the same number in words and the same number in pictures to support understanding and encourage independent thinking.

DEEPEN Deepen question **5** by asking: *Can you think why Astrid thinks that the second picture is made up of three blocks? What could you do to help her see her mistake? How would you show this to her?*

ASSESSMENT CHECKPOINT Questions **1** to **5** should help you assess children's one-to-one correspondence and their ability to count objects reliably, regardless of size, orientation or arrangement.

Question **6** should help you assess children's ability to order numbers and write numbers in digits and words correctly.

ANSWERS Answers for the **Practice** part of the lesson appear in the separate **Practice and Reflect answer guide**.

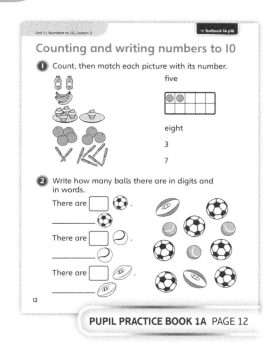

PUPIL PRACTICE BOOK 1A PAGE 12

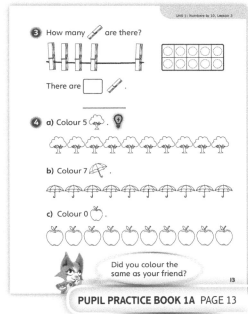

PUPIL PRACTICE BOOK 1A PAGE 13

Reflect

WAYS OF WORKING Pair work

IN FOCUS This **Reflect** activity allows children to reflect on the numbers they have learned about and pick one they would like to examine further. Children should now have enough experience with concrete amounts and the related abstract numbers that they are able to confidently pick a number, record the related digit and its written name, and offer more than one representation of it.

ASSESSMENT CHECKPOINT Assess if children use the correct digit and written name to represent an amount. Discuss their chosen way of representing the number by asking: *Could you have coloured the triangles in a different way and still have the same amount?* Assess if children can confidently explain that they could have done this.

ANSWERS Answers for the **Reflect** part of the lesson appear in the separate **Practice and Reflect answer guide**.

After the lesson ⏸

- Can children reliably count objects, regardless of the objects' size, orientation and arrangement?
- Can all children confidently recognise both the digit and written name of every number from 1 to 10?
- What representations or strategies could you use from this lesson to support counting backwards from 10 in Lesson 4?

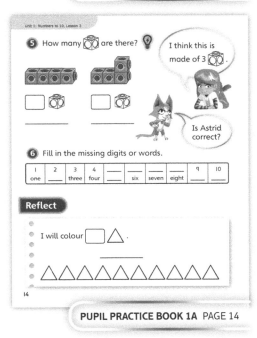

PUPIL PRACTICE BOOK 1A PAGE 14

Counting backwards from 10 to 0

Learning focus

In this lesson, children use their knowledge and understanding of counting forwards to 10 to help them count backwards from 10.

Small steps

→ Previous step: Counting and writing numbers to 10
→ **This step: Count backwards from 10 to 0**
→ Next step: Counting one more

NATIONAL CURRICULUM LINKS

Year 1 Number – Number and Place Value

Count to and across 100, forwards and backwards, beginning with 0 or 1, or from any given number.

ASSESSING MASTERY

Children can confidently count backwards to 0 from a given number up to, and including, 10. Children can use their knowledge of counting forwards and backwards to recognise patterns and complete sequences.

COMMON MISCONCEPTIONS

Children may be inclined to count forwards from a particular starting point as this may be what they are more comfortable with. Ask: *Which way are you counting today? Can you trace that direction on the number track with your finger? How is it different to counting forwards?*

Children may miscount and either count the same number twice or miss a number.

STRENGTHENING UNDERSTANDING

Give children number cards, each of which should show a numeral, the corresponding number in words and the corresponding number in pictures. These will support understanding throughout this lesson. Display a number track prominently in the classroom for children to refer to during the lesson.

Reinforce understanding by counting backwards during daily activities such as tidying up or crossing the classroom to sit on the carpet.

GOING DEEPER

Using number cards, children turn over a card and count backwards from that number to 0. Children could then turn over two number cards, identify which number is bigger and count backwards from the bigger number to the smaller one.

KEY LANGUAGE

In lesson: pattern, count back

Other language to be used by the teacher: 1, 2, 3, 4, 5, 6, 7, 8, 9, 10, how many, number, next, number track, pattern

STRUCTURES AND REPRESENTATIONS

Ten frames, counters, multilink cubes, number track

RESOURCES

Mandatory: ten frames, multilink cubes, number tracks, six-sided dice

Optional: number cards, a selection of real-life countable objects

Teaching Tools | In the eTextbook of this lesson, you will find interactive links to a selection of teaching tools.

Before you teach

- Are children ready to count backwards? How confident are they at counting forwards?
- How confident are children with the concept of 0?
- What real-life contexts could you use to frame this concept?

Discover

WAYS OF WORKING Pair work

ASK

- *Can you recognise a pattern in the numbers?*
- *When you count backwards, what number comes before 6?*
- *When you count backwards, what number comes after 3?*
- *How is this the same and how is this different to when you counted forwards?*

IN FOCUS Question ① a) could be supported by using a video of a rocket launch or by 'launching' a rocket that children make out of plastic bottles. The question should allow you to assess children's confidence when counting backwards.

Question ① b) provides an opportunity to discuss what number children should stop counting at. Are children confident when counting backwards to 0?

ANSWERS

Question ① a): The number 5 comes next.

Question ① b): You stop counting at 0.

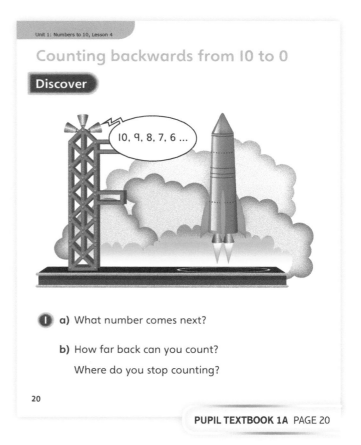

Counting backwards from 10 to 0

Discover

① a) What number comes next?

  b) How far back can you count?
  Where do you stop counting?

20

PUPIL TEXTBOOK 1A PAGE 20

Share

WAYS OF WORKING Whole class teacher led

ASK

- *Can you spot a pattern?*
- *What happens to the amount of blocks each time you count backwards?*
- *What amount is smaller than 1? Explain how you know.*
- *Could you show these numbers in a different way?*
- *How did you represent the numbers in the last lesson? Could you use that method again?*
- *How will you know what comes next?*

IN FOCUS Questions ① a) and ① b) support children's understanding of counting backwards and demonstrate how the amount decreases as they count backwards. The second representation also supports children in their understanding of 0 equalling nothing and what this looks like in comparison to the other amounts.

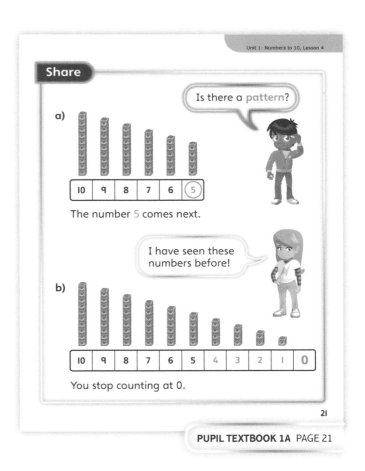

Share

Is there a **pattern**?

a)

| 10 | 9 | 8 | 7 | 6 | 5 |

The number 5 comes next.

I have seen these numbers before!

b)

| 10 | 9 | 8 | 7 | 6 | 5 | 4 | 3 | 2 | 1 | 0 |

You stop counting at 0.

21

PUPIL TEXTBOOK 1A PAGE 21

Think together

Whole class teacher led (I do, We do, You do)

ASK

- *What number comes next? How can you check?*
- *What did you use to help you count?*
- *How many blocks disappear with each number you count backwards?*
- *What can you do to help you count backwards from any number?*
- *Can you show your counting by drawing a picture?*

IN FOCUS Questions ③ and ④ require children to use the understanding of number they have gained so far to count backwards from a given number. These questions are presented in the abstract, so children will need to use the strategies and representations they have learned to complete these questions.

STRENGTHEN Have a number track available for children who are finding the process of counting backwards more challenging.

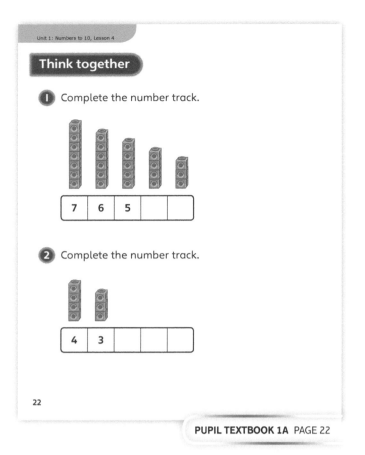

PUPIL TEXTBOOK 1A PAGE 22

DEEPEN Use Ash's statement to investigate this further. Ask: *Is there the same amount of numbers between 8 and 2? How about between 7 and 1? Why is this?* Can children prove their ideas by drawing pictures or using concrete materials?

ASSESSMENT CHECKPOINT Questions ③ and ④ should help you assess children's ability to recognise numerals and count backwards from them. Can children explain how they know what number comes next? Can they show how they know?

ANSWERS

Question ①: 7 6 5 **4 3**

Question ②: 4 3 **2 1 0**

Question ③: 9 **8 7 6 5 4 3**

Question ④: 8 **7 6 5 4 3 2 1**

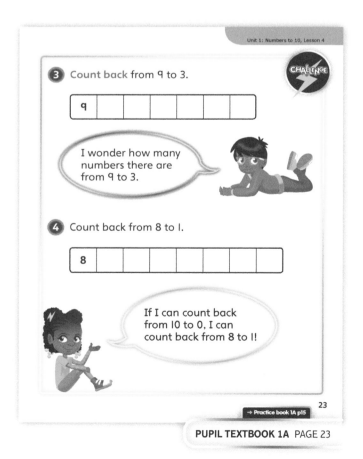

PUPIL TEXTBOOK 1A PAGE 23

Practice

WAYS OF WORKING Independent thinking

IN FOCUS Questions ① to ③ allow children to practise the skill of counting backwards from a given number. The questions are increasingly abstract, gradually requiring children to rely more on their own knowledge of number in order to solve them.

STRENGTHEN Provide a number track for children to refer to. Children could also have access to a ten frame and counters to build the numbers and take one counter away each time they count backwards.

DEEPEN Questions ④ and ⑤ challenge children to recognise whether a number sequence is counting forwards or backwards and complete it appropriately. Questions ④ a), b) and e) add further challenge by leaving the starting numbers blank, requiring children to work inverse to the pattern to solve it.

ASSESSMENT CHECKPOINT Questions ① to ③ should help you assess children's ability to count backwards from a given number and represent the sequences in different ways. Check that children are able to correctly represent the patterns in all forms of the numbers (as pictures, numerals and written names).

ANSWERS Answers for the **Practice** part of the lesson appear in the separate **Practice and Reflect answer guide**.

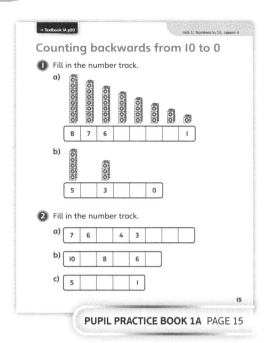

PUPIL PRACTICE BOOK 1A PAGE 15

PUPIL PRACTICE BOOK 1A PAGE 16

Reflect

WAYS OF WORKING Independent thinking

IN FOCUS At this point, children should be able to roll a random number below 10 and count forwards and backwards from it accurately and confidently. Ask children where they should put their number on the number track so that the 10 and 1 appear at the beginning and end of their number track. Can they explain their ideas?

ASSESSMENT CHECKPOINT This **Reflect** activity should help you assess if children are counting forwards and backwards confidently and fluently. Are there any numbers missing from their sequences?

ANSWERS Answers for the **Reflect** part of the lesson appear in the separate **Practice and Reflect answer guide**.

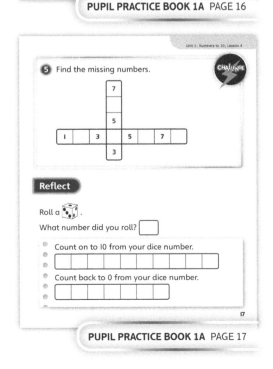

PUPIL PRACTICE BOOK 1A PAGE 17

After the lesson ⏸

- Do any children still have any misconceptions about counting backwards?
- Are children sufficiently confident and able to explain and show the differences between counting forwards and backwards?
- Is there anything that you will do differently when you approach this concept again in the future?

Counting one more

Learning focus

In this lesson, children will learn to find one more than a given number. They will investigate further the place value of numbers from 0 to 10 and consider what 'one more' means.

Small steps

→ Previous step: Counting backwards from 10 to 0
→ **This step: Counting one more**
→ Next step: Counting one less

NATIONAL CURRICULUM LINKS

Year 1 Number – Number and Place Value
- Given a number, identify one more and one less.
- Identify and represent numbers using concrete objects and pictorial representations including the number line, and use the language of: equal to, more than, less than (fewer), most, least.
- Count to and across 100, forwards and backwards, beginning with 0 or 1, or from any given number.

ASSESSING MASTERY

Children can reliably and confidently count one more from any given number between 0 and 10. Children can explain what 'one more' means in terms of a number's comparative place value.

COMMON MISCONCEPTIONS

Children may be able to recite counting forwards in ones but may not be able to explain how counting forwards one more actually changes the amount. Ask: *Can you use the cubes to show me what happens when you count one more? How has your collection of cubes changed?*

Children may count forwards from 0 or 1 instead of beginning at the number they are finding one more than. Ask:
- *What number did you want to count forwards from?*
- *Can you show me that number in cubes?*
- *How many more cubes will you have if you count one more?*
- *Can you show me that number on a number track? Where will you be on the number track if you count one more?*

STRENGTHENING UNDERSTANDING

Make sure that all representations that have been used in the previous lessons are available. Children should be confident using ten frames by now, so use ten frames to help scaffold children's understanding of having 'one more'.

GOING DEEPER

When children are confident explaining what happens when they count one more, ask them to explain what happens when they count 2 or 3 more. Ask: *Which numbers can you count forwards 3 from without the result being greater than 10? Which numbers can you count forwards 3 from and have a result greater than 10? Why does this happen?*

KEY LANGUAGE

In lesson: one more, one more than

Other language to be used by the teacher: how many, more, greater, value, increase, prove, represent

STRUCTURES AND REPRESENTATIONS

Multilink cubes, number track, ten frame, counters

RESOURCES

Mandatory: multilink cubes, number track, ten frame, counters, number cards

Optional: a selection of countable real-life objects

Teaching Tools In the eTextbook of this lesson, you will find interactive links to a selection of teaching tools.

Before you teach

- Do children have a preferred concrete material that they always choose to use when representing amounts?
- How will you provide scaffolding for the development of children's ability to reason about place value?

Discover

WAYS OF WORKING Pair work

ASK

- *How many dinosaurs have hatched and are out of their shells?*
- *What can you use to represent the hatched dinosaurs?*
- *What is going to happen with the dinosaur that is still hatching?*
- *How many more dinosaurs will you have once it has hatched?*
- *What happens if the final egg does not hatch? How many dinosaurs will you have?*
- *If another egg that you cannot see hatches, how many dinosaurs will you have now?*

IN FOCUS Questions **1** a) and **1** b) require children to visualise the increase in dinosaurs, especially in question **1** b) where the final egg is not shown hatching in the picture. This visualisation could be supported with toy dinosaurs or cubes to represent the dinosaurs. This is the first time that children will encounter the lesson's key language: 'one more'.

ANSWERS

Question **1** a): There are 5 🦕 now.

Question **1** b): There are 6 🦕 now.

PUPIL TEXTBOOK 1A PAGE 24

Share

WAYS OF WORKING Whole class teacher led

ASK

- *How do the blocks show that 5 is one more than 4?*
- *Can this be shown clearly as a picture?*
- *If you wanted to find one more than 3, at what number should you begin counting? Why?*

IN FOCUS Questions **1** a) and **1** b) reinforce the idea that it is not necessary to begin counting from 1 every time children want to find one more than another number. They do this in the number sentences on the right, by only showing the number that children are finding one more than, instead of showing all the numbers preceding it.

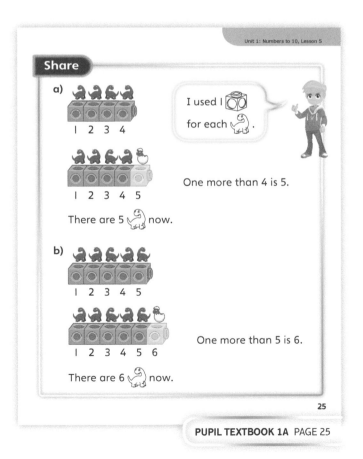

PUPIL TEXTBOOK 1A PAGE 25

Think together

Unit 1: Numbers to 10, Lesson 5

Think together

WAYS OF WORKING Whole class teacher led (I do, We do, You do)

ASK

- *What do you need to do first?*
- *What do you need to count?*
- *How will you prove what one more is?*
- *Could you show this in a picture?*
- *Which group of blocks has more blocks? How do you know?*
- *Is it sensible to start counting from 0 each time? Explain your ideas.*

STRENGTHEN Consider linking the concept to children's real-life experiences and support this with the representations used in previous lessons. For example, ask: *If you have 3 sweets and I give you 1 more, how many sweets do you have?* Children can arrange the first 3 sweets on a ten frame and then add 1 more. Discuss how many sweets there were and how many sweets there are now.

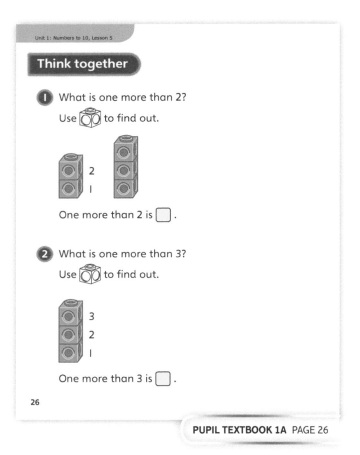

1 What is one more than 2?
Use [cubes] to find out.

2
1

One more than 2 is ☐ .

2 What is one more than 3?
Use [cubes] to find out.

3
2
1

One more than 3 is ☐ .

26

PUPIL TEXTBOOK 1A PAGE 26

IN FOCUS Question ❸ can be used to show that, when finding one more than 8, it is more efficient to start at 8 and count forwards one, rather than count forwards to 8 and then count forwards one more.

DEEPEN Children could choose two different number cards from a group of number cards numbered 0–10. Ask children to choose the smallest number. Ask: *How many times do you have to count one more before you reach the bigger number? Can you represent this using resources or a picture?*

ASSESSMENT CHECKPOINT Assess if children are showing an understanding of the principle that beginning at the number they are adding one more to is the most efficient method of counting forwards one more. Can they explain why this is, using concrete materials and visual proof to justify their ideas?

ANSWERS

Question ❶: One more than 2 is 3.

Question ❷: One more than 3 is 4.

Question ❸ a): One more than 8 is 9.

Question ❸ b): 8 is one more than 7.

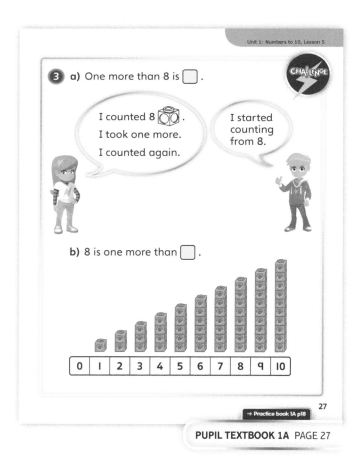

Unit 1: Numbers to 10, Lesson 5

CHALLENGE

3 a) One more than 8 is ☐ .

I counted 8 [cube].
I took one more.
I counted again.

I started counting from 8.

b) 8 is one more than ☐ .

| 0 | 1 | 2 | 3 | 4 | 5 | 6 | 7 | 8 | 9 | 10 |

27

→ Practice book 1A p18

PUPIL TEXTBOOK 1A PAGE 27

Practice

WAYS OF WORKING Independent thinking

IN FOCUS Question ① provides children with visual scaffolding to help them approach questions ① a), ① b) and ① c).

Question ④ offers an opportunity for problem solving as it requires children to begin thinking about the inverse of one more.

STRENGTHEN Make sure that the number track from question ① is available for children to refer to when answering all of the questions.

DEEPEN Question ⑤ provides an opportunity to develop children's reasoning. Ask children to explain how their representations prove that 8 is one more than 7 as though they were teaching this to someone who has not learned about it before.

ASSESSMENT CHECKPOINT Questions ③ and ④ should help you decide whether children are starting at the number they are counting forwards from or counting forwards from 0 each time.

Assess if children can explain how each number is different in value.

ANSWERS Answers for the **Practice** part of the lesson appear in the separate **Practice and Reflect answer guide**.

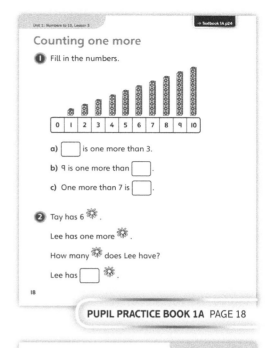

PUPIL PRACTICE BOOK 1A PAGE 18

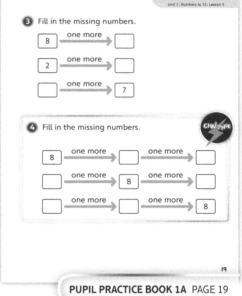

PUPIL PRACTICE BOOK 1A PAGE 19

Reflect

WAYS OF WORKING Independent thinking and pair work

IN FOCUS Children can begin by completing the statements. Use paired discussion to highlight where children have chosen different resources and representations to help them complete the statements. You could use this opportunity to discuss which representations are effective and why.

ASSESSMENT CHECKPOINT Assess if children can confidently and consistently find one more in an efficient way. Decide if children can explain what 'one more' means and equates to. Assess if children can justify and prove their ideas through confident use of different representations.

ANSWERS Answers for the **Reflect** part of the lesson appear in the separate **Practice and Reflect answer guide**.

After the lesson ⏸

- Are children able to explain clearly what 'one more' means?
- Are children able to recognise why counting on from the given number is more efficient?
- Which representation best demonstrated the idea of 'one more'? What made it work so well?

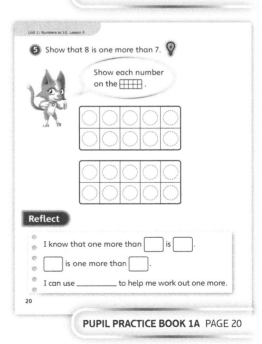

PUPIL PRACTICE BOOK 1A PAGE 20

Counting one less

Learning focus

In this lesson, children will learn to find one less than a given number. They will investigate further the place value of numbers from 0 to 10 and consider what 'one less' means.

Small steps

→ Previous step: Counting one more
→ **This step: Counting one less**
→ Next step: Comparing groups

NATIONAL CURRICULUM LINKS

Year 1 Number – Number and Place Value
- Given a number, identify one more and one less.
- Identify and represent numbers using concrete objects and pictorial representations including the number line, and use the language of: equal to, more than, less than (fewer), most, least.
- Count to and across 100, forwards and backwards, beginning with 0 or 1, or from any given number.

ASSESSING MASTERY

Children can reliably and confidently count one less from any given number between 1 and 10. Children can explain what 'one less' means in terms of a number's comparative place value.

COMMON MISCONCEPTIONS

Children may be able to recite counting backwards in ones but may not be able to explain how counting one less actually changes the amount. Ask:
- *Can you use the cubes to show me what happens when you count one less?*
- *How has your collection of cubes changed?*

Children may count forwards instead of backwards. Ask:
- *On a number track, can you show me with your finger which way you would go to count backwards?*

STRENGTHENING UNDERSTANDING

Make sure that all representations that have been used in the previous lessons are available. Children should be confident using ten frames by now, so use ten frames to help scaffold children's understanding of having 'one less'.

Use the concept of musical chairs (as shown in **Discover**). Children could play musical chairs with toys, discussing how many chairs will be left and how many toys would be able to sit down as each chair is taken away.

GOING DEEPER

When children are confident explaining what happens when they count backwards by 1, ask them to explain what happens when they count backwards 2 or 3. Ask: *Which numbers can you count backwards 3 from without the result being smaller than 0?*

KEY LANGUAGE

In lesson: one less, one less than

Other language to be used by the teacher: how many, another, pattern, fewer, value, less, decrease

STRUCTURES AND REPRESENTATIONS

Multilink cubes, number track

RESOURCES

Mandatory: multilink cubes, number tracks, ten frames, counters

Optional: a selection of countable real-life objects

Teaching Tools In the eTextbook of this lesson, you will find interactive links to a selection of teaching tools.

Before you teach ⏸

- In Lesson 5, how did children respond to the questions that required them to think inversely?
- How could you use this as a starting point for Lesson 6?

Discover

ASK

- *What is happening in the picture?*
- *What is the teacher doing?*
- *If a chair is taken away, can more children sit down or can fewer children sit down?*
- *If 1 chair is taken away, how many are left?*
- *If another chair is taken away, how many are left?*
- *Can every child in the picture sit down?*
- *Why is the number of children always one more than the number of chairs?*

IN FOCUS Questions ❶ a) and ❶ b) could be approached by playing musical chairs in an appropriate space. Children are likely to recognise the game of musical chairs, which provides a good introduction to the concept of 'one less'.

ANSWERS

Question ❶ a): There are 6 chairs left.

Question ❶ b): There are 5 chairs left now.

Counting one less

Discover

❶ a) There are 7 chairs.

I chair is removed.

How many are left?

b) Another chair is removed. How many are left?

28

PUPIL TEXTBOOK 1A PAGE 28

Share

ASK

- *How can you represent the number of chairs?*
- *How can you use cubes or counters to show that the number of chairs is one less?*
- *Can you have one less than 1? Can you prove it with resources or in a picture?*

IN FOCUS Questions ❶ a) and ❶ b) introduce children to the lesson's key language: 'one less than'. This provides an opportunity to link the concept of 'one less' to their knowledge and understanding of 'one more'. Discussing how it is similar but different should help to clarify the key differences between 'one more' and 'one less'. It should also help children to avoid counting forwards when asked to count backwards.

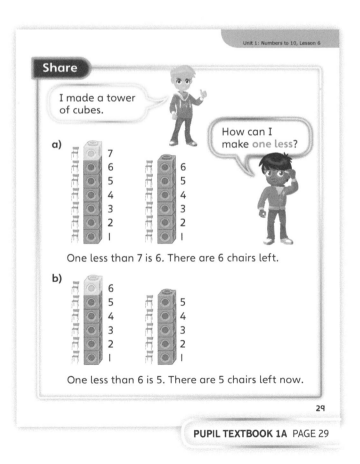

Share

I made a tower of cubes.

How can I make one less?

a)

One less than 7 is 6. There are 6 chairs left.

b)

One less than 6 is 5. There are 5 chairs left now.

29

PUPIL TEXTBOOK 1A PAGE 29

Think together

WAYS OF WORKING Whole class teacher led (I do, We do, You do)

ASK

- Question ❶: *Can you find 4 multilink cubes?*
- Question ❶: *What do you need to do to show one less than 4?*
- *Can you show it in another way?*
- Question ❶: *Which is more? Which is less? How do you know?*
- *Do you need to count forwards at all when finding one less? Explain your ideas.*
- *How is finding one less similar and different to finding one more? Explain your ideas.*

IN FOCUS Question ❸ challenges the need to start counting from any number other than the number that you are finding one less than. Discuss Astrid and Ash's comments to elicit children's understanding of the most efficient method of finding one less than a number.

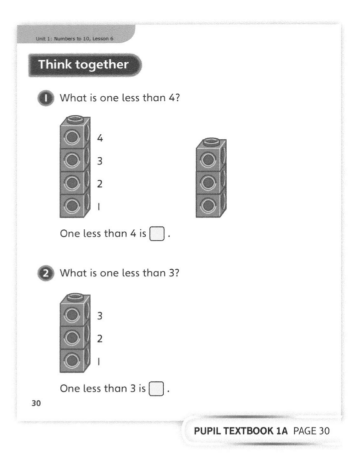

STRENGTHEN Consider linking the concept of 'one less' to the real-life experiences of children and support with the representations used in previous lessons. For example, ask: *If you have 3 sweets and I take 1 from you, how many do you have?* Children can arrange the first 3 sweets on a ten frame and then take 1 away. Discuss how many sweets there were and how many sweets there are now to help children understand the decrease in the number of sweets.

DEEPEN Refer to Ash's comments about patterns. Ask: *Are there any other patterns you can find? What happens if you count down two? How many fewer do you have now? How could you show that?*

ASSESSMENT CHECKPOINT Questions ❶ and ❷ provide the opportunity to assess whether children can show how to find one less than and explain how it affects the value of an amount.

Question ❸ provides an opportunity to assess if children can identify the most efficient way of finding one less than a number.

ANSWERS

Question ❶: One less than 4 is 3.

Question ❷: One less than 3 is 2.

Question ❸ a): One less than 9 is 8.

Question ❸ b): 9 is one less than 10.

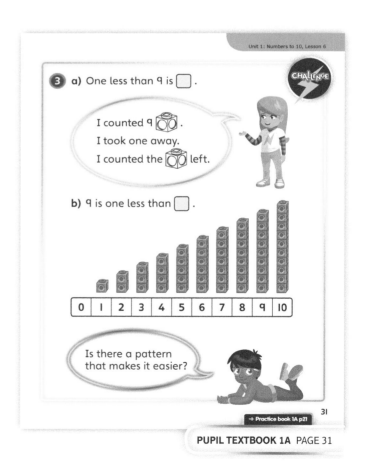

Practice

WAYS OF WORKING Independent thinking

IN FOCUS Question **1** provides a number track and multilink cubes as scaffolding for children to begin answering questions to do with finding one less. It also models the different ways the key language can be used in a sentence, which provides scaffolding for children to reason and justify their ideas.

STRENGTHEN Make sure the number track from question **1** is available for children to refer to when answering all of the questions in this section.

DEEPEN In question **5** use Sparks' comment about showing each number on the ten frame as a way to discuss other ways that children could show the numbers. Ask: *Do the different representations show the same patterns? Which do you think is the clearest representation of 'one more' and 'one less'? Explain your ideas.*

ASSESSMENT CHECKPOINT Questions **1**, **2** and **3** should help you to assess if children can find one less than a number. Assess children's understanding and expose potential misconceptions by asking: *How do you know? Can you prove this? Can you show me this another way?*

ANSWERS Answers for the **Practice** part of the lesson appear in the separate **Practice and Reflect answer guide**.

Reflect

WAYS OF WORKING Pair work

IN FOCUS Use Ash's comment to discuss how this lesson's learning is similar and linked to what children learned in the previous lesson. Can children use their knowledge of one more to help them find one less?

ASSESSMENT CHECKPOINT This **Reflect** activity should help you assess if children can confidently and consistently find one less in an efficient way. Assess if children can explain what 'one less' means and equates to. Are children confident discussing the links between finding one more and one less? Assess if children can justify and prove their ideas through confident use of different representations of the numbers shown on their fingers.

ANSWERS Answers for the **Reflect** part of the lesson appear in the separate **Practice and Reflect answer guide**.

After the lesson ⏸

- Do children clearly understand the links between the topics they have learned about in Lessons 5 and 6?
- Do children clearly understand the links between 'one more' and 'one less'?
- Are children more confident with 'one more' than they are with 'one less' or vice versa? How will you support them in the future so that they become equally confident with both?

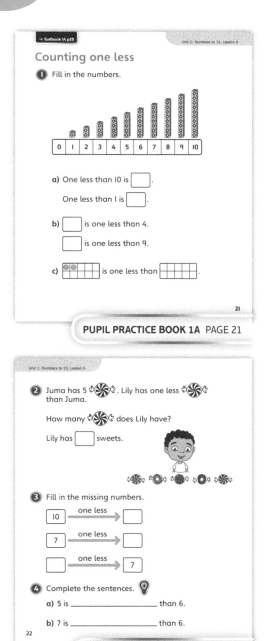

PUPIL PRACTICE BOOK 1A PAGE 21

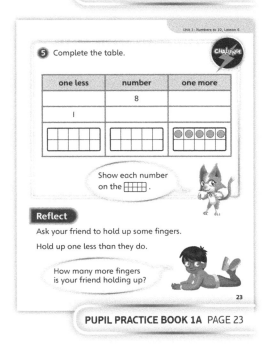

PUPIL PRACTICE BOOK 1A PAGE 22

PUPIL PRACTICE BOOK 1A PAGE 23

Comparing groups

Learning focus

In this lesson, children will compare groups of objects. Children will identify, when given two groups of objects, whether one group has more objects than the other.

Small steps

→ Previous step: Counting one less
→ **This step: Comparing groups**
→ Next step: Comparing numbers of objects

NATIONAL CURRICULUM LINKS

Year 1 Number – Number and Place Value

Identify and represent numbers using concrete objects and pictorial representations including the number line, and use the language of: equal to, more than, less than (fewer), most, least.

ASSESSING MASTERY

Children can recognise two groups of objects, count them and explain which group has more and which group has less. Children can justify their reasoning using concrete, pictorial and abstract representations.

COMMON MISCONCEPTIONS

Children may miscount the objects and so compare the groups inaccurately. Ask:
- *What could you use to help you count the objects?*

Children may say that a greater number is smaller or vice versa. Ask:
- *What could you use to help you compare?*
- *Could you show these numbers using multilink cubes?*

STRENGTHENING UNDERSTANDING

To strengthen understanding of counting and comparing, discuss the different representations that children could use. Ask: *Could you use a ten frame to help you visualise the amount? Could you use multilink cubes to help you compare? How could the number track help?*

Prepare pictorial representations of the flags, sandcastles, buckets and spades in the **Pupil Textbook** for children to manipulate, group and count when answering the questions.

GOING DEEPER

Ask children to investigate by how much a group is bigger or smaller than another group. Ask: *How many more of this object do you have than of that object? How do you know?*

KEY LANGUAGE

In lesson: matched, fewer

Other language to be used by the teacher: match, sorted, compare, count, equal, less than, fewer than, greater than, more than

STRUCTURES AND REPRESENTATIONS

Ten frame, 2D shapes (squares and circles)

RESOURCES

Mandatory: multilink cubes, 2D shapes (squares and circles), ten frame, counters

Optional: number tracks, a selection of countable real-life objects

Teaching Tools
In the eTextbook of this lesson, you will find interactive links to a selection of teaching tools.

Before you teach

- Are children confident counting forwards and backwards?
- What resources and representations will you make available from previous lessons to support their learning?

Discover

WAYS OF WORKING Pair work

ASK

- *Has each child made a sandcastle? How do you know?*
- *How many flags are standing up? Are there more flags or fewer flags lying down?*

IN FOCUS Question **1** a) prompts a discussion about the different representations and resources that children could use to help them compare groups of objects.

ANSWERS

Question **1** a): There are more ⚑ .

Question **1** b): Each person cannot have a 🪣 .

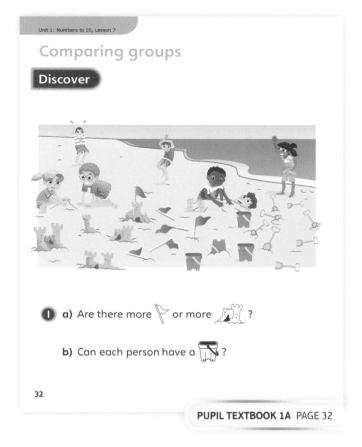

PUPIL TEXTBOOK 1A PAGE 32

Share

WAYS OF WORKING Whole class teacher led

ASK

- Question **1** a): *How is the matching made clear?*
- *Did anyone compare the objects in a different way?*
- Question **1** b): *How many more buckets do you need so that everyone can have a bucket?*

IN FOCUS Question **1** a) introduces children to the lesson's key language: 'matched'. Discuss the meaning of 'matched' and how it has helped Dexter decide whether there are more sandcastles or more flags.

PUPIL TEXTBOOK 1A PAGE 33

Think together

Think together

WAYS OF WORKING Whole class teacher led (I do, We do, You do)

ASK

- Question **1**: *What do you do with the buckets? What do you do with the sandcastles? How can you show where they match?*
- Question **3**: *What shape do you predict there are more of? Explain your idea. How could you make these shapes easier to count?*

IN FOCUS Question **1** provides scaffolding to help children compare the buckets and sandcastles and explain which group has more. Question **2** introduces children to the lesson's key language: 'fewer'. Children will use 'fewer' in their explanation and conclusion.

STRENGTHEN Represent the people and objects in the different groups using two different-coloured towers of multilink cubes. Children could count out multilink cubes to represent people and objects and then compare the two groups. Ask: *Which has more? Which has less? How can you tell?*

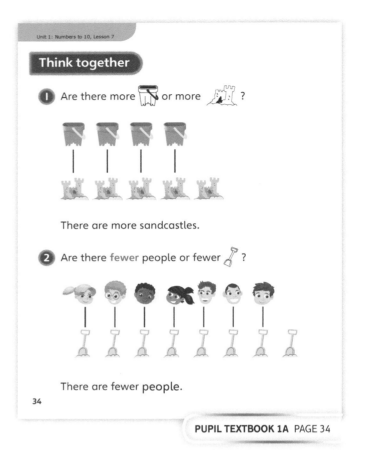

PUPIL TEXTBOOK 1A PAGE 34

DEEPEN Use Astrid and Flo's comments in question **3** to discuss which method is the most efficient and effective. Have children try both methods and decide which one they prefer. If two children think differently, have them work together in pairs to convince each other.

ASSESSMENT CHECKPOINT Question **3** should help you to decide if children can organise and count groups of objects. Assess if children can organise the groups to facilitate easy comparison and explain which group has more and which group has fewer.

ANSWERS

Question **1**: There are more sandcastles.

Question **2**: There are fewer people.

Question **3**: There are more ☐.

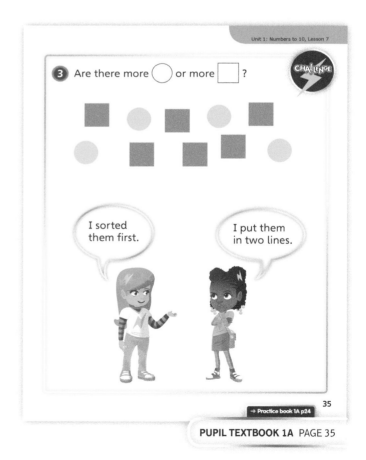

PUPIL TEXTBOOK 1A PAGE 35

Practice

WAYS OF WORKING Independent thinking

IN FOCUS Questions ❶ and ❷ support comparisons by arranging the objects in neat rows. Children can draw lines between corresponding objects. The objects in question ❸ are not arranged as neatly as the objects in the previous questions. Discuss with children how they could make the correspondence between the mice and the pieces of cheese clearer. What concrete materials could they use?

STRENGTHEN Use a number track and comparative amounts shown by towers of multilink cubes to help children order the amounts that they count in each group.

DEEPEN Question ❹ requires children to sort, group and order three different objects. Ask: *Have the groups been ordered as clearly as they could be? Explain your ideas. What if you put the triangles and circles into one group? Which two groups have the greatest difference between them? Which two groups have the least difference between them?*

ASSESSMENT CHECKPOINT Questions ❸ and ❹ should allow you to assess if children can suggest different ways to represent problems.

ANSWERS Answers for the **Practice** part of the lesson appear in the separate **Practice and Reflect answer guide**.

Reflect

WAYS OF WORKING Independent thinking

IN FOCUS This **Reflect** activity develops children's ability to reason and justify. It links the representation of the ten frame with the process of comparing groups. Ask children if there is a way of organising the ten frame so the comparison is clearer.

ASSESSMENT CHECKPOINT This **Reflect** activity should help you to decide if children can compare two groups confidently and draw conclusions about their comparative values. Assess if children can reason clearly, using the mathematical language of comparison to help them justify their ideas.

ANSWERS Answers for the **Reflect** part of the lesson appear in the separate **Practice and Reflect answer guide**.

After the lesson ⏸

- Are children able to confidently compare two groups?
- Can children use the language learned in the lesson to describe the comparisons?
- Are all children able to organise groups clearly and accurately?

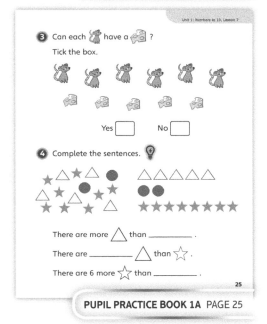

PUPIL PRACTICE BOOK 1A PAGE 24

PUPIL PRACTICE BOOK 1A PAGE 25

PUPIL PRACTICE BOOK 1A PAGE 26

Comparing numbers of objects

Learning focus

In this lesson, children will use the < > = symbols to compare two groups of objects. They will explain their comparisons using the correct mathematical language.

Small steps

→ Previous step: Comparing groups
→ **This step: Comparing numbers of objects**
→ Next step: Comparing numbers

NATIONAL CURRICULUM LINKS

Year 1 Number – Number and Place Value

Identify and represent numbers using concrete objects and pictorial representations including the number line, and use the language of: equal to, more than, less than (fewer), most, least.

ASSESSING MASTERY

Children can describe a number as greater than, less than or equal to another number and clearly explain how the < > = symbols are used. Children can demonstrate this knowledge using different representations.

COMMON MISCONCEPTIONS

Children are likely to confuse > (greater than) and < (less than). Ask: *Could you use multilink cubes to help you compare? How could the number track help you compare?*

STRENGTHENING UNDERSTANDING

To strengthen children's ability to count and compare, provide large versions of the > < = symbols. Ask:
- *Can you use these symbols to help you visualise the comparison?*

Encourage children to arrange different-sized towers of multilink cubes either side of each symbol. Ask:
- *Can you point to each amount and tell me the sentence you would say to compare?*
- *What side do you start reading from?*
- *Does the symbol begin with the bigger end or the smaller end?*

GOING DEEPER

Give children a number of multilink cubes. Encourage children to use them to investigate how many different ways they can partition a given number and then make comparisons between the different parts of the number using the symbols introduced in this lesson. Ask: *How many ways can you partition this number? Have you found all the comparisons you can make? Is there a pattern?*

KEY LANGUAGE

In lesson: greater than, >, less than, <, equal to, =

Other language to be used by the teacher: same, compare

STRUCTURES AND REPRESENTATIONS

Multilink cubes, ten frame, counters, 2D shapes (circles and triangles)

RESOURCES

Mandatory: multilink cubes

Optional: a selection of countable real-life objects such as tennis balls and footballs, large printed versions of the < > = symbols for children to hold and manipulate

Teaching Tools In the eTextbook of this lesson, you will find interactive links to a selection of teaching tools.

Before you teach

- Are children confident in their ability to recognise numbers that are bigger or smaller than one another?
- How will you make the difference between < and > as clear as possible?

Discover

WAYS OF WORKING Pair work

ASK

- *How many multilink cubes does Anya have?*
- *How else could you show the amounts in this picture?*
- *Can you order all the amounts from most to least?*

IN FOCUS Questions ❶ a) and ❶ b) ask children to compare two amounts. They move from comparing 'one more' and 'one less' to any amount more and less. Introduce the lesson's key language of comparison: 'less than' and 'greater than'.

ANSWERS

Question ❶ a): Tim has more than Lou.

Lou has fewer than Tim.

Question ❶ b): Tim and Anya have an equal number of .

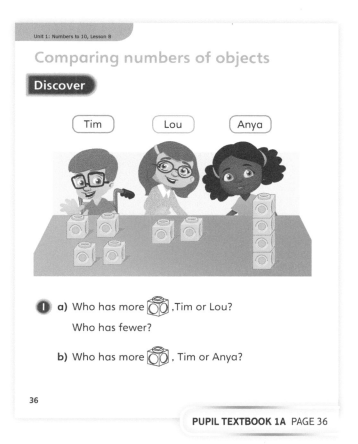

Comparing numbers of objects

Discover

Tim   Lou   Anya

❶ a) Who has more ,Tim or Lou?
Who has fewer?

b) Who has more , Tim or Anya?

36

PUPIL TEXTBOOK 1A PAGE 36

Share

WAYS OF WORKING Whole class teacher led

ASK

- *What could you use the > < = symbols to compare?*
- *How do the pictures show you how to use the symbols?*
- *How are > and < the same and how are they different?*
- *Can you show another two numbers that are equal?*

IN FOCUS Questions ❶ a) and ❶ b) introduce children to the lesson's key language. Use large printed versions of the < > = symbols for children to manipulate and arrange objects on.

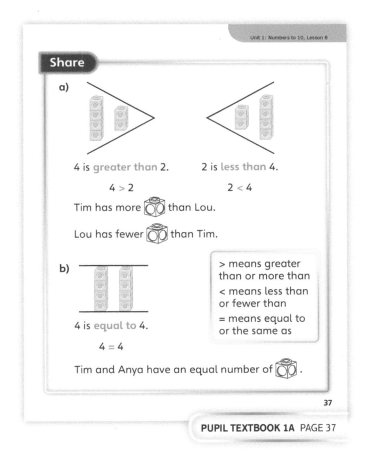

Share

a)

4 is greater than 2.   2 is less than 4.

$4 > 2$ $2 < 4$

Tim has more than Lou.

Lou has fewer than Tim.

b)

> means greater than or more than

< means less than or fewer than

= means equal to or the same as

4 is equal to 4.

$4 = 4$

Tim and Anya have an equal number of .

37

PUPIL TEXTBOOK 1A PAGE 37

Think together

WAYS OF WORKING Whole class teacher led (I do, We do, You do)

ASK

- Question **2**: *What do you need to do with the objects first?*
- *How could you represent the objects differently?*
- *Which symbol will you need to use? How do you know?*

IN FOCUS Question **2** reduces the amount of scaffolding provided to encourage children's use and understanding of the three symbols. Children do not have a picture of the symbol with blocks and the objects that they have to compare are different sizes.

STRENGTHEN Encourage children to arrange balls or cubes along a number track to help compare the two amounts in questions **1** and **2**.

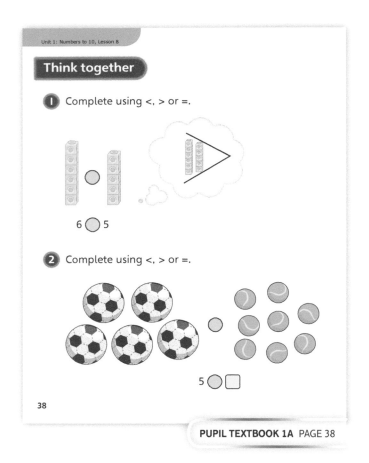

DEEPEN Use Ash's question in question **3** to discuss if there is more than one answer. Ask:
- *How many answers are there?*
- *Is it possible to find all the answers? Explain your ideas.*

ASSESSMENT CHECKPOINT Questions **2** and **3** should help you assess whether children can independently count and compare pictures or objects and numbers confidently or need the pictorial representations to support their use of the > < = symbols.

ANSWERS

Question **1**:

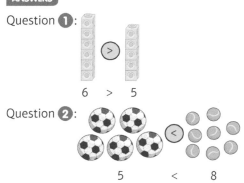

6 > 5

Question **2**:

5 < 8

Question **3**: For example, 5 > 4, 6 > 4 or 7 > 4.

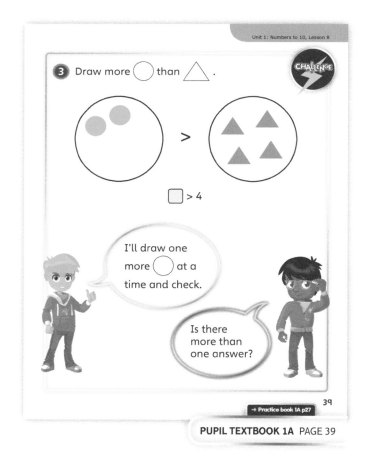

Practice

WAYS OF WORKING Independent thinking

IN FOCUS

- Question ❶ requires children to count, compare and record, using the symbols they have learned in this lesson.
- Question ❷ supports children's ability to reason and justify their ideas, demonstrating the kind of sentences that children can use to help explain their thoughts.

STRENGTHEN Encourage children to compare amounts by arranging blocks inside large printed versions of the > < = symbols. Ask: *How could you represent the objects? Do you recognise any of the representations in the pictures? What resources have you used before?*

DEEPEN Question ❺ develops children's ability to use and apply their understanding of the concepts taught in this lesson. Ask: *How can you prove that you have found all the possible solutions? Can you explain what you have found in a sentence using the language you have learnt?*

ASSESSMENT CHECKPOINT Questions ❶ to ❹ should help you to assess if children can describe comparisons between numbers using the > < = symbols.

ANSWERS Answers for the **Practice** part of the lesson appear in the separate **Practice and Reflect answer guide**.

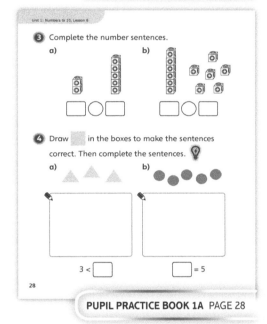

PUPIL PRACTICE BOOK 1A PAGE 27

PUPIL PRACTICE BOOK 1A PAGE 28

Reflect

WAYS OF WORKING Pair work

IN FOCUS This **Reflect** activity allows children to work with a partner to compare amounts and determine the correct number sentence, using the language and symbols they have learned in this lesson.

ASSESSMENT CHECKPOINT Assess children's use of the written language as well as the > < = symbols.

ANSWERS Answers for the **Reflect** part of the lesson appear in the separate **Practice and Reflect answer guide**.

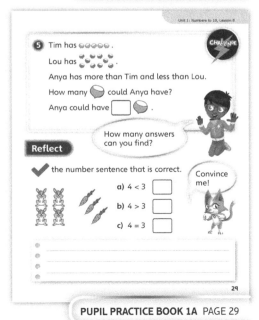

PUPIL PRACTICE BOOK 1A PAGE 29

After the lesson ⏸

- Are children using the > < = symbols accurately?
- Are children ready to use the > < = symbols in other contexts?

Comparing numbers

Learning focus

In this lesson, children will compare more abstract numbers where they are not given countable objects. Children will choose the best representation or resource to help them compare.

Small steps

→ Previous step: Comparing numbers of objects
→ **This step: Comparing numbers**
→ Next step: Ordering objects and numbers

NATIONAL CURRICULUM LINKS

Year 1 Number – Number and Place Value

Identify and represent numbers using concrete objects and pictorial representations including the number line, and use the language of: equal to, more than, less than (fewer), most, least.

ASSESSING MASTERY

Children can recognise numbers and link them to the amount they represent. Children can compare and order numbers represented in more abstract ways, using representations and resources they think most appropriate.

COMMON MISCONCEPTIONS

Children may confuse numerals and the amount they represent. Ask:
• *What tools have you used in the past to help you with what a number is worth?*

Children may confuse > (greater than) and < (less than). Ask:
• *Which side do you start reading from?*
• *Does the symbol begin with the bigger end or the smaller end?*

STRENGTHENING UNDERSTANDING

Provide number cards, each of which shows an amount represented using the number track or towers of multilink cubes, as well as the large > < = symbols used in Lesson 8.

GOING DEEPER

Give children two ten-sided dice each. Ask children to roll the dice and order the numbers that they have rolled using the < > = symbols.

KEY LANGUAGE

Other language to be used by the teacher: <, >, =, represent, more than, fewer than, greater than, how many same, compare

STRUCTURES AND REPRESENTATIONS

Multilink cubes

RESOURCES

Mandatory: multilink cubes, ten frames, counters, number tracks, bead strings

Optional: ten-sided dice, large printed versions of the < > = symbols for children to hold and manipulate, a selection of countable real-life objects such as pencils, a classroom display of the language and symbols of comparison

Teaching Tools In the eTextbook of this lesson, you will find interactive links to a selection of teaching tools.

Before you teach

• Are children ready to approach the abstract concepts in this lesson?
• What will you provide for those children still needing concrete materials or pictorial representations?

Discover

Pair work

ASK

• *Does Jess have 7 pencils? Where are her pencils?*
• *Whose pencils are easier to count? Why?*
• *How many pencils does Ted have?*
• *Who has the most pencils?*

IN FOCUS Question ❶ helps children to start recognising and comparing amounts using only numerals. The picture provides scaffolding for the journey from recognising concrete amounts (the pencils held by Bo), to reading the abstract numeral (the words spoken by Jess), to visualising an amount mentally (the pencils that Ted could have).

ANSWERS

Question ❶ a): Jess has more ✏ than Bo.

Question ❶ b): Ted could have 0, 1, 2 or 3 ✏ .

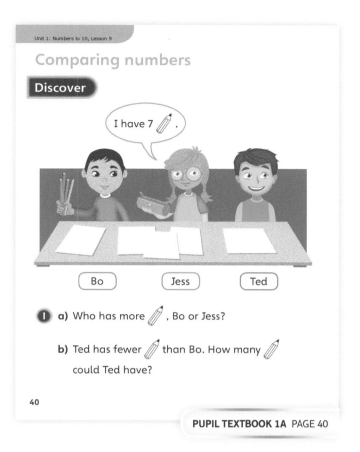

Share

Whole class teacher led

ASK

• *How do you know 7 is greater than 4?*
• *Why did Flo decide to represent pencils using multilink cubes?*
• *How does the number track help?*
• *How do the pictures in question ❶ b) help to prove the solutions?*
• *Would you use something different to represent the pencils? Why?*

IN FOCUS Questions ❶ a) and ❶ b) help children to move from comparing concrete amounts of pencils to the abstract comparison of the numerals. Use the pictures in question ❶ b) to discuss how children know that all the options have been found.

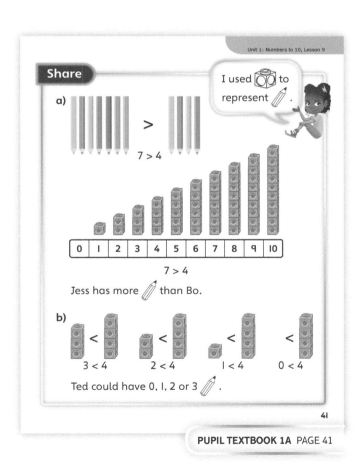

Think together

WAYS OF WORKING Whole class teacher led (I do, We do, You do)

ASK

- Question **1**: *What will you need to do first to compare the amounts of cookies?*
- Question **1**: *What symbol will you need to use? How can you prove that the symbol you have chosen is the correct one? Can you prove it in another way?*
- Question **2**: *How can you show your comparison of the scores?*

IN FOCUS Question **2** asks children to compare two scores. Be mindful of the potential misconceptions regarding the use of the > < = symbols and also recognising the value of the numerals. Reinforce children's use of different representations and the tools that they have used in previous lessons.

STRENGTHEN Have a display in the classroom that shows the language and symbols of comparison, so that children can refer to the display as a reminder.

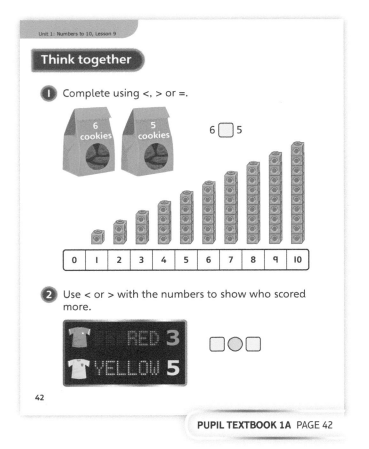

PUPIL TEXTBOOK 1A PAGE 42

DEEPEN Use Flo's comment about using multilink cubes to help her as an opportunity to discuss any other resources or representations that children might use. Using a variety of representations helps children to develop mathematical fluency and confidence.

ASSESSMENT CHECKPOINT Questions **2** and **3** will help you to decide if children can relate a numeral to the amount it represents. Can children compare the amounts in the questions and explain the comparison using the correct language and symbols?

ANSWERS

Question **1**: 6 > 5

Question **2**: 5 > 3, or 3 < 5

Question **3**: 8, 9 and 10 are greater than 7.

PUPIL TEXTBOOK 1A PAGE 43

Practice

WAYS OF WORKING Independent thinking

IN FOCUS Question ❶ helps children to practise comparing concrete amounts with abstract numerals. Questions ❷, ❸ and ❹ require children to compare only abstract numerals and to demonstrate their understanding of the related concrete amounts.

STRENGTHEN Ensure that children have access to all number resources and representations from the previous lessons to support their comparisons. Link the questions to contexts that children know and understand by asking questions, such as: *Would you rather have 6 sweets or 10 sweets? Why?*

DEEPEN Encourage children to work systematically to find all the solutions to Ash's question. Deepen their understanding by asking: *How many solutions can you find for '_ > 6'?*

ASSESSMENT CHECKPOINT Questions ❶ and ❷ should help you to assess if children can use the > < = symbols confidently and accurately. Questions ❸ and ❹ should help you to decide if children recognise and understand numerals.

ANSWERS Answers for the **Practice** part of the lesson appear in the separate **Practice and Reflect answer guide**.

Reflect

WAYS OF WORKING Whole class

IN FOCUS Develop this **Reflect** activity using different patterns. For example, you could use the following repeated pattern: 'bigger, bigger, smaller, bigger, bigger, smaller'. If children select 10 as the first 'bigger' in the repeated pattern, use this as an opportunity to begin discussing what is bigger than 10.

ASSESSMENT CHECKPOINT This **Reflect** activity should help you assess children's understanding of greater than and smaller than, as well as their understanding and fluency with numbers to 10.

ANSWERS Answers for the **Reflect** part of the lesson appear in the separate **Practice and Reflect answer guide**.

After the lesson ⏸

- Did moving from concrete materials and pictorial representations to the abstract concepts in this lesson result in any unexpected misconceptions?
- How will you approach these misconceptions in Lesson 10?

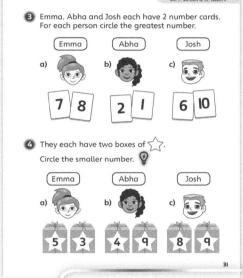

PUPIL PRACTICE BOOK 1A PAGE 30

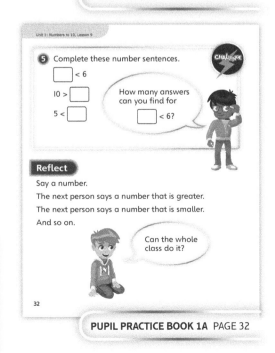

PUPIL PRACTICE BOOK 1A PAGE 31

PUPIL PRACTICE BOOK 1A PAGE 32

Ordering objects and numbers

Learning focus

In this lesson, children will compare three or more groups of objects or numbers and order them in both ascending and descending order.

Small steps

→ Previous step: Comparing numbers
→ **This step: Ordering objects and numbers**
→ Next step: First, second, third…

NATIONAL CURRICULUM LINKS

Year 1 Number – Number and Place Value

Identify and represent numbers using concrete objects and pictorial representations including the number line, and use the language of: equal to, more than, less than (fewer), most, least.

ASSESSING MASTERY

Children can confidently count groups of objects and recognise the comparative place values of numbers to 10. Children can compare more than two amounts and can arrange these amounts in both ascending and descending order, justifying their ideas using pictorial representations and concrete materials.

COMMON MISCONCEPTIONS

Children may arrange numbers in ascending order when asked to arrange them in descending order. Ask:
• *What does 'most' mean?*
• *Which number is the greatest?*

STRENGTHENING UNDERSTANDING

Provide number cards that show pictured examples of the concrete materials used in the lesson. For example, a card could show the numeral, the appropriate face of a dice, the number represented on a ten frame and so on. Link these number cards to a large number track displayed in the classroom.

GOING DEEPER

When children are confident ordering numbers and amounts in both ascending and descending order, ask: *What is the greatest difference you could find using the numbers 1–10? How can you prove your ideas?*

KEY LANGUAGE

In lesson: most, least, fewest, greatest

Other language to be used by the teacher: compare, order

STRUCTURES AND REPRESENTATIONS

Multilink cubes, ten frame, six-sided dice

RESOURCES

Mandatory: multilink cubes, ten frames, six-sided dice

Optional: a selection of countable real-life objects, three dolls, a bag of sweets

Teaching Tools In the eTextbook of this lesson, you will find interactive links to a selection of teaching tools.

Before you teach

• What challenges will you set children who can already compare more than two groups?
• Is there a representation of amounts that children are relying on more than other representations? How could you increase their confidence with the other representations?

Discover

WAYS OF WORKING Pair work

ASK

- *Who do you predict has more stickers? Explain.*
- *How many more stickers does Kat need before she has the same amount as Josh?*
- *How many fewer stickers does Josh have in comparison to Em?*
- *Can you order the amounts of stickers from greatest to least?*

IN FOCUS Questions ❶ a) and ❶ b) introduce the lesson's key language: 'most' and 'least'. Discuss ordering amounts from least to greatest and from greatest to least.

ANSWERS

Question ❶ a): Em has the most ⭐ .

Question ❶ b):

4	6	7
Kat	Josh	Em

Ordering objects and numbers

Discover

| Kat | Em | Josh |

❶ a) Who has the most ⭐ ?

b) Order the children from the one who has the least ⭐ to the one who has the most.

44

Share

WAYS OF WORKING Whole class teacher led

ASK

- *What should you do before you compare the amounts?*
- *Why has Astrid chosen to use multilink cubes?*
- *What will you use to represent the numbers? Explain why.*
- *What can you tell me about the numbers?*
- *Can you make a number sentence using the > < = symbols you have learnt about?*

IN FOCUS Questions ❶ a) and ❶ b) encourage children to order amounts from least to greatest when comparing amounts. Refer to Flo's question to assess if children can explain what 'most' means.

Share

I will use 🎲 to compare them.

What does most mean?

a)

Em has the most ⭐ .

b)

4	6	7
Kat	Josh	Em

45

Think together

Whole class teacher led (I do, We do, You do)

ASK

- *What clues can you use to find out how many stars Bob and Adam have?*
- *Who do you predict has the most stars? Explain your prediction.*
- *How could you order the amounts?*
- *Which is the greatest? How can you prove it?*
- *How many different ways can you show that amount?*

IN FOCUS Question ② introduces children to the key language: 'fewest'. It also develops their understanding that amounts can be sorted from greatest to least, as well as least to greatest. Question ③ introduces the key language: 'greatest'.

STRENGTHEN In question ①, support children making the link between the amount of cubes and the amount of stars that each child has by asking: *Why does Erin have four blocks above her? How many stars will Adam have? How do you know?*

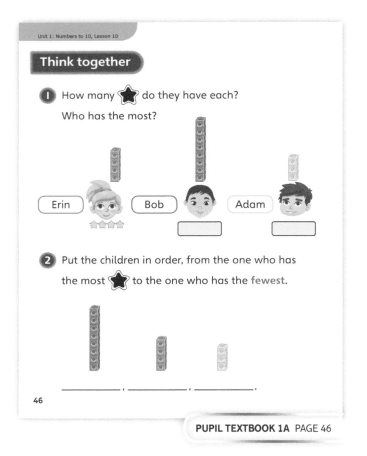

PUPIL TEXTBOOK 1A PAGE 46

DEEPEN Refer to Astrid's suggestion in question ③ and discuss other ways in which children could approach the question. Does Astrid use the only possible approach or can the numbers be shown using other resources, like a picture?

ASSESSMENT CHECKPOINT

- Questions ① and ② should help you decide if children can order amounts in both ascending and descending order.
- Question ③ should help you to assess if children can compare more than two amounts and discuss different ways of ordering them.

ANSWERS

Question ①: Erin has 4 ⭐, Bob has 8 ⭐, Adam has 3 ⭐. Bob has the most ⭐.

Question ②: Bob, Erin, Adam

Question ③ a): Toby rolled the greatest score.

Question ③ b): Eve rolled the least.

PUPIL TEXTBOOK 1A PAGE 47

Practice

WAYS OF WORKING Independent thinking

IN FOCUS Questions ❶ and ❷ allow children to demonstrate their understanding of greatest and least. The questions move from pictorial representations of objects to the abstract numerals. Question ❸ requires children to order numbers in ascending and descending order and use the lesson's key language and its meaning.

STRENGTHEN Display three dolls and give the dolls different amounts of sweets based on the numbers in question ❸. Ask: *Which doll has the most? Which has the least? Can you order the dolls so the one with the greatest number comes first? Can you order the dolls so the one with the least number comes first?*

DEEPEN In question ❺ use Flo's question to discuss why she thinks all of the towers might be the same. Encourage children to prove to her that they are different.

ASSESSMENT CHECKPOINT Question ❸ should help you decide if children are confident in their ability to order three or more numbers in both ascending and descending order. Assess whether children can explain the difference between ascending and descending order and how this difference affects the order of numbers.

ANSWERS Answers for the **Practice** part of the lesson appear in the separate **Practice and Reflect answer guide**.

Reflect

WAYS OF WORKING Pair work

IN FOCUS This **Reflect** activity allows children to discuss with a partner how they approached the problem. Highlight any similarities and differences in approaches, then discuss whether any one method is more efficient and why.

ASSESSMENT CHECKPOINT Assess if children are confident in their use of all of the lesson's language. Can children confidently explain their approach to the **Reflect** activity and justify it?

ANSWERS Answers for the **Reflect** part of the lesson appear in the separate **Practice and Reflect answer guide**.

After the lesson ⏸

- Did increasing the number of groups being compared create any unexpected issues? If so, what were the issues and how did they change your lesson?
- Are children able to arrange numbers in both ascending and descending order?

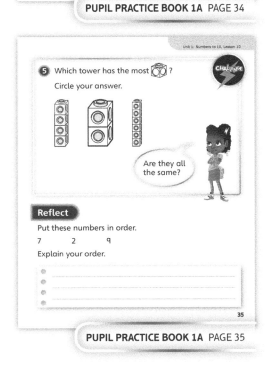

PUPIL PRACTICE BOOK 1A PAGE 33

PUPIL PRACTICE BOOK 1A PAGE 34

PUPIL PRACTICE BOOK 1A PAGE 35

First, second, third...

Learning focus

In this lesson, children will learn to describe the order and position of objects using ordinal numbers. They will develop their understanding of the difference between a numeral representing the number of objects and the ordinal position of something.

Small steps

→ Previous step: Ordering objects and numbers
→ **This step: First, second, third...**
→ Next step: The number line

NATIONAL CURRICULUM LINKS

Year 1 Number – Number and Place Value

Identify and represent numbers using concrete objects and pictorial representations including the number line, and use the language of: equal to, more than, less than (fewer), most, least.

ASSESSING MASTERY

Children can describe the position of an object in a set using ordinal numbers. Children can confidently describe how a number representing an amount is different to a number representing an ordinal position.

COMMON MISCONCEPTIONS

Children may confuse cardinal numbers and ordinal numbers, such as 5 and 5th. For example, when asked to colour the fifth object, children may colour five objects in. Ask:
• *Can you point to the first object in the list?*
• *Can you point to the second object in the list?*
• *When you pointed to the fifth position, how many objects were you pointing at?*

Children may start counting from the wrong end of a collection of objects. Ask:
• *Can you point to the first word of a sentence? Where is the second word?*

STRENGTHENING UNDERSTANDING

Strengthen understanding by having children take part in races outside. Ask: *How do you know who won the race? How can you describe the person who follows the winner? What about the next person after them?*

GOING DEEPER

Design simple riddles for children to solve. For example, ask: *Can you order where everyone finished in the race? Tim finished behind Milly. John finished in front of Tim. Milly was first.*

KEY LANGUAGE

In lesson: 1st, first, 2nd, second, 3rd, third, 4th, fourth, 5th, fifth, 6th, sixth, 7th, seventh, 8th, eighth, 9th, ninth, 10th, tenth
Other language to be used by the teacher: order

STRUCTURES AND REPRESENTATIONS

Counters, 2D shapes (triangle, circle, square, rectangle)

RESOURCES

Optional: a selection of orderable and countable objects, number cards displaying ordinal numbers, number tracks listing ordinal numbers in order, cards displaying the four images in question 1 from the **practice book**

Teaching Tools In the eTextbook of this lesson, you will find interactive links to a selection of teaching tools.

Before you teach

• Have any children had experience with ordinal numbers outside of school, such as in competitions?
• How could you use this experience to engage children's interest in the concept from the beginning?

Discover

WAYS OF WORKING Pair work

ASK

• *What subject do you think the children are doing?*
• *How have the activities been ordered?*
• *How can you tell which activity is the first activity? How can you tell which activity is the fourth activity?*

IN FOCUS Questions **1** a) and **1** b) give children their first experience of the ordinal language that they will use throughout the lesson. Discuss other places where children may have heard this language before, such as in sports competitions.

ANSWERS

Question **1** a): The second activity is throwing a bean bag into a bucket.

Question **1** b): The fourth activity is jumping over some cones.

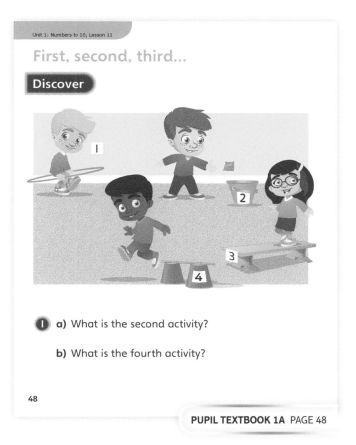

Share

WAYS OF WORKING Whole class teacher led

ASK

• *How has the order of the activities been made clearer in this picture?*
• *What else can you say about the order that the children are in?*
• *In what place is the girl balancing on a bench?*
• *How many children are doing the fourth activity?*

IN FOCUS Questions **1** a) and **1** b) provide an opportunity to address the misconception that the ordinal number has to match the amount that is in that position. Approach this by discussing how many children are doing each activity. For example, fourth position does not have to mean that four children are doing the activity.

77

Think together

WAYS OF WORKING Whole class teacher led (I do, We do, You do)

ASK

- *Where do you begin counting from?*
- *Can you begin counting in the middle of the group?*
- Question ❶: *How can you tell which is third place?*
- Question ❶: *If you are looking for the third position should you keep counting to the fifth position?*
- Question ❷: *How far do you need to count if you are looking for the fourth position?*

IN FOCUS Questions ❶ and ❷ develop children's recognition of and ability to count in ordinal numbers. Ensure that children are comfortable and confident with where to begin counting along an organised group.

STRENGTHEN Provide a number track with ordinal numbers positioned on it for children who are still developing their ability to recognise and use ordinal numbers.

PUPIL TEXTBOOK 1A PAGE 50

DEEPEN When approaching question ❸, discuss what is meant by 'after the sixth person' and why Dexter thinks there is more than one person. Ask: *Is Ash's idea a useful one? Would circling sixth place help you?*

ASSESSMENT CHECKPOINT Question ❸ should help you to assess if children can use the ordinal numbers to describe the positions of objects within an ordered group.

ANSWERS

Question ❶: The third child is May.

Question ❷: The fourth pizza's topping is meat.

Question ❸: Jack and Lola come after the sixth person.

PUPIL TEXTBOOK 1A PAGE 51

Practice

WAYS OF WORKING Independent thinking

IN FOCUS

- Question **2** requires children to recognise that ordinal number and cardinal number do not have to be the same. For example, in question **2** a), colour the fourth object does not mean 'colour in four objects'.
- Question **3** requires children to recognise that objects can be counted from different starting points.

STRENGTHEN

- When approaching question **1**, provide the pictures available as individual cards for children to manipulate and arrange.
- When approaching question **3**, ensure that children recognise the shapes within the picture by having them build the picture using concrete 2D shapes.

DEEPEN If children use and apply their understanding of ordinal numbers correctly when answering questions **4** and **5**, encourage them to create similar puzzles for themselves.

ASSESSMENT CHECKPOINT Question **2** should help you assess whether children are confidently identifying which end of the group to start counting from and recognising that the amount of objects that fills a position is not necessarily the same as the position's ordinal number.

ANSWERS Answers for the **Practice** part of the lesson appear in the separate **Practice and Reflect answer guide**.

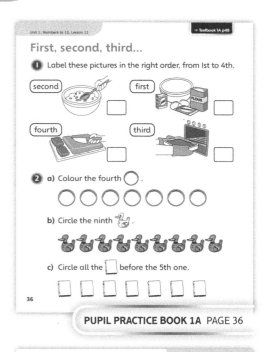

PUPIL PRACTICE BOOK 1A PAGE 36

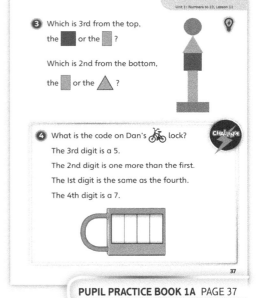

PUPIL PRACTICE BOOK 1A PAGE 37

Reflect

WAYS OF WORKING Pair work

IN FOCUS This **Reflect** activity gives children the opportunity to practise using the language of ordinal numbers with a partner.

ASSESSMENT CHECKPOINT Assess whether children can assess their partner's use of ordinal language and reason and justify their own ideas.

ANSWERS Answers for the **Reflect** part of the lesson appear in the separate **Practice and Reflect answer guide**.

After the lesson

- Are children fully able to recognise the difference between cardinal numbers and ordinal numbers?
- Did you encounter any misconceptions in this lesson that you didn't expect to encounter? How will you approach these misconceptions in Lesson 12?

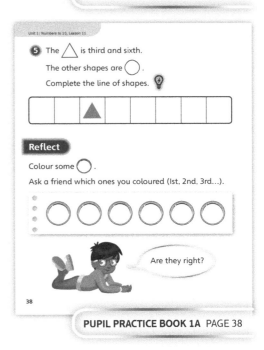

PUPIL PRACTICE BOOK 1A PAGE 38

The number line

Learning focus

In this lesson, children will learn to recognise and use the representation of a number line to help them answer questions based on all of the learning in this unit.

Small steps

→ Previous step: First, second, third…
→ **This step: The number line**
→ Next step: The part-whole model (1)

NATIONAL CURRICULUM LINKS

Year 1 Number – Number and Place Value

Identify and represent numbers using concrete objects and pictorial representations including the number line, and use the language of: equal to, more than, less than (fewer), most, least.

ASSESSING MASTERY

Children can use a number line to help them answer questions based on the learning that has taken place throughout Unit 1. Children can explain how a number line works, how it represents numbers and amounts and how it helps them to compare, order and count up and down from different numbers.

COMMON MISCONCEPTIONS

Children may not recognise that a number line features 0 as an amount. This is different to the number track and the ten frame that children have met so far, because these representations only start recording amounts at 1. Ask: *What number does the number track start at? What number does the number line start at? How are they different?*

Give children groups that contain different amounts of objects and ask children to point to the correct number on the number line. Give them a group of 0 things and ask: *Where would you place this group on a number line? Could you represent this group on the number line if the 0 wasn't on the number line?*

STRENGTHENING UNDERSTANDING

To introduce the concept of the number line, play a simple dice game along a number line. Start at 0 and roll a six-sided dice to move up the number line. This game could be played outside with a large number line drawn in chalk on the ground.

GOING DEEPER

Give children a template to create their own missing number questions for a partner to complete using a number line. Ensure that children check their own questions before giving them to their partner.

KEY LANGUAGE

In lesson: number line

Other language to be used by the teacher: order, greater, one more, one less

STRUCTURES AND REPRESENTATIONS

Number line, multilink cubes

RESOURCES

Mandatory: number line, multilink cubes, six-sided dice, a printed example of a correct number line to show children

Optional: six-sided dice, chalk, ten frames, number tracks, a selection of countable real-life objects such as bags or pencil cases

 In the eTextbook of this lesson, you will find interactive links to a selection of teaching tools.

Before you teach

- How will you make the links between this representation and the previous representations clear?
- Could these links be displayed in the classroom to help provide scaffolding for children's understanding?

Discover

WAYS OF WORKING Pair work

ASK

- *What numbers do you recognise?*
- *What numbers are missing?*
- *Do the numbers match how many bags there are?*

IN FOCUS Questions ① a) and ① b) offer children their first opportunity to work with numbers on a number line. Question ① a) recaps their understanding of cardinal numbers by requiring them to recognise the missing numbers.

ANSWERS

Question ① a): 4, 8 and 9 are missing.

Question ① b): 3 is upside-down. 6 and 7 are in the wrong order.

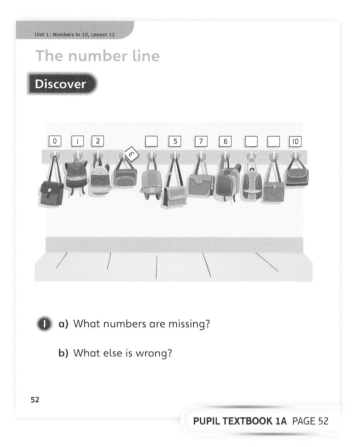

The number line

Discover

① a) What numbers are missing?

b) What else is wrong?

52

PUPIL TEXTBOOK 1A PAGE 52

Share

WAYS OF WORKING Whole class teacher led

ASK

- *How did you know what numbers were missing?*
- *How did you know that 6 and 7 were in the wrong order?*
- *Why is this called a number line?*
- *How is this number line similar to the representations you have used before? What is different about it?*
- *Can you see any patterns in the number line?*

IN FOCUS Flo introduces the lesson's key language: 'number line'. Discuss the fact that the number line begins at 0.

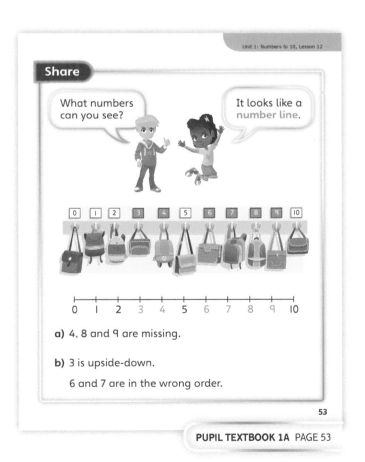

Share

What numbers can you see?

It looks like a number line.

a) 4, 8 and 9 are missing.

b) 3 is upside-down.

6 and 7 are in the wrong order.

53

PUPIL TEXTBOOK 1A PAGE 53

Think together

WAYS OF WORKING Whole class teacher led (I do, We do, You do)

ASK

- Question **1**: *How do you know where the missing numbers are?*
- Question **1**: *How can you tell what the missing numbers are?*
- Question **2**: *How many multilink cubes would be above the number 0?*

IN FOCUS Question **1** reinforces children's understanding of how a number line is constructed and what patterns can be found. Question **2** links this lesson's representation to children's previous learning.

STRENGTHEN Link the number line to other representations from previous lessons, such as the ten frame and the number track. Ask: *How are the representations the same? How are they different?*

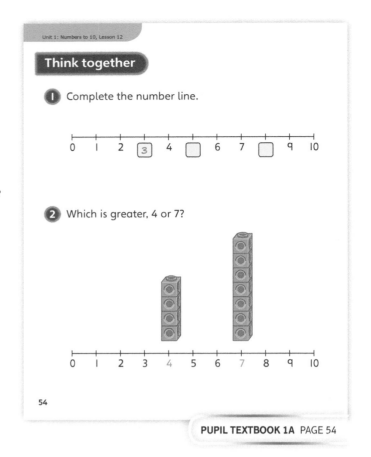

DEEPEN To deepen their understanding and fluency with the concept of 'one more' and 'one less', children could challenge each other with a guessing game. Ask children to choose a number but to keep it secret (alternatively, they could pick a number card and keep it hidden). They should tell their partner which number is one more than their mystery number and which is one less. Can their partner guess their number based on the clues given to them?

ASSESSMENT CHECKPOINT Question **1** should help you to assess whether children can recognise a number line and explain the way the numbers are arranged along it. Question **2** should help you to decide whether children can use the number line to help them compare the size of numbers to 10. Question **3** should show whether children can use the number line to count forwards and backwards by one.

ANSWERS

Question **1**: 5 and 8 are missing.

Question **2**: 7 is greater than 4.

Question **3** a): 7 is one more than 6.

Question **3** b): 5 is one less than 6.

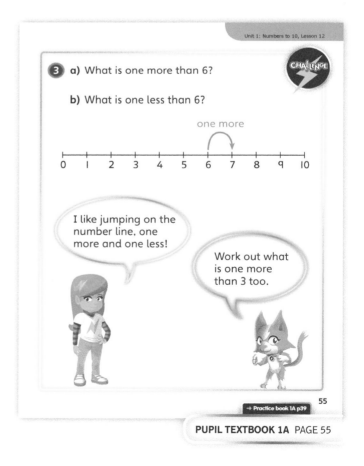

Practice

WAYS OF WORKING Independent thinking

IN FOCUS Questions **1** and **2** allow children to demonstrate their understanding of the number line and how numbers are arranged along it. The questions provide decreasing levels of scaffolding and require children to visualise more of the numbers on the unlabelled divisions. Questions **3** and **4** allow children to use the number line to practise skills learned in previous lessons.

STRENGTHEN If children complete the number line in question **1** incorrectly, show them a printed example of a correct number line and ask them to identify what is the same and what is different between their line and the printed line.

DEEPEN In question **6** use Flo's comment to discuss whether circling the numbers on the number line is a useful thing to do. Ask: *Will it help you? How?*

ASSESSMENT CHECKPOINT Questions **3** to **5** should help you assess whether children can use the number line fluently to compare the size of numbers to 10 and to count forwards and backwards by 1 or more.

ANSWERS Answers for the **Practice** part of the lesson appear in the separate **Practice and Reflect answer guide**.

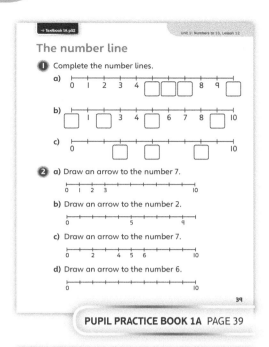

PUPIL PRACTICE BOOK 1A PAGE 39

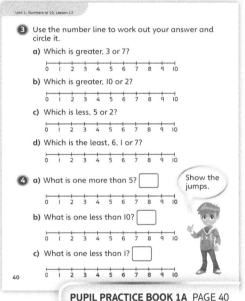

PUPIL PRACTICE BOOK 1A PAGE 40

Reflect

WAYS OF WORKING Independent thinking

IN FOCUS This **Reflect** activity allows children to reflect on what they have learnt in this lesson and link it to concepts that they have learnt throughout Unit 1. Discuss what children feel they have learnt to use the number line to do. Point out the different uses that children mention.

ASSESSMENT CHECKPOINT Assess whether children can identify uses for the number line and confidently use the appropriate language to explain their ideas.

ANSWERS Answers for the **Reflect** part of the lesson appear in the separate **Practice and Reflect answer guide**.

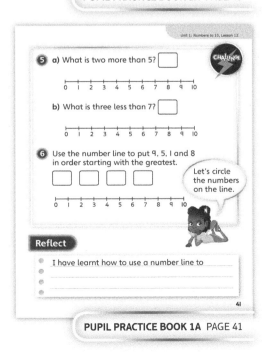

PUPIL PRACTICE BOOK 1A PAGE 41

After the lesson ⏸

- Are children able to confidently apply their knowledge and understanding to the new representation? Did this lesson highlight any lingering misconceptions around the concepts taught in previous lessons?
- Did children have enough opportunities to explain their reasoning about number lines?

End of unit check

Don't forget the End of unit check proforma (page 56)!

WAYS OF WORKING Group work – adult led

IN FOCUS
- Questions **1**, **3** and **5** focus on children's understanding of counting forwards and backwards from numbers up to 10.
- Question **2** assesses children's understanding of the ten-frame representation of numbers up to 10.
- Question **4** assesses children's ability to compare two numbers and describe their relationship to each other.

Think!

WAYS OF WORKING Pair work or small groups

IN FOCUS This question assesses children's ability to recognise and compare numbers to 10. They should be able to recognise that 6 has been partitioned in two different ways, giving three amounts to compare (the red balloons, the yellow balloons and all the balloons). Ask:
- *What is the same and different about the two sets of balloons?*
- *What numbers can you see in the pictures?*
- *Who has more red balloons? How do you know?*

Draw children's attention to the words at the bottom of the My journal page and encourage them to use them in their answers.

Encourage children to think through or discuss how many balloons Bea and Seth have, and what they can say about those balloons, before writing their answer in My journal.

ANSWERS AND COMMENTARY Children will demonstrate mastery in this concept by recognising and comparing the different numbers they can see in the picture. They will count reliably and fluently and use language such as 'more', 'less' and 'equal'. If asked to, they should be able to choose an appropriate representation for the balloons and use this to help prove their comparisons.

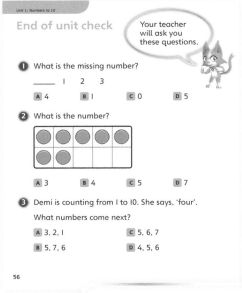

PUPIL TEXTBOOK 1A PAGE 56

PUPIL TEXTBOOK 1A PAGE 57

Q	A	WRONG ANSWERS AND MISCONCEPTIONS	STRENGTHENING UNDERSTANDING
1	C	Choosing B suggests that the child is not confident with the concept of 0.	To help children gain fluency in counting on and back, give them a number track or number line and ask: • *Can you point to the number you are starting at?* • *Which way will you move along the track/line if you are counting forward/back?* Give children opportunities to compare numbers using concrete resources. Ask: • *How could you represent the numbers?* • *What do you notice about them?* • *Which number is greater? How do you know?*
2	D	Choosing A suggests that the child has counted the blank spaces.	
3	C	Choosing D indicates that the child has recognised they need to count forward but has started at 4, not the number following it.	
4	D	Choosing A or B could indicate a lack of understanding of the value of the numbers or the vocabulary of 'more' and 'less' (also Q5 B, C).	
5	A	Choosing C suggests that the child has counted one less, rather than one more.	

My journal

WAYS OF WORKING Independent thinking

ANSWERS AND COMMENTARY

What is the same?
• Each child has six balloons.
• Both children have red and yellow balloons.

What is different?
• Bea has 2 more red balloons than Seth.
• Seth has 2 fewer red balloons than Bea.
• Bea has 5 red balloons and Seth has 3.
• Seth has 2 more yellow balloons than Bea.
• Bea has 2 fewer yellow balloons than Seth.
• Bea has 1 yellow balloon and Seth has 3.

If children are finding it difficult to articulate anything but surface similarities and differences (for example, 'They are different colours.'), ask:
• *Do they have the same number of red/yellow balloons? How do you know?*
• *Who has more red/yellow balloons? Can you prove it?*

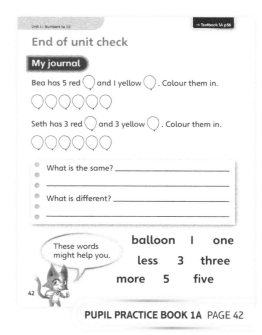

PUPIL PRACTICE BOOK 1A PAGE 42

Power check

WAYS OF WORKING Independent thinking

ASK
• *How confident do you feel when counting up/back to/from 10?*
• *Do you prefer using a number track or a number line? Why?*

Power play

WAYS OF WORKING Pair work or small groups

IN FOCUS Use this Power play to assess whether children are fluent making numbers up to 10 using the ten frame. Children should be able to recognise and demonstrate that any number below ten can be arranged in different ways and still be worth the same amount.

ANSWERS AND COMMENTARY Children should realise that 9 is the biggest number they can make. They will show through their discussion that they can compare two numbers, explaining how they know which is bigger and which is smaller. They will recognise that a number can be presented in different ways on a ten frame but still keep its same value.

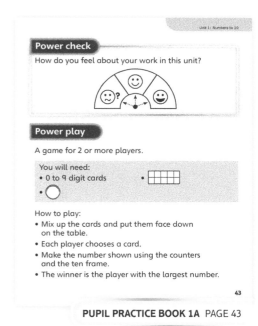

PUPIL PRACTICE BOOK 1A PAGE 43

After the unit ⏸

• In what other areas of the curriculum could you use the skills learned in this unit? For example: comparisons of measurements in science, counting down to start a race in P.E.
• Were children honest in their assessment of their own ability? How could you develop their ability to self-assess in future lessons?

Strengthen and *Deepen* activities for this unit can be found in the Power Maths online subscription.

Unit 2
Part-whole within 10

Mastery Expert tip! "When I taught this unit I found it was worth spending a good amount of time ensuring children could confidently identify the parts and the whole before starting to deal with finding missing numbers. Taking my time with the early lessons meant my children ended up making more rapid progress in the later lessons."

Don't forget to watch the unit 2 video!

WHY THIS UNIT IS IMPORTANT

This is one of the most important units of work to teach in maths. Children who have a solid grasp of numbers to 10 are able to apply this knowledge to so many other areas, including numbers to 20, numbers to 50 and beyond, and addition and subtraction.

Conversely, children who are not secure with the idea of partitioning within 10 may end up constantly playing catch up, due to the vast number of topics that rely on this knowledge. It is therefore worth spending time exploring this concept in depth.

WHERE THIS UNIT FITS

→ Unit 1: Numbers to 10
→ **Unit 2: Part-whole within 10**
→ Unit 3: Addition and subtraction within 10 (1)

This unit, which builds on Unit 1: Numbers to 10, introduces children to the part-whole model, focusing on different ways of partitioning numbers to 10. Children use the part-whole model to help them write and compare number bonds. They will continue to use these skills in Unit 3, which focuses on addition and subtraction.

Before they start this unit, it is expected that children:
- know how to sort and compare objects to 10
- understand how to count forwards and backwards within 10
- can order a set of numbers and use the vocabulary 'less than', 'more than' and 'equal to'.

ASSESSING MASTERY

Children who have mastered this unit will be able to confidently partition numbers within ten using a part-whole model. They can write the associated number sentences and be flexible with where they write the = symbol; for example, they know that 3 + 2 = 5 and 5 = 3 + 2 represent the same fact.

As children gain in confidence, they can compare number sentences using the <, > and = symbols, and use a systematic approach to solve problems.

COMMON MISCONCEPTIONS	STRENGTHENING UNDERSTANDING	GOING DEEPER
Children may confuse the parts and the whole, particularly when the part-whole model is oriented differently.	Allow children to spend time recognising and identifying the parts and the whole in a part-whole model without any numbers in it. This means children only have one thing to focus on and learn.	Children could explore part-whole models with more than two parts. It is important to ensure that the whole remains within 10.
Children may write incorrect number sentences based on confused part-whole thinking; for example, thinking that 4 + 6 = 2 is the same as 4 + 2 = 6.	Encourage children to use cubes to prove their answers and reinforce the meaning of the = symbol.	Ask children more open-ended questions, such as: The whole is 8, what could the parts be? How many different number sentences can you write?

WAYS OF WORKING

Introduce the unit using teacher-led discussion. Give children time to discuss each question in small groups or pairs and then discuss their ideas as a class.

STRUCTURES AND REPRESENTATIONS

Part-whole model: This model helps children understand that two or more parts combine to make a whole. It also helps to strengthen children's understanding of number.

Five frame and ten frame: The five and ten frames help to give children a sense of the numbers, and support their understanding of number bonds to 5 and 10. They also play a key role in helping children to recognise the structure of other numbers, and to understand what happens when you add two numbers together.

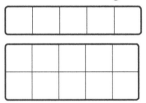

Bead string: The bead string is a great way of introducing children to patterns and helping them be systematic in their approach. They can find answers by moving one bead at a time, each time recording the number sentence they have represented.

KEY LANGUAGE

There is some key language that children will need to know as part of the learning in this unit.

- → part-whole model, part, whole, groups
- → number sentence, number bonds
- → plus
- → equal to
- → more than, less than

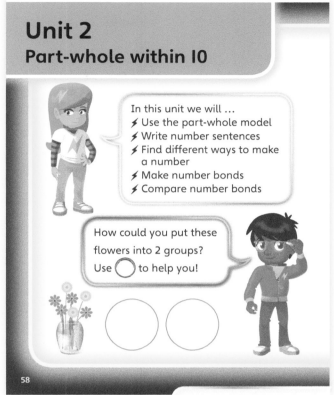

**Unit 2
Part-whole within 10**

In this unit we will ...
- ⚡ Use the part-whole model
- ⚡ Write number sentences
- ⚡ Find different ways to make a number
- ⚡ Make number bonds
- ⚡ Compare number bonds

How could you put these flowers into 2 groups? Use ◯ to help you!

58

PUPIL TEXTBOOK 1A PAGE 58

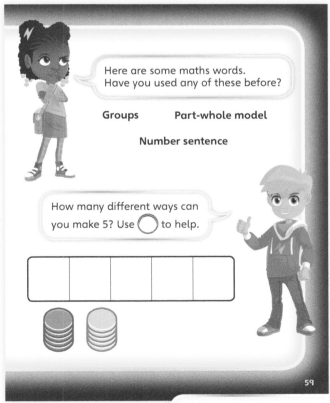

Here are some maths words. Have you used any of these before?

Groups   Part-whole model

Number sentence

How many different ways can you make 5? Use ◯ to help.

59

PUPIL TEXTBOOK 1A PAGE 59

The part-whole model ❶

Learning focus

In this lesson children learn that a number can be partitioned into two parts using a part-whole model. Children explore that numbers can be partitioned in different ways.

Small steps

→ Previous step: The number line
→ **This step: The part-whole model 1**
→ Next step: The part-whole model 2

NATIONAL CURRICULUM LINKS

Year 1 Number – Number and Place Value

Represent and use number bonds and related subtraction facts within 20.

ASSESSING MASTERY

Children can partition numbers to ten using a part-whole model.

COMMON MISCONCEPTIONS

Children may get the numbers mixed up. For example, they may write 5 as the whole and 6 and 1 as the parts. This is most likely to happen if the part-whole model is orientated differently. Ask:
• *In these part-whole models can you point to the whole? Can you point to the parts?*
• *Where should the biggest number go?*

STRENGTHENING UNDERSTANDING

Use hoops in the playground to introduce the idea of the part-whole model. Children can stand in the hoops and experiment with different combinations. If 7 is the whole, how many different ways can children stand in the hoops?

GOING DEEPER

To extend the practical activity above, children can decide what they should do if one child steps out of one of the hoops. Can the other children stay where they are? Does someone have to leave both of the other hoops or just one of them? What if two children leave each part? How many children need to leave the hoop representing the whole?

KEY LANGUAGE

In lesson: group, part-whole model, whole, part, diagram, different

Other language to be used by the teacher: partition, biggest, true, false

STRUCTURES AND REPRESENTATIONS

Part-whole model, cubes

RESOURCES

Mandatory: part-whole model

Optional: counters, hoops, teddy bears, selection of countable objects

Teaching Tools | In the eTextbook of this lesson, you will find interactive links to a selection of teaching tools.

Before you teach ❚❚

• Are all children secure with the idea of one-to-one correspondence used in numbers to ten?
• What resources will you provide for children who are still developing these ideas?

Discover

WAYS OF WORKING Pair work

ASK

- *Can you use any of the equipment on your table to show what the picture shows?*
- *Do you both agree with the number that is missing in the part-whole model?*
- *Can you explain to your partner how you got your answer?*

IN FOCUS In this part of the lesson children begin to learn about the idea that a number can be partitioned into two groups. They should think about and discuss with their partner what number goes in the missing part of the part-whole model.

ANSWERS

Question ① a): There are 6 children. There are 2 children in one group and 4 children in the other group.

Question ① b):

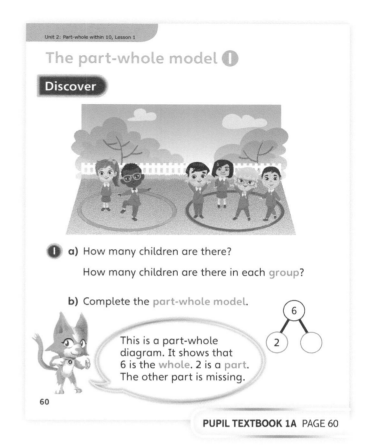

PUPIL TEXTBOOK 1A PAGE 60

Share

WAYS OF WORKING Whole class teacher led

ASK

- *What did you use to show the part-whole model of the children?*
- *Which number represents the whole?*
- *Which numbers represent the parts?*
- *Would it still work if you put the 4 in the red circle and the 2 in the blue circle? Is this still correct?*
- *Can I swap the 2 and 6 around? Is the part-whole model still correct?*

IN FOCUS Here children are looking at the part-whole model in more detail. They should be able to recognise which number is the whole and which numbers represent the parts. They also begin to experiment with which numbers can be moved and which numbers cannot.

PUPIL TEXTBOOK 1A PAGE 61

Think together

Think together

WAYS OF WORKING Whole class teacher led (I do, We do, You do)

ASK

- Question **1**: *Can you use counters or cubes to represent the children?*
- Question **1**: *If both parts are 3, is the whole 3?*
- Question **2**: *Does it matter which way around we draw our part-whole model?*
- Question **2**: *Which numbers can move and which numbers cannot?*
- Question **2**: *Can you move one of the numbers so that the part-whole model is no longer correct?*
- Question **3**: *How many ways can you find?*
- Question **3**: *Can you show me a way where one of the numbers is zero? Are the children now in two groups or are they still in one group?*

IN FOCUS In this part of the lesson children are learning that part-whole models can be presented in different ways. Children need to have a thorough grasp of the concept of the parts and the whole in order to complete part-whole diagrams in different orientations.

STRENGTHEN All of the activities can be done practically outside using big hoops or chalk circles. Let children experiment then encourage them to find all the combinations in a systematic way. For example, if the whole is 7, children could start with one circle empty and the other with all 7 in. They could move 1 child into the empty circle so that there is 1 and 6, move another so that there is 2 and 5, and so on until the other circle is empty.

DEEPEN To deepen understanding and expand thinking, ask children: *How do you know you have found all the possible ways of filling the part-whole model? Can you prove it using cubes?*

ASSESSMENT CHECKPOINT Questions **1** and **2** assess children's understanding of the part and the whole. In question **1**, children could easily fall into the trap of thinking the whole is 3 if they don't really understand that two parts make up a whole.

ANSWERS

Question **1**:

Question **2**: Yes, each of the part-whole models is correct.

Question **3**: Children could be arranged as:
- 1 and 7, or 7 and 1
- 2 and 6, or 6 and 2
- 3 and 5, or 5 and 3
- 4 and 4
- In this situation, we cannot use 0 and 7 as the children would then still be in one group, but it would be correct for an abstract part-whole.

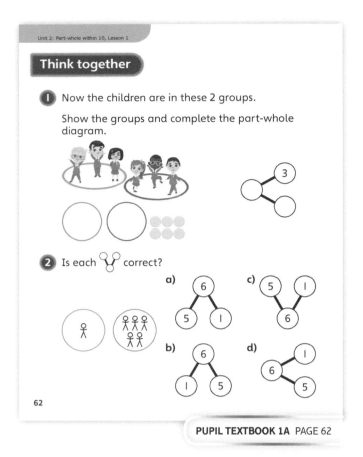

PUPIL TEXTBOOK 1A PAGE 62

PUPIL TEXTBOOK 1A PAGE 63

Practice

WAYS OF WORKING Independent thinking

IN FOCUS Children move between pictorial and abstract to partition numbers to ten using a part-whole model. Questions are presented in a variety of orientations to ensure children have a thorough understanding of the whole and the parts.

STRENGTHEN Encourage children to use cubes or counters to make each part-whole model. The questions could be linked to familiar situations to help them understand groups. For example, at a teddy bears' picnic, three teddy bears sit in one group and four teddy bears sit in another group. How many teddy bears are there altogether? Use actual teddy bears to show the groups.

DEEPEN Give children a number and ask them to show you all the possible part-whole models they can for this number. Ask: *Will each number make the same number of part-whole models? Which number (to 10) makes the greatest number of part-whole models? Is it possible to make a part-whole model for the number 1?*

ASSESSMENT CHECKPOINT Questions ❶, ❷ and ❸ check that children can read and interpret a part-whole model. Check that children are able to link a picture to an abstract model.

The numbers in question ❹ have been chosen purposely. The whole is the same in the first two models with one missing part, so children may be tempted to fill the empty circles with 3 and 6 if they do not fully understand the parts and the whole.

ANSWERS Answers for the **Practice** part of the lesson appear in the separate **Practice and Reflect answer guide**.

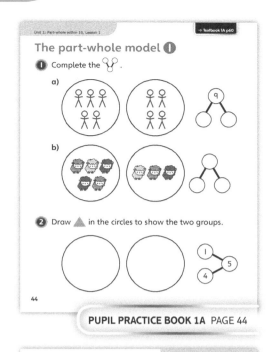

PUPIL PRACTICE BOOK 1A PAGE 44

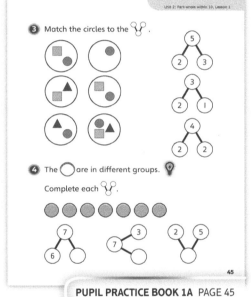

PUPIL PRACTICE BOOK 1A PAGE 45

Reflect

WAYS OF WORKING Independent thinking

IN FOCUS Children stretch their thinking on part-whole models in this part of the lesson. In all but one situation the whole will always be the biggest number as it is made up of two parts.

ASSESSMENT CHECKPOINT Have a show of hands to see who thinks the Reflect statement is true and who thinks it is false. Can children explain their reasons? Most children are likely to say that it is true unless they are thinking of the number 1; this is the only case where the whole is not bigger than the parts.

ANSWERS Answers for the **Reflect** part of the lesson appear in the separate **Practice and Reflect answer guide**.

After the lesson ⏸

- Did any of the children become confused when the part-whole model was presented in a different orientation?
- Were children able to find all the possible part-whole models for a specific number? Did they include examples with zero?

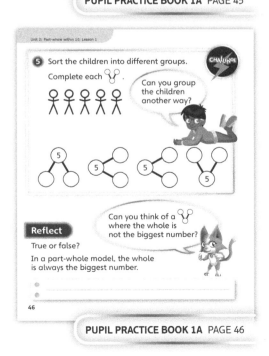

PUPIL PRACTICE BOOK 1A PAGE 46

The part-whole model ②

Learning focus

In this lesson children continue to use part-whole models to partition numbers to ten. They move their learning on by linking their part-whole models to an addition sentence.

Small steps

→ Previous step: The part-whole model 1
→ **This step: The part-whole model 2**
→ Next step: Related facts – number bonds

NATIONAL CURRICULUM LINKS

Year 1 Number – Number and Place Value

• Read, write and interpret mathematical statements involving addition (+), subtraction (–) and equals (=) signs.
• Represent and use number bonds and related subtraction facts within 20.

ASSESSING MASTERY

Children can partition numbers to ten and represent them in a part-whole model. They can link their part-whole model to a number sentence using the + and = symbols and write their number sentences with the = symbol in different places.

COMMON MISCONCEPTIONS

Children often think that the calculation has to come first, then the = symbol, then the answer. For example, 3 + 4 = 7. They also may not realise that they can use zero in their part-whole models or their number sentences. Ask:
• *Can you say this number sentence out loud? 'Three plus four is equal to seven.'*
• *If I say seven is equal to three plus four, is that the same? What is different about the two sentences?*
• *Can you think of an example using zero?*

STRENGTHENING UNDERSTANDING

Children can set up the first activity in question ① for themselves using pencils from the classroom. This will also help them to consolidate their counting.

GOING DEEPER

To deepen learning, encourage children to find different ways of writing number sentences using both digits and words. For example: 9 = 5 + 4, 9 = 4 + 5, 4 + 5 = 9, 5 + 4 = 9, nine is equal to five plus four, etc.

KEY LANGUAGE

In lesson: how many, **number sentence**, **equal to**, **plus**, groups, +, =

Other language to be used by the teacher: part-whole model, partition, part, whole, equal to, same, different

STRUCTURES AND REPRESENTATIONS

Part-whole model, cubes

RESOURCES

Mandatory: part-whole model, cubes

Optional: countable objects such as pencils, hoops, teddy bears, etc.

Teaching Tools In the eTextbook of this lesson, you will find interactive links to a selection of teaching tools.

Before you teach

• Are children secure with the idea of the parts and the whole?
• Are children confident using the language: part, whole and partition?

Discover

Unit 2: Part-whole within 10, Lesson 2

WAYS OF WORKING Pair work

ASK

• *Can you draw a picture to represent the pencils?*
• *Can you draw a part-whole model to represent the pencils?*
• *Is there more than one way of drawing the part-whole model?*

IN FOCUS This part of the lesson introduces children to the idea of linking parts and wholes to a number sentence. Children will also link the words 'equal to' and 'plus' to the correct symbols.

ANSWERS

Question ① a): There are four ✏ on the desk.

There are three ✏ in the tin.

Children use concrete materials or draw a picture to show the groups.

Question ① b): 7 ✏ is equal to 4 ✏ plus 3 ✏.

$7 = 4 + 3$

Accept answers where the 4 and the 3 are the other way around.

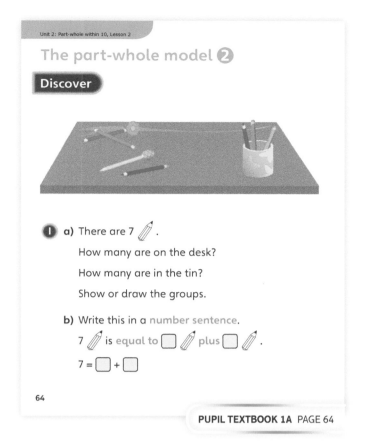

The part-whole model ❷

Discover

① a) There are 7 ✏.

How many are on the desk?

How many are in the tin?

Show or draw the groups.

b) Write this in a number sentence.

7 ✏ is equal to ▢ ✏ plus ▢ ✏.

7 = ▢ + ▢

64

PUPIL TEXTBOOK 1A PAGE 64

Share

WAYS OF WORKING Whole class teacher led

ASK

• *Does it matter which circles the 4 and the 3 go in?*
• *Does it matter which circle the 7 goes in?*
• *Can anyone write the number sentence in a different way?*

IN FOCUS Children need to see the journey from the concrete through to the pictorial and onto the abstract calculation. This activity links this learning together, helping children embed what the + and = symbols mean.

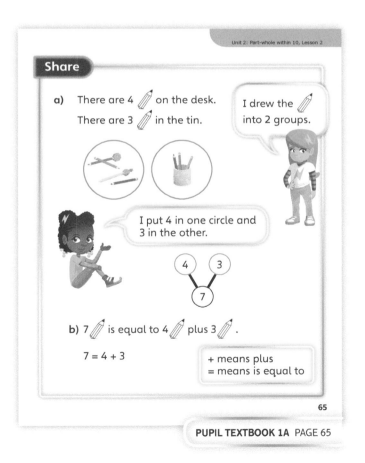

Unit 2: Part-whole within 10, Lesson 2

Share

a) There are 4 ✏ on the desk.
There are 3 ✏ in the tin.

I drew the ✏ into 2 groups.

I put 4 in one circle and 3 in the other.

4   3
 7

b) 7 ✏ is equal to 4 ✏ plus 3 ✏.

$7 = 4 + 3$

+ means plus
= means is equal to

65

PUPIL TEXTBOOK 1A PAGE 65

Think together

WAYS OF WORKING Whole class teacher led (I do, We do, You do)

ASK

- Question ❶: *Did you all draw the same picture?*
- Question ❷: *How many mistakes did you find?*
- Question ❷: *Is that the only way to write the number sentences?*
- Question ❸: *How many groups have you found? Do you think you have found them all?*

IN FOCUS Children look at examples that are correct and examples that are not correct. If children can recognise both correct representations and incorrect representations, it demonstrates a deeper understanding of the concept.

STRENGTHEN Encourage children to use practical equipment throughout. They should use a variety of resources – some that match the pictures, such as pencils, and others that represent the pictures, such as cubes or counters.

DEEPEN Encourage children to find multiple answers to the questions. How can children record all their different answers? Could they use a table? When they have recorded all the ways of partitioning 3 and 4, can they predict how many ways they could partition 5 and 6? Ask them to use cubes to check if they are correct. Can they now predict how many different ways they could partition 9?

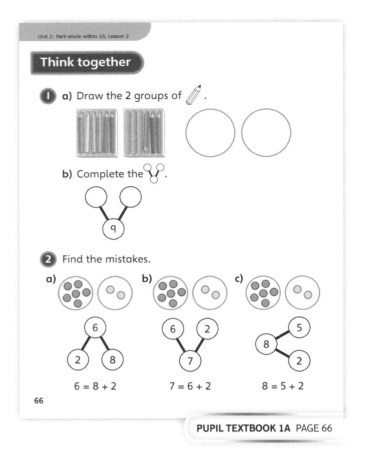

PUPIL TEXTBOOK 1A PAGE 66

ASSESSMENT CHECKPOINT Question ❷ a) should help assess if children have a good understanding of the part-whole model as, at first glance, this question looks correct. Children need a thorough understanding of parts and wholes to spot this mistake.

ANSWERS

- Question ❶ a): Children draw 6 pencils and 3 pencils.
- Question ❶ b):

- Question ❷ a): 8 should be the whole and 6 and 2 should be the parts.
- Question ❷ b): 6 and 2 should be the parts, 8 is the whole.
- Question ❷ c): 8 should be the whole, 6 and 2 are the parts.
- Question ❸ a): Possible groups are: 1 and 6, 2 and 5, 3 and 4, in any order.
- Question ❸ b): A completed part-whole model that represents the child's groups from question ❸ a).
- Question ❸ c): A number sentence that represents the child's groups from question ❸ a), such as 7 = 1 + 6 or 7 = 6 + 1.

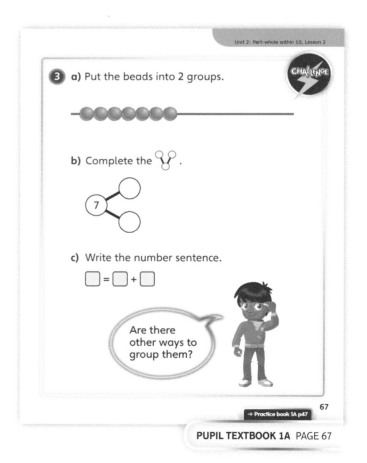

→ Practice book 1A p47

PUPIL TEXTBOOK 1A PAGE 67

Practice

WAYS OF WORKING Independent thinking

IN FOCUS The exercise presents questions in a variety of ways to check whether children are confident with the concepts of parts and wholes and linking these with abstract number sentences. Children need to be able to use the plus (+) and equal to (=) symbols and understand that number sentences can be written in different orders.

STRENGTHEN Children can use concrete materials throughout to support their understanding. All of the questions could also be set up in the classroom using large circles of string to represent the part-whole model, or outside in the playground using chalk circles or hoops.

DEEPEN Encourage children to think about how they record their results when a question has multiple answers. Can they see a pattern between the number they start with and the number of ways it can be partitioned?

ASSESSMENT CHECKPOINT Question ④ gives children the opportunity to be creative, thinking of their own part-whole models and number sentences. Question ⑤ checks that children are able to find all the different ways of partitioning 4. Check how they have completed this. Have they filled in the part-whole models randomly or been systematic in their approach?

ANSWERS Answers for the **Practice** part of the lesson appear in the separate **Practice and Reflect answer guide**.

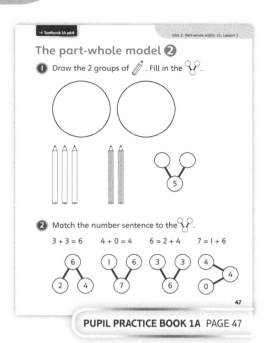

PUPIL PRACTICE BOOK 1A PAGE 47

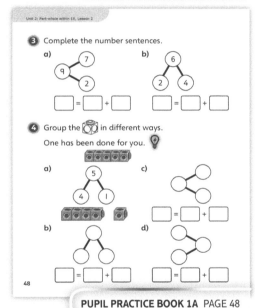

PUPIL PRACTICE BOOK 1A PAGE 48

Reflect

WAYS OF WORKING Independent thinking

IN FOCUS The activity explores the order of number sentences in more detail. Children need to be able to recognise which part of the number sentence can change and which part cannot.

ASSESSMENT CHECKPOINT Check that children are using the correct vocabulary. For example, 'the **whole** has stayed the same'.

ANSWERS Answers for the **Reflect** part of the lesson appear in the separate **Practice and Reflect answer guide**.

After the lesson

- Are children confident using the + and = symbols?
- Do they understand which part of the number sentence represents the whole and which part represents the parts?

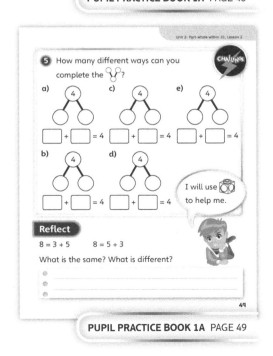

PUPIL PRACTICE BOOK 1A PAGE 49

Related facts – number bonds

Learning focus

In this lesson children consolidate their learning on part-whole models while looking in more detail at number sentences. They explore related facts and how if they know one fact, they also know others.

Small steps

→ Previous step: The part-whole model 2
→ **This step: Related facts – number bonds**
→ Next step: Finding number bonds

NATIONAL CURRICULUM LINKS

Year 1 Number – Number and Place Value

- Read, write and interpret mathematical statements involving addition (+), subtraction (–) and equals (=) signs.
- Represent and use number bonds and related subtraction facts within 20.

ASSESSING MASTERY

Children can write all the possible number sentences for any part-whole model and can make their own number sentences. Children can recognise that there are four different ways of writing an addition sentence.

COMMON MISCONCEPTIONS

Children may get their numbers mixed up and write more number sentences than there are. For example, for 4 + 2 = 6 they may be tempted to write 4 + 6 = 2 or 2 + 6 = 4. Ask:
- *Can you prove that 4 + 6 = 2 is correct using cubes?*
- *What have you done wrong?*
- *What is 4 + 6 actually equal to? How can you tell?*

It is too soon to link this to subtraction sentences, so ensure that you are only discussing what the total is with the children to prove why their sentence is incorrect.

STRENGTHENING UNDERSTANDING

Give children access to blocks, cubes or counters and ask them to use these resources to represent simple number sentences. Ask them to move the resources around, as illustrated below, to prove that the = symbol can go in different places and the number sentence remains correct. For example:

  + =   = +

3 + 1 = 4   4 = 1 + 3

GOING DEEPER

To deepen learning, children could look at partitioning numbers into three parts instead of two. For example, they could write 7 = 1 + 2 + 4 or 2 + 2 + 3 = 7. Ask children to partition different numbers to 10 into three parts.

KEY LANGUAGE

In lesson: groups, number sentence, same, different

Other language to be used by the teacher: part-whole model, partition, part, whole, equal to, plus

STRUCTURES AND REPRESENTATIONS

Part-whole model, cubes

RESOURCES

Mandatory: part-whole model, cubes, blocks, counters

Optional: plastic food and flowers, hoops, teddy bears, toys, etc

Teaching Tools In the eTextbook of this lesson, you will find interactive links to a selection of teaching tools.

Before you teach ⏸

- Do children understand what the + and = symbols mean?
- Do children understand that numbers can be partitioned in different ways?

Discover

Pair work

ASK

• *How can you find out which numbers to put in the part-whole model?*
• *How can you check that you have eight altogether?*

IN FOCUS Children compare the same number sentence written in different ways.

ANSWERS

Question ❶ a):

Children could write 8 = 3 + 5, 8 = 5 + 3, 3 + 5 = 8 or 5 + 3 = 8.

Question ❶ b): Accept all sensible answers here, including:
• They all have the same three numbers: 8, 3, 5.
• They all use the same symbols: + and =.
• Two of the number sentences show 3 + 5.
• The other two number sentences show 5 + 3.

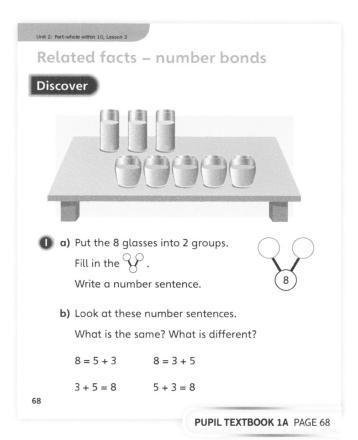

Related facts – number bonds

Discover

❶ a) Put the 8 glasses into 2 groups.
   Fill in the ⅄.
   Write a number sentence.

   b) Look at these number sentences.
   What is the same? What is different?

   8 = 5 + 3   8 = 3 + 5

   3 + 5 = 8   5 + 3 = 8

68

PUPIL TEXTBOOK 1A PAGE 68

Share

Whole class discussion

ASK

• *Compare your number sentence with the rest of the group. Have you all written it the same way?*
• *How many different ways has your group written it?*
• *Do you think there are any more ways?*

IN FOCUS Children share their ideas and come to the conclusion that there are four different addition sentences that can be written about one part-whole diagram.

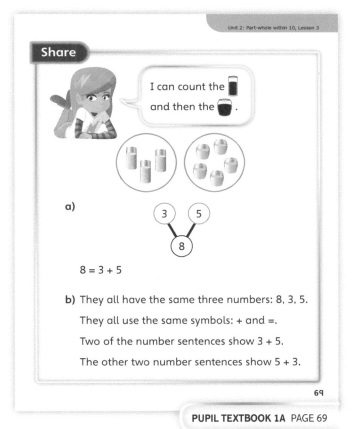

Share

I can count the 🥛 and then the 🥛.

a)

8 = 3 + 5

b) They all have the same three numbers: 8, 3, 5.
   They all use the same symbols: + and =.
   Two of the number sentences show 3 + 5.
   The other two number sentences show 5 + 3.

69

PUPIL TEXTBOOK 1A PAGE 69

Think together

WAYS OF WORKING Whole class teacher led (I do, We do, You do)

ASK

- Question **①**: *Do you think everyone will have filled in the number sentence in the same way? What are the two possible ways of filling in the blanks?*
- Question **②**: *How many mistakes did you find?*
- Question **③**: *What different groups can you see in the image?*
- Question **③**: *How can you work out the number that is the whole?*

IN FOCUS Children work towards seeing an image and then being able to represent this in a part-whole diagram and four different addition sentences.

STRENGTHEN In question **③**, children can use concrete materials to represent the flowers. Use different colours to represent the different coloured flowers, further scaffolding their understanding here if necessary.

DEEPEN Can children draw a picture of some flowers that they could partition in three ways? For example, they could draw purple flowers, blue flowers and pink flowers, then make their own part-whole models and number sentences to represent their drawings.

ASSESSMENT CHECKPOINT Question **③** brings all the main learning points together. Check that children interpret the pictures correctly into part-whole models and then write all four addition sentences accurately.

ANSWERS

Question **①**:

2 + 4 = 6 or 4 + 2 = 6

Question **②** a): 2 + 3 = 5

Question **②** b):

2 + 4 = 6

Question **③** a):

Question **③** b): 5 + 2 = 7

Question **③** c): 7 = 5 + 2

Question **③** d): 2 + 5 = 7

Question **③** e): 7 = 2 + 5

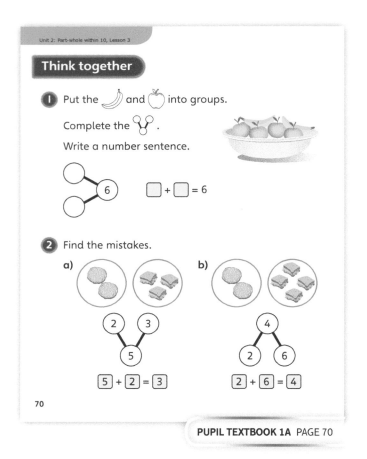

PUPIL TEXTBOOK 1A PAGE 70

PUPIL TEXTBOOK 1A PAGE 71

Practice

WAYS OF WORKING Independent thinking

IN FOCUS Children begin to write number sentences with less scaffolding and later with no scaffolding. They consolidate the idea that for every addition fact they know, they can write down three more.

STRENGTHEN Give children a number sentence and ask them to draw a picture of what this sentence could represent. Make sure that they are given number sentences written in a variety of ways.

DEEPEN To deepen understanding, children could make their own questions for others to answer. They could make questions that start with a picture, such as three cats and six dogs, and ask their partner to complete a part-whole diagram and number sentences to match the picture. To further extend learning, ask children to write some questions that start with a part-whole model, and their partner could then draw a picture and write the matching number sentences.

ASSESSMENT CHECKPOINT

- Question ❸ requires children to write the addition symbol for the first time. Check that they recognise that the different-shaped missing box means they should put a symbol there.
- In question ❹, check that children have written all the different addition sentences and not simply repeated one that they already have. Would writing them in a certain order help them to ensure they have them all?

ANSWERS Answers for the **Practice** part of the lesson appear in the separate **Practice and Reflect answer guide**.

Reflect

WAYS OF WORKING Independent thinking

IN FOCUS This activity ensures that children have made the link between a part-whole model and the four addition sentences that go with it.

ASSESSMENT CHECKPOINT Check that children have written a part-whole model that makes sense. Have they put the numbers in the correct place? Check that they have written all four sentences correctly.

ANSWERS Answers for the **Reflect** part of the lesson appear in the separate **Practice and Reflect answer guide**.

After the lesson ⏸

- Are children confident writing four number sentences for one part-whole model?
- Are children confident at various starting points? For example, can they start with the number sentence and work backwards to a diagram? Can they start with a part-whole model, then draw a diagram representing it and then write four number sentences?
- How can you build this into future learning?

PUPIL PRACTICE BOOK 1A PAGE 50

PUPIL PRACTICE BOOK 1A PAGE 51

PUPIL PRACTICE BOOK 1A PAGE 52

Finding number bonds

Learning focus

In this lesson children are learning about number bonds within ten. Children learn strategies for organising their thinking and begin to spot patterns.

Small steps

→ Previous step: Related facts – number bonds
→ **This step: Finding number bonds**
→ Next step: Comparing number bonds

NATIONAL CURRICULUM LINKS

Year 1 Number – Number and Place Value

- Represent and use number bonds and related subtraction facts within 20.

ASSESSING MASTERY

Children can work systematically to find all the number bonds of a number within ten.

COMMON MISCONCEPTIONS

Children may work in a random way and therefore miss or duplicate answers. Children may also forget or disregard number bonds, including zero. Ask:
- *Can you think of a different way of working to make sure you don't miss any number bonds?*
- *You have missed one of the number bonds. Can you think what you may have missed?*

STRENGTHENING UNDERSTANDING

Using practical equipment in two different colours, such as counters, cubes or bead strings, will help children see patterns and understand when they have found all of their number bonds. For example, here we can see the number bonds for 4:

⬤⬤⬤⬤ 4 + 0
⬤⬤⬤◯ 3 + 1
⬤⬤◯◯ 2 + 2
⬤◯◯◯ 1 + 3
◯◯◯◯ 0 + 4

By changing one block at a time, children can see that they have found all the number bonds.

GOING DEEPER

Children could expand their thinking by working on more complex problems involving number bonds. For example:

If the circle has the **same** value in each calculation, what must the value of the square be?

◯ + 5 = 7
☐ + ◯ = 5

KEY LANGUAGE

In lesson: how many, same, different, number sentence

Other language to be used by the teacher: number bond, part-whole model, partition, part, whole, equal to, sequence

STRUCTURES AND REPRESENTATIONS

Ten frame, bead string

RESOURCES

Mandatory: ten frame, bead string

Optional: cubes, counters

Teaching Tools In the eTextbook of this lesson, you will find interactive links to a selection of teaching tools.

Before you teach

- Do children understand that 3 + 1 is the same as 1 + 3?
- Do children understand that the equal to symbol can be put in different places, such as 3 + 1 = 4 and 4 = 3 + 1?

Discover

Pair work

ASK

- *How many different colours are used?*
- *How many red counters are there and how many yellow? How many are there in total?*

IN FOCUS Children experiment with different ways to make five.

ANSWERS

Question ❶ a): Children could have completed this activity in various ways. For example, 1 yellow counter and 4 red counters.

Question ❶ b): Depending on their answer to question ❶ a), children could have found 3 yellow counters and 2 red counters, and 4 yellow counters and 1 red counter.

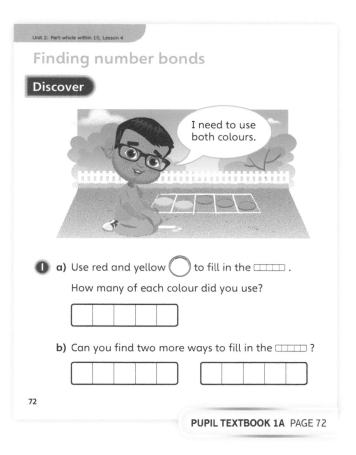

Share

WAYS OF WORKING Whole class teacher led

ASK Refer to what Sparks is saying at the bottom of page 73 of the **Pupil Textbook**. Ask:
- *Did everyone complete the activity the same way?*
- *How do we know we have found all the ways?*
- *Should we start with all the same-coloured counters, then swap a counter one by one?*

IN FOCUS Children share ideas and begin to think of strategies to ensure they have found all the different ways of filling in the five frame.

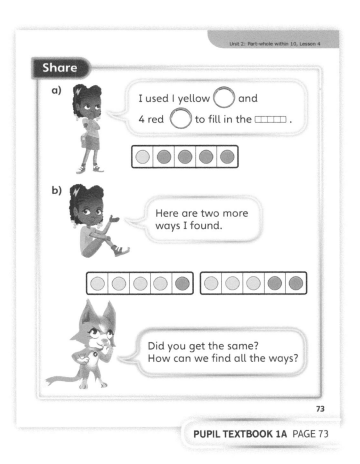

Think together

WAYS OF WORKING Whole class teacher led (I do, We do, You do)

ASK

- Question ❶: *Are you sure you have found all the ways? How do you know?*
- Question ❷: *Explain your method to a partner. Did they do it the same way?*
- Question ❸: *Do you think you have found all the different ways of showing the 6 beads? How did your method make it easy to do?*

IN FOCUS Children focus on being systematic with their method for finding number bonds using a variety of representations.

STRENGTHEN This activity could be done practically using boys and girls to represent number bonds. Ask five boys to stand at the front, and then swap a boy for a girl (so there are now four boys and one girl). Then repeat this until there are five girls instead of five boys. The other children could use counters, cubes or a bead string to illustrate what is happening.

DEEPEN Extend learning by encouraging children to experiment with partitioning numbers in three ways. Encourage them to think of ways of making sure they have found all possible number bond combinations. For example, for 7 they could make:

7 + 0 + 0	5 + 2 + 0	4 + 2 + 1
6 + 1 + 0	4 + 1 + 2	4 + 3 + 0
5 + 1 + 1		

ASSESSMENT CHECKPOINT Questions ❷ and ❸ should highlight whether or not children understand the link between the model, the part-whole diagram and the number sentence.

ANSWERS

Question ❶:

Question ❷ b):

Question ❷ c):

Question ❷ d):

Question ❷ e):

Question ❸: 6 = 3 + 3
6 = 4 + 2
6 = 5 + 1

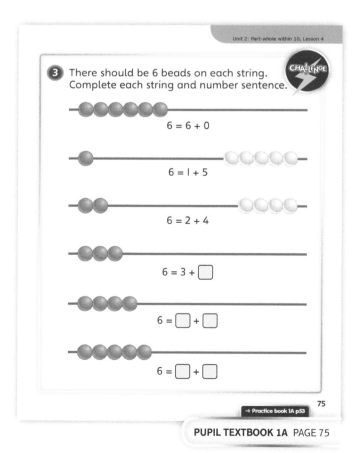

Think together

❶ Use ◯ to find all the ways to fill in the ▭▭▭ .

❷ How many different ways can you arrange 4 ◯ ?
Fill in the ▭▭▭ and the ⅋ .

a)

Be organised with your method.

b)

c)

d)

e)

74

PUPIL TEXTBOOK 1A PAGE 74

CHALLENGE

❸ There should be 6 beads on each string. Complete each string and number sentence.

6 = 6 + 0

6 = 1 + 5

6 = 2 + 4

6 = 3 + ▢

6 = ▢ + ▢

6 = ▢ + ▢

75

→ Practice book 1A p53

PUPIL TEXTBOOK 1A PAGE 75

Practice

Independent thinking

IN FOCUS Children practise finding number bonds independently. Children should look for patterns and be able to see mistakes in patterns or sequences.

STRENGTHEN Encourage children to represent the pictures with the actual equipment throughout. For question **4**, allow children to choose which equipment they would prefer to use to represent the number sentences.

DEEPEN Extend learning by giving children some open-ended problems to solve such as:

 + ◯ + △ = 9

Ask: *What could the value of* ▢ *,* ◯ *and* △ *be? How many different answers can you find?*

Ask children to create some of their own problems similar to those in question **4**. Can they make some using three different shapes rather than two?

ASSESSMENT CHECKPOINT In question **2** look out for children who do not understand the word 'sequence'. This question highlights whether children can see the patterns.

Question **5** checks if children have understood that different numbers have a different number of possible number bonds. Can children spot that the higher the number the more combinations it is possible to find?

ANSWERS Answers for the **Practice** part of the lesson appear in the separate **Practice and Reflect answer guide**.

Reflect

Independent thinking

IN FOCUS Children prove that they have understood the lesson by drawing beads to show number bonds. You should expect to see children being organised in their approach.

ASSESSMENT CHECKPOINT Check that children have drawn their beads systematically, not randomly.

ANSWERS Answers for the **Reflect** part of the lesson appear in the separate **Practice and Reflect answer guide**.

After the lesson ⏸

- Have children been systematic with their approach to finding number bonds?
- Are they able to show number bonds using pictures, a part-whole model and a number sentence?
- Have children made use of zero throughout the lesson?

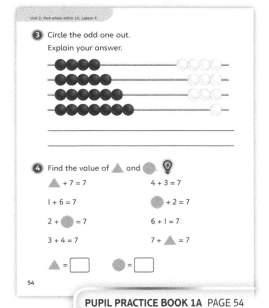

PUPIL PRACTICE BOOK 1A PAGE 53

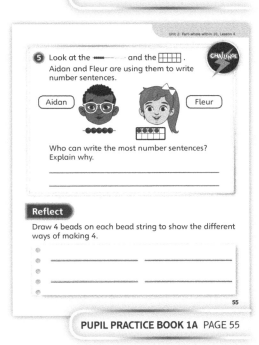

PUPIL PRACTICE BOOK 1A PAGE 54

PUPIL PRACTICE BOOK 1A PAGE 55

Comparing number bonds

Learning focus

In this lesson children compare number sentences within ten using the <, > and = symbols. Children compare without working out answers to additions each time.

Small steps

→ Previous step: Finding number bonds
→ **This step: Comparing number bonds**
→ Next step: Finding the whole – adding together

NATIONAL CURRICULUM LINKS

Year 1 Number – Number and Place Value

• Represent and use number bonds and related subtraction facts within 20.

ASSESSING MASTERY

Children can use the < and > symbols to compare number bond sentences. Children can tackle questions with multiple answers and be systematic with their approach.

COMMON MISCONCEPTIONS

Children may write the symbols the wrong way around. Ask:
• *Can you draw a picture to help you remember which way around the symbols go?*

Children may start counting again for each number sentence rather than look for links in the numbers. For example, 2 + 5 is clearly greater than 2 + 1, so there is no need to add them up. Ask:
• *Do you need to add up each number sentence to see which is bigger?*
• *How can you tell which is smaller without counting?*

STRENGTHENING UNDERSTANDING

When comparing numbers or number bonds, children often struggle more with understanding which way around the symbol goes rather than understanding which number bond is bigger or smaller. The following activity can help children understand how the symbols are used and gives them a strong visual they can always refer to if they get stuck. Use cubes and straws to show the symbols <, > and =, and cubes to represent the numbers.

Move on to drawing the cubes and lines on a mini whiteboard. The next step is to encourage children to visualise the cubes and straws in their head. This will help children remember which way around the symbols go when comparing number bonds.

GOING DEEPER

To expand thinking in this lesson, ask children to work through number problems with multiple answers. Write some calculations on the whiteboard and ask: *Which numbers could go in the boxes?* For example:

$5 + \boxed{} < \boxed{} + 3$

KEY LANGUAGE

In lesson: number, symbol, number sentence, in total, more than, <, >, =

Other language to be used by the teacher: part-whole model, partition, part, whole, equal to, compare, replace, number bond

STRUCTURES AND REPRESENTATIONS

Cubes

RESOURCES

Mandatory: cubes

Optional: straws, selection of countable objects from the classroom

Teaching Tools In the eTextbook of this lesson, you will find interactive links to a selection of teaching tools.

Before you teach ⏸

• Are children confident with number bonds of numbers within ten?
• Can children read the greater than > and less than < symbols?

Discover

WAYS OF WORKING Pair work

ASK

- *Shall we add up all the cubes to check who has the most?*
- *Is there a quicker way?*
- *Can you remember seeing the < symbol before? Who can say what it means in words?*

IN FOCUS Children are immediately encouraged to reason how they know who has the most cubes. They do not need to count the total number of cubes to work the answer out.

ANSWERS

Question ❶ a): Marta has more. Tom and Marta have an equal number of cubes under the cup, but Marta has more cubes on the table.

Question ❶ b): 1 + 4 < 3 + 4 or 4 + 1 < 4 + 3

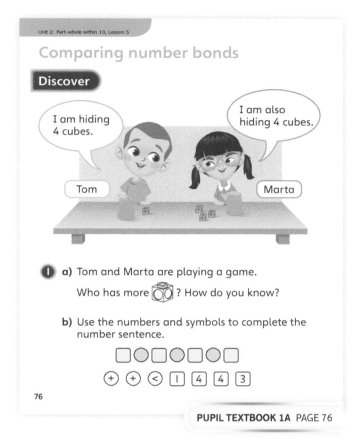

Share

WAYS OF WORKING Whole class teacher led

ASK

- *Did you all work out if Tom or Marta had the most cubes the same way? Share the way you worked it out with the children on your table.*
- *Who had the quickest way of working it out?*

IN FOCUS Children use their reasoning skills to decide who has the most cubes. Both Tom and Marta have the same amount under the cup. Three is greater than one, therefore Marta must have the most. Children can prove their answer by counting the total number of cubes each person has, but it is important that they do not count from one each time. You should expect children to count from four as they know there are four cubes under each cup.

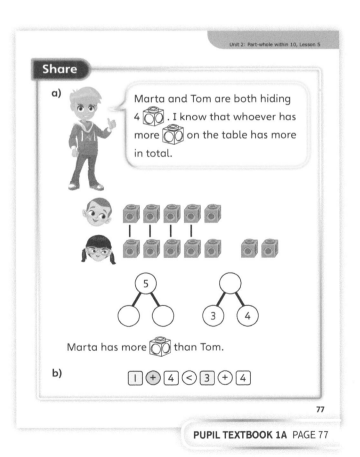

Think together

WAYS OF WORKING Whole class teacher led (I do, We do, You do)

ASK

- Question **1**: *Explain to your partner how you know who has the most. Did you work it out the same way or differently?*
- Question **2**: *What is different about this problem?*
- Question **3**: *Why are the first two questions easier than the last two?*
- Question **3**: *What strategy did you use to answer the last two questions?*

IN FOCUS Children are asked to compare number bonds in a variety of ways. Sometimes one of the numbers is the same, which makes them easy to compare. At other times none of the numbers are the same. Encourage children to discuss different strategies for working these out.

STRENGTHEN Recreate the practical activity in the **Discover** section to strengthen understanding. Ask children to line cubes up to see who has the most. This will help children see clearly which number bond is greater and help them to see that they don't need to begin to counting from one each time.

DEEPEN Children could answer more open-ended problems. This will show that children have fully grasped the concept and gives them the opportunity to experiment with efficient methods for finding multiple answers to a problem. For example: *How many possible answers are there for this number sentence?*

$\boxed{} + 6 > \boxed{} + 1$

To secure and extend learning, ask:
- *Are you sure you have all possible answers?*
- *Did you use a system to check you found all the answers?*
- *Have you included zero?*

ASSESSMENT CHECKPOINT Question **2** is worded differently to all the other examples so far. In this case the number of cubes hidden is different, but the number of cubes on the table is the same. Check that children have recognised this or if they have reverted back to counting.

Check how children tackle the last two questions in question **3**. Can children find a way to answer the question without working the additions out?

ANSWERS

Question **1**: Chen has more.

Question **2**: Molly has more.

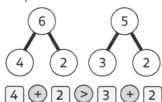

Question **3**: 2 + 5 $<$ 2 + 7
5 + 3 $<$ 6 + 3
2 + 6 $=$ 3 + 5
5 + 1 $>$ 3 + 2

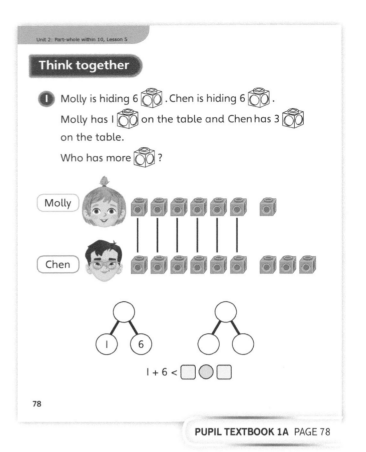

PUPIL TEXTBOOK 1A PAGE 78

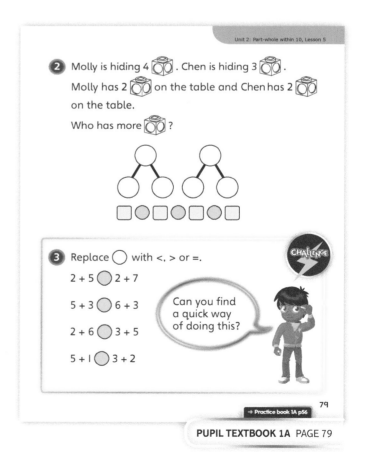

PUPIL TEXTBOOK 1A PAGE 79

Practice

WAYS OF WORKING Independent thinking

IN FOCUS This section brings numerous concepts together. Children are expected to write and interpret number bonds, complete part-whole models, use <, > and = symbols and work systematically to solve problems.

STRENGTHEN Encourage children to use cubes to recreate the calculations. This way, children can build the number problems and physically see the size of the numbers. Ask children to discuss their strategies for solving the calculations with a partner.

DEEPEN Extend thinking on question **5** with question prompts:
- *How many possible answers are there for △, ◯ and ▢?*
- *How could you change the question so that there are more possible answers?*
- *How could you change the question so that there are fewer possible answers?*
- *Can you make up a question of your own like this?*

ASSESSMENT CHECKPOINT Check how children are completing question **3**. Are they working out each side of the number sentence or are they looking for links in the numbers?

Observe how children answer question **4**. Have they chosen the next available number or chosen a random number?

ANSWERS Answers for the **Practice** part of the lesson appear in the separate **Practice and Reflect answer guide**.

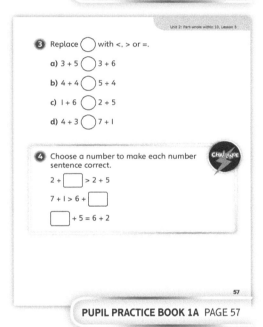

PUPIL PRACTICE BOOK 1A PAGE 56

PUPIL PRACTICE BOOK 1A PAGE 57

Reflect

WAYS OF WORKING Pair work

IN FOCUS Children are given the opportunity to experiment with their number sentence and share their thinking with others.

ASSESSMENT CHECKPOINT Encourage children to compare using words as well as symbols. This will help you to assess whether there are any areas that need further consolidation. For example, if a child says 1 + 2 is smaller than 1 + 5 but writes the number sentence 1 + 2 > 1 + 5, you know the issue is in their understanding of the symbol, not their ability to compare the size of number sentences.

ANSWERS Answers for the **Reflect** part of the lesson appear in the separate **Practice and Reflect answer guide**.

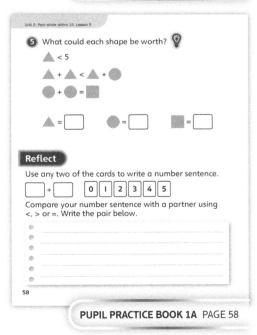

PUPIL PRACTICE BOOK 1A PAGE 58

After the lesson ⏸

- Were children confident using the <, > and = symbols?
- Were children able to compare number sentences by seeing links in the numbers or did they want to work out each number sentence first?

End of unit check

Don't forget the End of unit check proforma (page 80)!

WAYS OF WORKING Group work – adult led

IN FOCUS

- Question **4** includes a number bond where one of the numbers is 0.
- Questions **2** , **4** and **5** require a secure understanding of the = symbol.

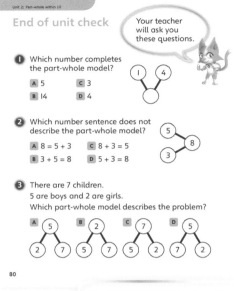

PUPIL TEXTBOOK 1A PAGE 80

Think!

WAYS OF WORKING Pair work or small groups

IN FOCUS This activity gives children more than one thing to think about: they need to think about the parts and the whole whilst also considering which numbers will fit where. Check how children approach the problem. How confident are they, faced with an unfamiliar problem without an immediate answer? Do they use a systematic approach or try numbers at random? Challenge children who tackle this problem well by asking them to find more solutions.

Draw children's attention to the key vocabulary at the bottom of the **My journal** page.

Encourage children to think through or discuss possible numbers for all three part-whole models before writing their answer in **My journal**.

ANSWERS AND COMMENTARY Children who have mastered the concepts of this unit will recognise the part-whole model and be able to explain what each number represents. They can use the part-whole model to write the four addition facts that the model represents and they are beginning to learn the number bonds to ten.

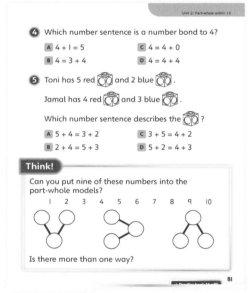

PUPIL TEXTBOOK 1A PAGE 81

Q	A	WRONG ANSWERS AND MISCONCEPTIONS	STRENGTHENING UNDERSTANDING
1	A	C suggests that children think they need to subtract; they may not yet have a secure understanding of how the part-whole model works, whereas D suggests that children think they just need to choose the largest number.	Allow children to use cubes to check and prove their answers as they work.
2	D	A suggests that children think the = sign should always come at the end of the number sentence.	
3	C	Any wrong answer indicates that children do not have a secure understanding of the total or whole.	
4	C	Any wrong answer indicates that children do not recognise 4 = 4 + 0 as a correct number fact because it includes zero.	
5	D	Any wrong answer suggests that children do not have a thorough understanding of the = symbol.	

My journal

WAYS OF WORKING Independent thinking

ANSWERS AND COMMENTARY

There are 10 unique solutions:
$10 = 9 + 1, 8 = 6 + 2, 7 = 4 + 3$
$10 = 9 + 1, 8 = 5 + 3, 6 = 4 + 2$
$10 = 8 + 2, 9 = 6 + 3, 5 = 4 + 1$
$10 = 8 + 2, 9 = 5 + 4, 7 = 6 + 1$
$10 = 8 + 2, 7 = 4 + 3, 6 = 5 + 1$
$10 = 7 + 3, 9 = 8 + 1, 6 = 4 + 2$
$10 = 7 + 3, 5 = 4 + 1, 8 = 6 + 2$
$10 = 6 + 4, 9 = 8 + 1, 7 = 5 + 2$
$10 = 6 + 4, 9 = 7 + 2, 8 = 5 + 3$
$10 = 6 + 4, 8 = 7 + 1, 5 = 3 + 2$

Observe what strategies children use to tackle this question. It is easiest to start with 10 and work backwards (for example, $10 = 9 + 1$, $8 = 6 + 2$ and $7 = 4 + 3$). Support children by giving them whiteboards so that they can try combinations then rub numbers out if they go wrong, by giving them 1–9 digit cards to move about, or by giving them cubes so they can experiment with sharing them out between part-whole models. Children should be prepared to make mistakes and try again until they find a solution.

Power check

WAYS OF WORKING Independent thinking

ASK

- *What did you find the most difficult?*
- *What pictures do you make in your mind to help you answer the questions?*

Power play

WAYS OF WORKING Pair work or small groups

IN FOCUS Use this Power play to see if children can work in pairs to complete a part-whole model. Children will need to think carefully about whether to place one or two counters to try to ensure their opponent does not win.

ANSWERS AND COMMENTARY Answers will depend on what number children choose as their whole. Consider pairing up children with varying levels of confidence so that more confident children can support less confident children.

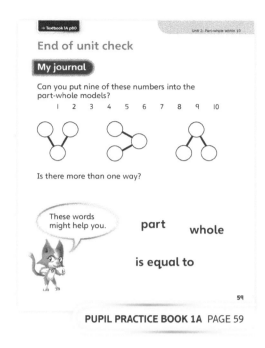

→ Textbook 1A p80

End of unit check

My journal

Can you put nine of these numbers into the part-whole models?

1 2 3 4 5 6 7 8 9 10

Is there more than one way?

These words might help you.

part **whole**

is equal to

PUPIL PRACTICE BOOK 1A PAGE 59

Unit 2: Part-whole within 10

Power check

How do you feel about your work in this unit?

Power play

A game for 2 players.

You will need:
- counters
- part-whole model

How to play:
- Choose a number between 5 and 10.
- This number is the whole. Put that many counters onto a part-whole model.
- Take it in turns to place 1 or 2 counters in one of the parts.
- If you make the whole, you win a point.
- If you don't make the whole, the next player goes.
- The first to 5 points is the winner.

PUPIL PRACTICE BOOK 1A PAGE 60

After the unit ⏸

- How confident were children identifying the parts and the whole and writing number sentences?
- Can children find number bonds without counting on?

Strengthen and *Deepen* activities for this unit can be found in the Power Maths online subscription.

Unit 3
Addition and subtraction within 10 ①

Mastery Expert tip! "When I taught this unit, I used the characters within the Pupil Books to encourage children to talk about the different methods they were using. This worked well and helped us explore different ways of working. It also encouraged children to talk openly about mistakes."

Don't forget to watch the Unit 3 video!

WHY THIS UNIT IS IMPORTANT

This unit focuses on number bonds within 10 and number bonds to 10. It is important that over time children become fluent in these facts because they are the foundation for future number facts.

Within this unit, children are introduced to formal addition for the first time through the idea of 'count all' and 'count on' strategies. A 'count all' strategy is when all parts are added together to make a whole. A 'count on' strategy asks children to start with a number and count on.

As well as introducing children to some of the key language associated with addition, children will also begin to develop an understanding of the commutativity of addition – the idea that addition calculations can be performed in any order.

WHERE THIS UNIT FITS

→ Unit 2: Part-whole within 10
→ **Unit 3: Addition and subtraction within 10 (1)**
→ Unit 4: Addition and subtraction within 10 (2)

This unit builds on Unit 2: Part-whole within 10, which introduced children to the idea that a whole can be separated into parts of various sizes. Unit 3 is the first of two 'Addition and subtraction within 10' units. Unit 3 focuses on addition, and Unit 4 will focus on subtraction.

Before they start this unit, it is expected that children:
• can use the part-whole model to partition a number to 10
• can write and compare number bonds to 10.

ASSESSING MASTERY

Children who have mastered this unit will be able to relate each number in a calculation to what it represents. Children will be able to use a variety of manipulatives to represent addition within ten, including cubes, ten frames, number lines and part-whole models.

Children's confidence in knowing and recognising number facts and number pairs will also start to increase, and children will start to use these to answer simple calculations without manipulatives.

Additionally, children showing mastery would be able to rearrange the order of a calculation to work efficiently, using their knowledge of commutativity.

COMMON MISCONCEPTIONS	STRENGTHENING UNDERSTANDING	GOING DEEPER
Children may not apply number facts and therefore resort to a 'count all' or 'count on' strategy.	Repeat the number fact after counting objects, and remind children that they do not need to count each time.	Ask children to solve missing number problems or to create their own number story.
Children may struggle with the transition from a 'count all' to a 'count on' strategy.	Remind children that we start at the first number, but then count on from there. Count each jump together.	Remember to use numbers within 10. It is important to deepen learning rather than moving children on.

WAYS OF WORKING

Use these pages to introduce the unit focus to children. You can use the characters to explore different ways of working too!

STRUCTURES AND REPRESENTATIONS

Part-whole model: This model helps children understand that two or more parts combine to make a whole. It also helps to strengthen children's understanding of number bonds within 10.

Number line: Number lines help children learn about addition as counting on. They allow children to identify the starting point, the number counted on and the end point.

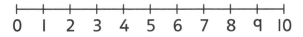

Ten frame: The ten frame helps to give children a sense of ten, and supports their understanding of number bonds to 10. It also plays a key role in helping children to recognise the structure of other numbers, and to understand what happens when you add two numbers together.

KEY LANGUAGE

There is some key language that children will need to know as part of the learning in this unit.

→ part, whole and part-whole
→ altogether, in total, total, sum
→ add, added, plus, or +
→ count, count on
→ missing, missing part
→ number bonds, number pairs
→ number stories

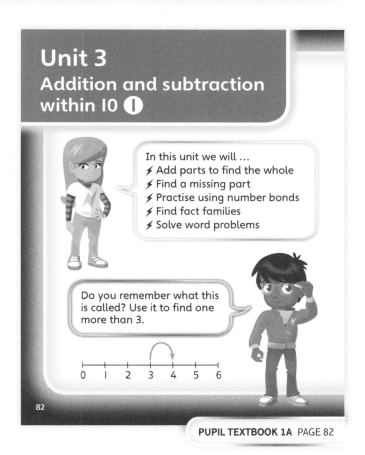

PUPIL TEXTBOOK 1A PAGE 82

PUPIL TEXTBOOK 1A PAGE 83

Finding the whole – adding together

Learning focus

In this lesson, children will combine two parts into a whole and understand how the part-whole diagram represents addition. Children will make links between concrete representations, part-whole models, ten frames and abstract addition calculations.

Small steps

→ Previous step: Comparing number bonds
→ **This step: Finding the whole – adding together**
→ Next step: Finding the whole – adding more

NATIONAL CURRICULUM LINKS

Year 1 Number – Addition and Subtraction

Represent and use number bonds and related subtraction facts within 20.

ASSESSING MASTERY

Children can correctly identify the different parts of the part-whole model and relate them to different pictorial representations or structures. Children can understand that the same whole can be made up of different parts.

COMMON MISCONCEPTIONS

Children may put numbers into the part-whole model incorrectly. They may put the whole as one of the parts, or vice versa. Ask:
• *Which two numbers show the parts? Which number shows the whole?*

Children may also grapple with the idea that the same whole can be made up of different parts. To support understanding, model this with physical resources and ask:
• *The whole is how many cubes there are altogether. If I move the cubes into two different piles and keep changing them, will the whole ever change?*

Children may find it initially confusing that the equals (=) sign appears first in some calculations. Ask:
• *What does the symbol '=' mean? Does it mean something different if it comes first?*

STRENGTHENING UNDERSTANDING

You can strengthen understanding by encouraging children to make number bonds using objects around the classroom. Look for children to split the whole into the two parts correctly.

GOING DEEPER

Encourage children to work systematically to find all the ways to make a whole. You could also expose children to equivalent addition calculations, for example 4 + 2 = 5 + 1. This is particularly tricky, as there is no defined whole and so the numbers cannot be put straight into a part-whole model.

KEY LANGUAGE

In lesson: altogether, add , in total, plus, '+', added / adding / addition, parts, whole

Other language to be used by the teacher: sum, part-whole model, equal / equals

STRUCTURES AND REPRESENTATIONS

Part-whole model, ten frame

RESOURCES

Mandatory: blank part-whole model, blank ten frames, cubes or counters to put in each of these
Optional: any physical resources to make parts of a whole (for example, cubes, counters, teddies, cars)

Teaching Tools In the eTextbook of this lesson, you will find interactive links to a selection of teaching tools.

Before you teach

• Based on teaching of the part-whole model in Unit 2, are there any additional misconceptions that need to be addressed?
• How will you support children when moving from structured addition (for example 3 + 4 = __) to writing a calculation based on a pictorial representation (for example __ + __ = __)?

Discover

WAYS OF WORKING Pair work

ASK

- Question ❶ a): *Which numbers are the parts?*
- Question ❶ b): *What happens to the total number of bowling pins when one is knocked over?*

IN FOCUS In this part of the lesson, we first want children to understand how the real-life problem can give numbers that are parts and wholes. The word 'altogether' is used repeatedly to promote understanding that the two parts can combine to make a whole.

DEEPEN Question ❶ b) provides a good opportunity to ensure that children understand that one more bowling pin being knocked over means the parts have changed but the whole has not.

ANSWERS

Question ❶ a): 6 ⚲ are left up. 4 ⚲ are knocked over.

There are 10 ⚲ altogether.

Question ❶ b): There are 10 ⚲ altogether.

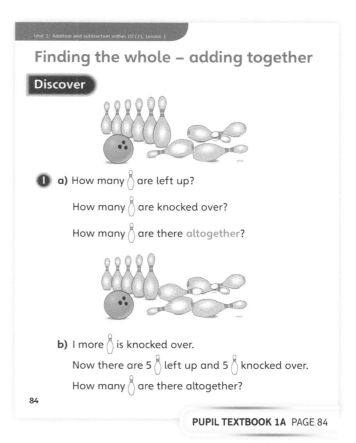

Finding the whole – adding together

Discover

❶ a) How many ⚲ are left up?

How many ⚲ are knocked over?

How many ⚲ are there altogether?

b) 1 more ⚲ is knocked over.

Now there are 5 ⚲ left up and 5 ⚲ knocked over.

How many ⚲ are there altogether?

84

PUPIL TEXTBOOK 1A PAGE 84

Share

WAYS OF WORKING Whole class teacher led

ASK

- Question ❶ a): *What part of the part-whole model shows how many bowling pins are standing?*
- Question ❶ a): *How many bowling pins have fallen over?*
- Question ❶ a): *How many are there altogether?*
- Question ❶ b): *Why is the total the same for both questions?*

IN FOCUS In this part of the lesson, the concrete representations are being linked to the part-whole model and abstract calculation. The addition symbol, '+', is being introduced in context. Use the characters to introduce this idea.

ASSESSMENT CHECKPOINT Assess whether the children can point to the two different parts on the part-whole model. In question ❶ b) it is important to distinguish that, even though the parts (5 and 5) are the same, they represent different things. Refer back to the picture in question ❶ a) so they can make the distinction.

Share

There are two parts.

To add we need to put the two parts together and count the whole.

a) There are 6 ⚲ left up.

There are 4 ⚲ knocked over.

There are 10 ⚲ altogether.

$6 + 4 = 10$

b) There are 5 ⚲ left up.

There are 5 ⚲ knocked over.

There are 10 ⚲ altogether.

$5 + 5 = 10$

85

PUPIL TEXTBOOK 1A PAGE 85

Think together

Think together

WAYS OF WORKING Whole class teacher led (I do, We do, You do)

ASK

- Question ❶: *What does 'total' mean? Where would you find it on the part-whole model?*
- *How are the bowling pins represented in the part-whole models?*
- *How could you find the total using counters to represent the bowling pins?*

IN FOCUS In question ❶, children should be able to explain how the counters represent the bowling pins, and show that they can be used to make it easier to represent the calculation, rather than having to draw bowling pins every time.

STRENGTHEN Refer to the definition of 'total'. To embed this new vocabulary, ask children to point to the place the total should appear in the part-whole model. Make the link between the words 'altogether' and 'whole'.

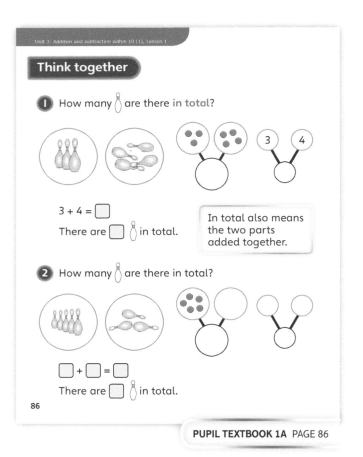

PUPIL TEXTBOOK 1A PAGE 86

DEEPEN Question ❸ provides a good opportunity to ensure that children are able to use their new knowledge of the '+' symbol and what the parts and wholes are to create different calculations. When moving the '=' symbol, there may be confusion as to where the numbers go and what they represent.

ASSESSMENT CHECKPOINT Ask children to represent question ❸ using their blank part-whole model and counters or cubes. Assess whether children correctly represent each number as a part or a whole, and if they are able to distinguish that the whole has now changed but the method to find it has stayed the same.

ANSWERS

Question ❶ 3 + 4 = 7

There are 7 🎳 in total.

Question ❷ 5 + 3 = 8

There are 8 🎳 in total.

Question ❸ 5 + 2 = 7

PUPIL TEXTBOOK 1A PAGE 87

Practice

WAYS OF WORKING Independent thinking

IN FOCUS Throughout this section, children will be exposed to different part-wholes. In question ❸, the '=' sign is at the start of the calculation, in a different place to where they have seen it previously.

STRENGTHEN In question ❸, one of the parts has stayed the same but the other part and the whole have changed. Can children continue this pattern of keeping one part the same, and then adding one more to the other part? See if the children can spot a pattern in what happens to the whole each time.

DEEPEN In question ❹ a), children have freedom over what the different parts of 9 could be. Once they have found two ways, additional ten frames could be provided for children to continue to find the different ways to make 9.

ASSESSMENT CHECKPOINT In question ❹, ascertain whether children colour in the parts of the ten frame in different colours to represent their two parts.

ANSWERS Answers for the **Practice** part of the lesson appear in the separate **Practice and Reflect answer guide**.

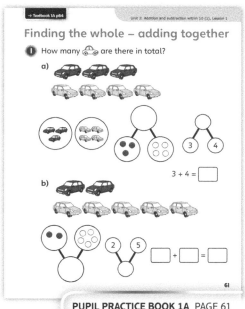

PUPIL PRACTICE BOOK 1A PAGE 61

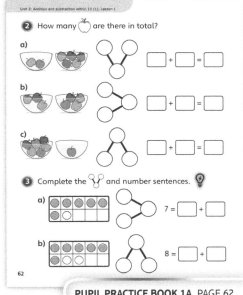

PUPIL PRACTICE BOOK 1A PAGE 62

Reflect

WAYS OF WORKING Pair work, Whole class

IN FOCUS Refer to what Flo is saying and what she is showing the children. Ask if children can name these models and explain how each of them helps to work out the total.

ASSESSMENT CHECKPOINT Assess whether children are able to name the models and images that Flo is showing them, and which they have used in this lesson. Ask them to explain the difference between them, or articulate how each helps them to find the total. Assess whether children are able to use language such as 'total', 'whole' and 'altogether' in their explanations.

ANSWERS Answers for the **Reflect** part of the lesson appear in the separate **Practice and Reflect answer guide**.

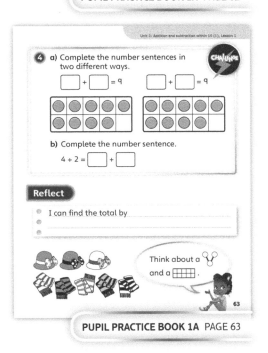

PUPIL PRACTICE BOOK 1A PAGE 63

After the lesson ⏸

- Are children secure using the part-whole model and ten frame before moving on?
- Are children confident with what each of the numbers in each structure represents, and can they move between them and the concrete examples?

Finding the whole – adding more

Learning focus

In this lesson, children will be able to find a total by counting on from one amount rather than having to start at zero.

Small steps

→ Previous step: Finding the whole – adding together
→ **This step: Finding the whole – adding more**
→ Next step: Finding a part

NATIONAL CURRICULUM LINKS

Year 1 Number – Addition and Subtraction

Represent and use number bonds and related subtraction facts within 20.

ASSESSING MASTERY

Children can accurately count on from an amount, and represent this on a number line to show the amount being added on as a number of jumps. Children can also develop their understanding of the commutative law of addition: for example, $2 + 7 = 7 + 2$.

COMMON MISCONCEPTIONS

Children may incorrectly use their starting number as their first count. When calculating the answer to $5 + 2$, for example, children may count the number 5 as their first count. They need to know that each count is in a one-one relationship with the objects being added. To support understanding, model this with physical resources and ask:
• *If I have 5 cubes to start with, and add two more, what number is my first count?*

Children may also lose track of how many they are counting on, as they have to hold the number they are counting on in their head as well as counting out loud from another number. One way of overcoming this is to ask:
• *Can you hold up fingers to match the number that you are counting on?*

STRENGTHENING UNDERSTANDING

To strengthen understanding, you can encourage children to count on from any given number to 10. Pairs could take it in turns to pick a number under 10, and ask their partner to count on 5 / count up to 10.

GOING DEEPER

You can encourage children to deepen understanding by building on prior learning of 'more than' or 'less than'. For example, model expressing $5 + 2 = 7$ as '2 *more than* 5 is 7'.

KEY LANGUAGE

In lesson: count on, add / added / adding / addition, plus, '+', in total

Other language to be used by the teacher: add more, starting point, total, altogether, jumps

STRUCTURES AND REPRESENTATIONS

Ten frame, number line

RESOURCES

Mandatory: blank ten frame, number line, dice, marbles/cubes and a jar
Optional: number track, bead string, multilink cubes

Teaching Tools In the eTextbook of this lesson, you will find interactive links to a selection of teaching tools.

Before you teach

• Based on teaching of the part-whole model and '+' symbol in Lesson 1, are there any remaining misconceptions that need to be addressed?
• How will you explore common mistakes, such as counting on from the starting number instead of the next number? Can children be encouraged to circle their starting number on a number line before counting on?

Discover

Pair work

ASK

- Question ① a): *How many are in the jar to start?*
- Question ① b): *How many are in the jar to start now? Why has this amount changed?* (Because 2 more were added in question ① a).)

IN FOCUS In this part of the lesson, children are presented with a real-life context for 'adding on' a certain amount when starting from an amount above zero. The language 'are added' is used repeatedly in question ①, to promote understanding that there is a starting quantity.

ANSWERS

Question ① a): 7 ⚪ are in the jar now.

Question ① b): 10 ⚪ are in the jar now.

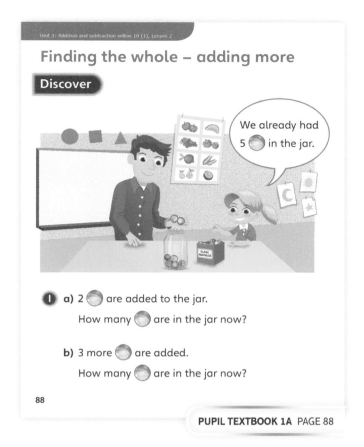

PUPIL TEXTBOOK 1A PAGE 88

Share

WAYS OF WORKING Whole class teacher led

ASK

- Question ① a): *What do the 5 and 2 refer to?*
- Question ① a): *Why did we count on from 5?*
- Question ① a): *Why did we count two jumps?*
- Question ① a): *Why did we count on … 6 …7… instead of … 5 … 6 …?*

IN FOCUS This part of the lesson lends itself to being very practical and sensory, as children can learn to count on using sounds. Tell children there are 5 cubes/marbles to begin with, and then ask them to count on with every sound they hear (as each cube/marble is dropped into a jar). This reinforces one-to-one correspondence.

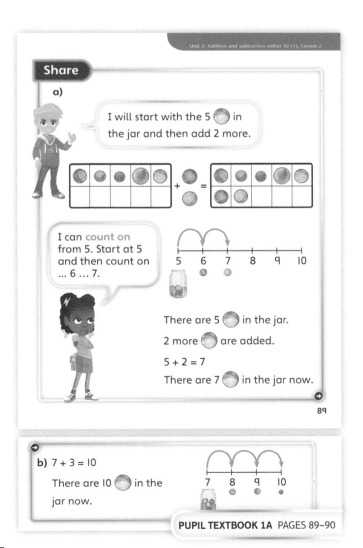

DEEPEN This part of the lesson provides a good opportunity to encourage children to be flexible with the numbers in the calculation. Ask: *What would the number line would look like if we started with 2 marbles and added 5?* Then ask children to start counting at 2, to arrive at the same answer.

PUPIL TEXTBOOK 1A PAGES 89–90

Think together

WAYS OF WORKING Whole class teacher led (I do, We do, You do)

ASK

- Question **1**: *What is our starting point? How many were in the jar to start with? Where do we see this number on the number line?*
- Question **1**: *How many are being added? Where is that shown on the number line?*
- Question **3**: *Does it make most sense to start counting from the smallest or the largest number in this calculation?*

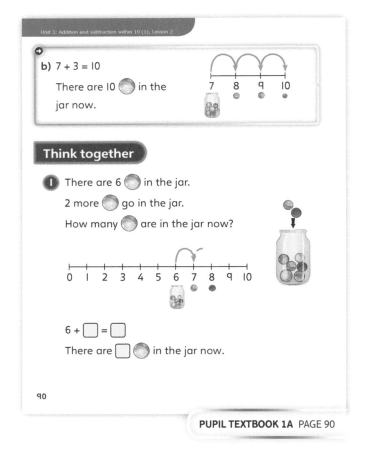

IN FOCUS Question **3** encourages children to think carefully about the most efficient strategy, and to decide from which number to count on: the smallest or the largest. Refer to Ash asking where to start. Ask children to point to the starting point on the number line.

STRENGTHEN For question **3**, you could use multilink cubes or bead strings to reinforce the practice of counting on: children can represent the calculation by physically moving the number of multilink cubes or beads they need to add on.

DEEPEN This part of the lesson provides a good opportunity to ensure that children can check their answers by counting backwards.

ASSESSMENT CHECKPOINT Assess whether children are able to relate the parts of a calculation to the number line accurately. For example, in question **2**, 5 is the starting point and 3 more are added. Therefore, 5 should be the starting point on the number line and there should be 3 jumps.

ANSWERS

Question **1**: $6 + 2 = 8$

There are 8 ⬤ in the jar now.

Question **2**: $5 + 3 = 8$

There are 8 ⬤ in the jar now.

Question **3**: $2 + 7 = 9$

Practice

WAYS OF WORKING Independent thinking

IN FOCUS In questions ❶ and ❷, the starting point has been given to children in the calculation. In question ❸, children need to find the starting point for themselves, and then count on.

STRENGTHEN In question ❹, a deliberate mistake has been made: Tom counts on from the starting number. Allow children to identify the mistake and explain, in their own words, what has gone wrong. Listen for children using the language 'starting point' or 'counted on wrong' in their explanations.

In question ❻, children could make the number bonds physically, placing multilink cubes onto a staggered number line.

DEEPEN Question ❻ provides a good opportunity for children to apply what they have learned. When the calculations have been matched to their correct places on the number line, ask children to make up their own calculations for the numbers that have no calculations attached.

ASSESSMENT CHECKPOINT Check that children are starting on the correct point in the number line, and counting on the correct amounts. Children should not be starting at zero to work out the overall total, even if their answers are correct.

ANSWERS Answers for the **Practice** part of the lesson appear in the separate **Practice and Reflect answer guide**.

Reflect

WAYS OF WORKING Pair work, Whole class

IN FOCUS This activity allows you to discuss the commutativity of addition as a class. The discussion should expose that there is less chance of making an error if you start from the larger number.

ASSESSMENT CHECKPOINT Assess whether children can identify that the total will be the same, no matter which is their starting number. Look for children using the number-line structures from the lesson to explain counting on.

ANSWERS Answers for the **Reflect** part of the lesson appear in the separate **Practice and Reflect answer guide**.

After the lesson ⏸

- Have children mastered counting on, rather than counting from zero, to find a total?
- Did children recognise when their approach was correct but took longer, for example by starting with the smaller part and counting on the larger?

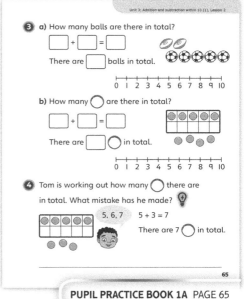

PUPIL PRACTICE BOOK 1A PAGE 64

PUPIL PRACTICE BOOK 1A PAGE 65

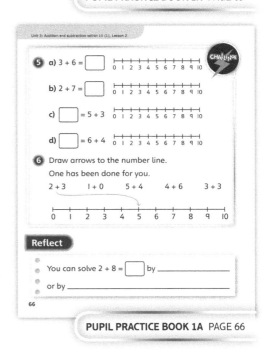

PUPIL PRACTICE BOOK 1A PAGE 66

Finding a part

Learning focus

In this lesson, children will find a missing part by counting on from another part to the whole.

Small steps

→ Previous step: Finding the whole – adding more
→ **This step: Finding a part**
→ Next step: Finding and making number bonds

NATIONAL CURRICULUM LINKS

Year 1 Number – Addition and Subtraction

Represent and use number bonds and related subtraction facts within 20.

ASSESSING MASTERY

Children can count on from one part to the total, in order to find the missing part. Children can identify that the missing part is the number of jumps (or the difference) between the two parts.

COMMON MISCONCEPTIONS

Children may not know when to stop counting, as they may lose track of what the whole is. Encourage children to circle the starting point and end point on their number lines, so they do not have to hold the total in their head as they are counting. Ask:
• *What is your starting point? What is your end point?*

Children may also make the mistake of adding the part to the whole. Ask children to differentiate between the two:
• *What is the total? Which part do we know?*

STRENGTHENING UNDERSTANDING

You can support children to embed understanding of a known whole and unknown part through activities outside of the lesson. For example, on a giant number line in the playground, children can take turns starting at different points and counting how many jumps they need to do to get to the end. This reinforces the idea that there is a fixed end point where counting needs to stop, and the missing part is found through the physical act of counting.

GOING DEEPER

Finding a missing part by counting on is an important skill, as it allows children to solve missing-number problems and sets the foundation for understanding the link between addition and subtraction. At the end of the lesson, deepen children's understanding by encouraging them to write a missing-number calculation based on a number line.

KEY LANGUAGE

In lesson: missing part, in total, altogether

Other language to be used by the teacher: part of the whole, more

STRUCTURES AND REPRESENTATIONS

Part-whole model, number line

RESOURCES

Mandatory: blank part-whole model, number line
Optional: bead string, number track, PE equipment

Teaching Tools In the eTextbook of this lesson, you will find interactive links to a selection of teaching tools.

Before you teach

• Do children have a thorough understanding of the part-whole model, and understand how the counting on method works in relation to it?
• How did children respond to using the number line in the previous lesson?
• Are children confident in recognising their starting number and what they should be counting on?

Discover

Pair work

ASK

- Question ❶ a): *How many apples are there? Is this the whole or the part?*
- Question ❶ a): *How many children are there? Is this the whole or the part?*
- Question ❶ a): *What is missing? How can we use counting to help us work it out?*

IN FOCUS In this part of the lesson, the concept of having one part and a known whole, and having to find the missing part, is introduced through a concrete story. Reinforce the fact that the *whole*, or *total*, is known.

ANSWERS

Question ❶ a): 3 children get a 🍌.

There are 3 🍌.

Question ❶ b): 4 children will get an 🍎.

There are 4 🍎.

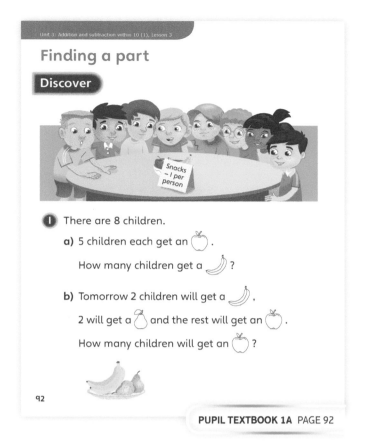

PUPIL TEXTBOOK 1A PAGE 92

Share

Whole class teacher led

ASK

- Question ❶ a): *Why did we count on from 5?*
- Question ❶ a): *How many jumps were there?*
- *Why do we need 8 pieces of fruit in total?*
- *How is our method similar to adding by counting on? How is it different?*

IN FOCUS In this section, the concrete story is applied to a number line. Children need to count the number of jumps from the part to the whole, to find the missing part.

STRENGTHEN With a number line in front of them, children can locate the starting number. Strengthen their understanding by asking children to use counters to count on until they reach the whole, and to represent the jumps underneath the number line.

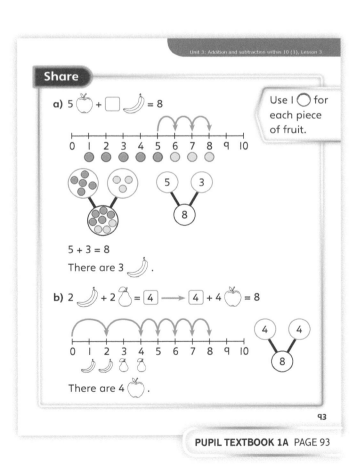

PUPIL TEXTBOOK 1A PAGE 93

Think together

WAYS OF WORKING Whole class teacher led (I do, We do, You do)

ASK

- Question **①**: *What part of the whole do we already know? What is it representing?*
  (Ask children to link this back to the concrete examples of strawberries and apples.)
- Question **②**: *What is the whole? Where will you stop counting on the number line?*

IN FOCUS Scaffolding is reduced in question **②**, so children have to identify the starting point on the number line for themselves.

STRENGTHEN Support children's understanding by using bead strings alongside the number line. Show the starting number and then physically count on as children move each bead across.

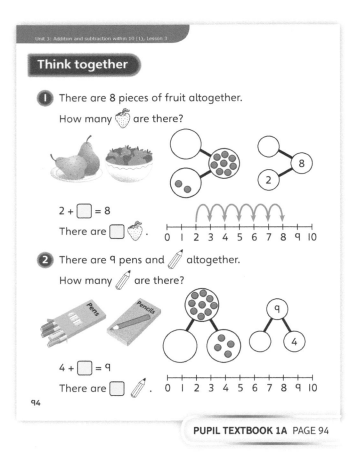

PUPIL TEXTBOOK 1A PAGE 94

DEEPEN In question **③** a), draw attention to the fact that both calculations' answers are the same. Then encourage them to apply this deepened knowledge to answer question **③** b).

ASSESSMENT CHECKPOINT Assess whether children can recognise that the number of jumps on the number line is the missing part of a calculation, and put it into the part-whole model with numbers.

ANSWERS

Question **①**: $2 + 6 = 8$
          There are 6 🍓.

Question **②**: $4 + 5 = 9$
          There are 5 ✏.

Question **③** a): $5 + 2 = 7$
          $2 + 5 = 7$

Question **③** b): $3 + 4 = 7$
          $4 + 3 = 7$

PUPIL TEXTBOOK 1A PAGE 95

Practice

WAYS OF WORKING Independent thinking

IN FOCUS In question **5**, the missing part is represented in different parts of the calculation. In question **5** b), children will have to use 3 as their starting point, even though it is the second part of the calculation.

STRENGTHEN In question **4** you can strengthen children's understanding by asking them to show the correct representation of 3 + 5, using concrete objects and correcting the calculation accordingly.

DEEPEN Deepen understanding by exploring the two ways to correct the mistake in question **4**. Children could correct the calculation by switching 5 to form the part, leaving the missing number as the whole. However, children could also keep the calculation as their basis, and make the 5 the whole in the part-whole model. The missing part would then be 2.

ASSESSMENT CHECKPOINT Assess whether children are able to use counting on to work out the missing part, or whether they are using another strategy. In question **6**, gauge whether children are using their answers from the previous question to help them answer the next one, as only one part of the calculation has been changed each time: one is added to the part or to the whole.

ANSWERS Answers for the **Practice** part of the lesson appear in the separate **Practice and Reflect answer guide**.

Reflect

WAYS OF WORKING Pair work, Whole class

IN FOCUS Before starting, ask children to label each number in the calculation as 'part' or 'whole'. Give pairs an opportunity to talk about their strategies for solving the problem before they feed back to the class. Discuss similarities and differences.

STRENGTHEN The skill of finding a missing part is going to form the basis for subtracting in later lessons. Strengthen children's understanding of this skill by pointing out some of the many every-day situations in which a whole and only one part are known.

ASSESSMENT CHECKPOINT Assess how confident children are regarding where to start and stop counting on number lines. Are they able to count jumps correctly, to find a missing part and count on? Are they able to represent this calculation using other resources, or physically act it out?

ANSWERS Answers for the **Reflect** part of the lesson appear in the separate **Practice and Reflect answer guide**.

After the lesson ⏸

- How did the children respond mathematically to the introduction of a missing-number question?
- Were the missing-number calculations too abstract for children to represent their mathematical thinking? If so, consider spending time with children, modelling calculations using concrete apparatus to strengthen conceptual understanding.

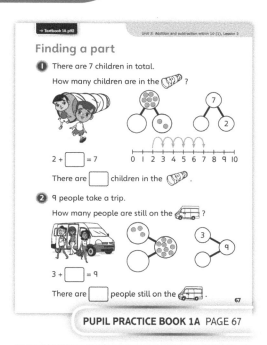

PUPIL PRACTICE BOOK 1A PAGE 67

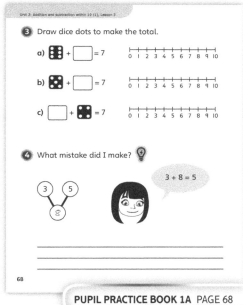

PUPIL PRACTICE BOOK 1A PAGE 68

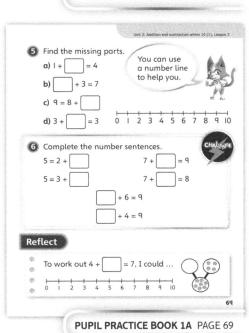

PUPIL PRACTICE BOOK 1A PAGE 69

Finding and making number bonds

Learning focus

In this lesson, children will find and represent number bonds to 10. The lesson builds on the previous one, on finding a missing part.

Small steps

→ Previous step: Finding a part
→ **This step: Finding and making number bonds**
→ Next step: Finding addition facts

NATIONAL CURRICULUM LINKS

Y1 Number – Addition and Subtraction

Represent and use number bonds and related subtraction facts within 20.

ASSESSING MASTERY

Children can use instant recall of number bonds to 10, and represent them in a ten frame and a part-whole model. Children can use this knowledge to answer missing-number problems without having to count on.

COMMON MISCONCEPTIONS

Children may not make the link between instant recall of number bonds to 10 and solving missing-number problems. They may revert to counting on, even if they know the answer. If children revert back to working out the number bond, use different mathematical structures to represent calculations. Ask:
• *Can you highlight the numbers that are the same?*

STRENGTHENING UNDERSTANDING

You can reinforce learning by encouraging children to work systematically to find all of the number bonds to 10. Suggest that they show this working on a resource such as a bead string.

GOING DEEPER

You can deepen learning by encouraging children to generate their own calculations based on their knowledge of number bonds to 10. Scaffolds, such as '_ + _ = 10', could be given.

When confident, children can create their own missing-number calculations in which the whole is always 10. For example, 8 + _ = 10. Remember to explore 0 + 10, as this is a number bond children should know.

KEY LANGUAGE

In lesson: add / added / adding / addition, plus, '+', altogether, in total, sum, number bonds
Other language to be used by the teacher: whole, part

STRUCTURES AND REPRESENTATIONS

Part-whole model, ten frame

RESOURCES

Mandatory: blank part-whole model, blank ten frame, counters or cubes
Optional: bead string

Teaching Tools In the eTextbook of this lesson, you will find interactive links to a selection of teaching tools.

Before you teach

• Based on teaching of finding a missing part in Lesson 3, are there any difficulties or misconceptions that need to be tackled before starting this lesson?
• Using your knowledge of how children have worked with number bonds to 10 in previous lessons, are there any adaptations or links you can make to this lesson?
• How could you prompt children to use their fingers to help them during this lesson?

Discover

WAYS OF WORKING Pair work

ASK

- Question **1** a): *How many cans are standing?*
- Question **1** a): *How many cans are on the floor?*
- Question **1** a): *How many cans are there in total?*

IN FOCUS In this part of the lesson, children are exposed to a real-life practical context surrounding number bonds to 10. Question **1** introduces a concrete story as illustration of the calculation. Focus on the picture. Ask: *What do you see? What do you think the problem could be?*

STRENGTHEN Strengthen children's understanding by acting out the story in the classroom, moving some of ten objects off a classroom table. Encourage children to play with and record the number bonds they find.

ANSWERS

Question **1** a): Tom hit 3 🥫.

Question **1** b): There are 5 🥫 left up.

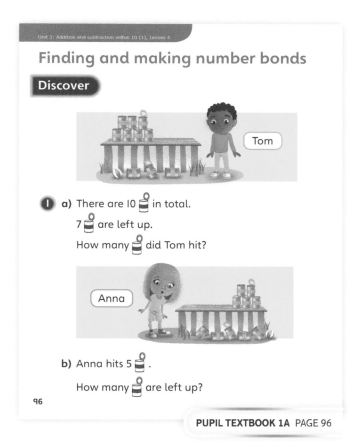

Finding and making number bonds

Discover

1 a) There are 10 🥫 in total.

7 🥫 are left up.

How many 🥫 did Tom hit?

b) Anna hits 5 🥫.

How many 🥫 are left up?

96

PUPIL TEXTBOOK 1A PAGE 96

Share

WAYS OF WORKING Whole class teacher led

ASK

- *What role does 10 have, in these calculations?*
- *What can we use to find bonds to 10?*
- *Why is a ten frame useful?*
- *On a ten frame, what numbers can you see easily?*

IN FOCUS This part of the lesson encourages children to share different strategies for finding number bonds to 10, based on structures and representations used in previous lessons.

STRENGTHEN If children struggle to recall different representations, strengthen their understanding by talking together about the different ways you can find the answer to 3 + 7. Ask: *What is the same about these methods, and what is different? Does the whole remain the same? Where are the parts 3 and 7? Does it matter which way around they go?*

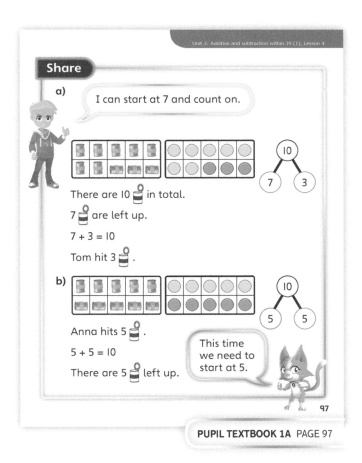

Share

a) I can start at 7 and count on.

There are 10 🥫 in total.

7 🥫 are left up.

7 + 3 = 10

Tom hit 3 🥫.

b) Anna hits 5 🥫.

5 + 5 = 10

There are 5 🥫 left up.

This time we need to start at 5.

97

PUPIL TEXTBOOK 1A PAGE 97

Think together

WAYS OF WORKING Whole class teacher led (I do, We do, You do)

ASK

- Question ❶: *Can you point to how many cans were hit in the picture? What number is shown in the ten frame – the number of cans that were left up, or the number of cans that were hit?*
- Question ❷: *What two parts of the part-whole model do you need to fill in?*

IN FOCUS In question ❶, 6 cans are shown standing, and 4 are shown on their sides. This illustration reinforces the number bond 6 + 4 = 10. Children can work out the answer to the calculation by using their number bond knowledge or by referring to the artwork.

Draw attention to what Astrid points out after question ❸, about using hands as a way to remember 5 + 5 = 10.

In question ❸, there is systematic progression in finding the number bonds to 10. This can be reinforced by working concretely with 10 objects and moving one at a time.

STRENGTHEN Strengthen children's understanding of how to tackle question ❷ by modelling looking at the picture to find which cans were hit.

DEEPEN In question ❸, six number bonds to 10 are found. Deepen children's understanding by explaining how they can use these bonds to work out other bonds to 10. For example, if they know that 9 + 1 = 10, they also know that 1 + 9 = 10.

ASSESSMENT CHECKPOINT In questions ❷ and ❸, there are blank ten frames to fill in. Up to this point, children have been presented with filled-in ten frames. Assess how children draw on separate parts for themselves. Will they use different-coloured pens, different-sized dots or another method? Point out what Dexter said about working in order, and ask children to explain what this means in relation to what they have just done.

ANSWERS

Question ❶: 6 + 4 = 10   4 🥫 were hit.

Question ❷: 8 + 2 = 10   2 🥫 were hit.

Question ❸: 8 + 2 = 10
7 + 3 = 10
6 + 4 = 10
5 + 5 = 10

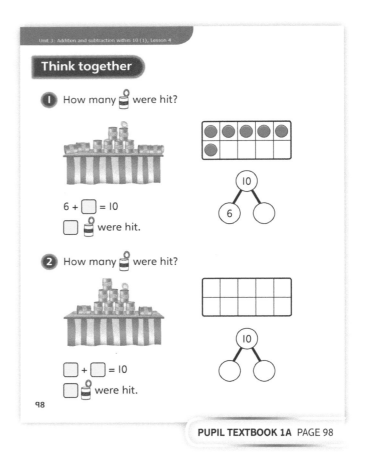

Think together

❶ How many 🥫 were hit?

6 + ☐ = 10

☐ 🥫 were hit.

10
6 ☐

❷ How many 🥫 were hit?

10

☐ + ☐ = 10

☐ 🥫 were hit.

98

PUPIL TEXTBOOK 1A PAGE 98

❸ Complete the diagrams and number sentences.   CHALLENGE

10 + 0 = 10

9 + 1 = 10

8 + ☐ = ☐

7 + ☐ = ☐

6 + ☐ = ☐

5 + ☐ = ☐

I worked in order.

I remember 5 + 5 = 10. ✋

→ Practice book 1A p70

99

PUPIL TEXTBOOK 1A PAGE 99

Practice

WAYS OF WORKING Independent thinking

IN FOCUS Question ③ involves adding 0. Reinforce understanding that adding 0 means adding nothing, and the original number has not changed.

STRENGTHEN Strengthen children's understanding by inviting them to show the different number bonds using different physical resources: for example, a bead string.

DEEPEN Deepen understanding of question ④ by challenging children to come up with different shapes for each of the numbers up to 10, and to make up their own shape calculations.

ASSESSMENT CHECKPOINT Look out for any children who count the number of circles needed to fill the ten frame, or who rely on their fingers to check or count, rather than trusting their number-bond knowledge.

ANSWERS Answers for the **Practice** part of the lesson appear in the separate **Practice and Reflect answer guide**.

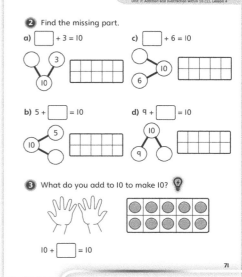

PUPIL PRACTICE BOOK 1A PAGE 70

PUPIL PRACTICE BOOK 1A PAGE 71

Reflect

WAYS OF WORKING Whole class

IN FOCUS The **Reflect** question reinforces different strategies children can use to remember number bonds to 10. Ask children to remember what other structures they have used to show these bonds.

ASSESSMENT CHECKPOINT Assess to what extent children are using instant recall. Do they have to use their fingers or the ten frames to help them work out the bonds? If so, do they represent the different parts in the ten frame using different colours or shapes?

ANSWERS Answers for the **Reflect** part of the lesson appear in the separate **Practice and Reflect answer guide**.

After the lesson ⏸

- Are children secure enough in number bonds to 10 to move on to finding addition facts in the next lesson, or is further reinforcement required?
- Did children recognise when their calculation strategies were inefficient, and were they able to modify their strategies based on your intervention?

PUPIL PRACTICE BOOK 1A PAGE 72

Finding addition facts

Learning focus

In this lesson, children will continue to find number bonds within 10 and link them to addition calculations. They will explore the commutativity of addition, through recognition of number pairs to 10.

Small steps

→ Previous step: Finding and making number bonds
→ **This step: Finding addition facts**
→ Next step: Solving word problems – addition

NATIONAL CURRICULUM LINKS

Year 1 Number – Addition and Subtraction
- Represent and use number bonds and related subtraction facts within 20.
- Read, write and interpret mathematical statements involving addition (+), subtraction (–) and equals (=) signs.

ASSESSING MASTERY

Children can solve both parts of addition pair calculations, without needing to calculate both parts (using the commutative law of addition). Children can use their growing knowledge of number bonds to help them to answer questions that are worded slightly differently: for example, *How many are missing?*

COMMON MISCONCEPTIONS

Children may not be familiar with the terminology of questions such as 'How many are missing?', and may answer with how many there *are*. Ask:
- *What does the word 'missing' mean? Can we see something that is 'missing'?*
Relate to any real-life context of something not being there, and therefore not being seen.

Children should be aware at this point that, even when numbers in an addition calculation are 'swapped', the calculation's answer will remain the same. Check that children don't swap out the answer of the calculation rather than one of the parts. Ask:
- *I can see numbers in the calculation have been switched around. Is it the parts that have been switched around?*
- *Can you show me this calculation using the part-whole model? Does it make sense? Which number is the whole?*

STRENGTHENING UNDERSTANDING

To strengthen understanding, set up a large-scale practical activity (perhaps using PE equipment) so children can explore number bonds to 10 in concrete form. Children can then demonstrate calculations individually, using building blocks, cubes or marbles.

GOING DEEPER

When a number bond can be recalled, deepen understanding by asking children to write down the *four* calculations that can be made from it. Scaffolds could be given initially:

_ + _ = _   _ + _ = _   _ + _ = _   _ + _ = _

KEY LANGUAGE

In lesson: in total, missing, '+', '='
Other language to be used by the teacher: add / added / adding / addition, altogether, plus, sum, number bond, part, whole, pairs

STRUCTURES AND REPRESENTATIONS

Ten frame, number line, part-whole model

RESOURCES

Mandatory: blank ten frame, blank part-whole model
Optional: PE equipment, building blocks, cubes, marbles

Teaching Tools In the eTextbook of this lesson, you will find interactive links to a selection of teaching tools.

Before you teach

- As this is not the first time children will be learning about number bonds to 10, what will you do in this lesson to improve fluency and accurate recall?
- How can you develop and refine children's representations of number bonds to 10?
- How might questions be scaffolded for those children who do not see addition pairs, but instead work out calculations?

Discover

WAYS OF WORKING Pair work

ASK

• Question ❶ a): *How many flowers are there in the tub, before the seeds are planted?*
• Question ❶ a): *How many seeds are there altogether?*

IN FOCUS The questions here ask children to use their acquired knowledge from previous lessons, to distinguish between parts and wholes.

ANSWERS

Question ❶ a): 10 🌼 will grow in total.

Question ❶ b): 3 seeds are still to grow.

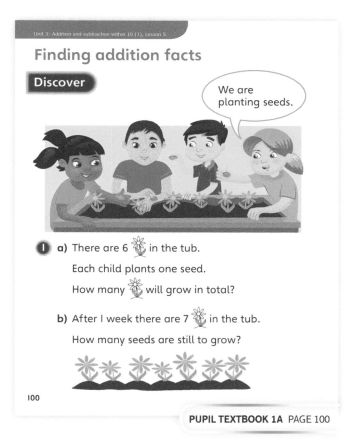

Share

WAYS OF WORKING Whole class teacher led

ASK

• Question ❶ a): *What do the 6, the 4 and the 10 show?*
• Question ❶ a): *Is adding the best way to solve this calculation?*
• Question ❶ a): *In what other ways could you solve it?*

IN FOCUS Before question ❶ a), Dexter says that the calculation can be represented on a ten frame. Ask children to make links between the concrete and pictorial representations, and to explain which counters represent flowers and seeds.

ASSESSMENT CHECKPOINT In question ❶ a), the number line starts at 6. Assess whether children understand why this is, listening for explanations involving counting on and not needing to start from zero.

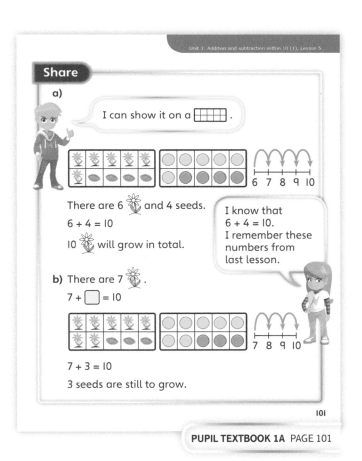

Think together

Whole class teacher led (I do, We do, You do)

ASK

- Question ❶: *How many gardening forks are there now?*
- Question ❶: *How many are needed to make 10?*
- Question ❶: *What strategies have you used before, to work this out?* (For example, counting on a number line, counting objects into a ten frame.)

IN FOCUS In question ❷, there is less scaffolding than in question ❶. Children now need to represent how many watering cans there are already, and then calculate how many are missing.

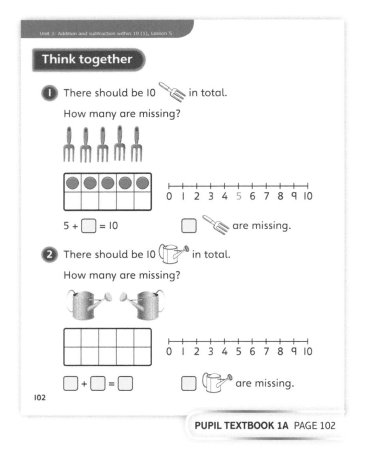

PUPIL TEXTBOOK 1A PAGE 102

STRENGTHEN Strengthen children's understanding of question ❸ by asking them to show the number bonds 7 + 3 and 3 + 7 using different-coloured multilink cubes, alongside the picture of the gardening spades. Encourage children to tell you which shows 7 + 3 and which shows 3 + 7.

DEEPEN This part of the lesson provides a good opportunity for children to come up with their own context for the number bond 7 + 3. Ask them to articulate an example and then to challenge a partner to use a different context for this same number bond.

ASSESSMENT CHECKPOINT

- In question ❷, assess whether children grasp that they should represent the 2 and 8 differently in the ten frame. Will they use different-coloured pens, different-sized dots or another method?
- In question ❸, look for any children who still need to calculate each separate fact rather than applying knowledge of the first addition pair to fill in the second.

ANSWERS

Question ❶: 5 + 5 = 10

        5 🍴 are missing.

Question ❷: 2 + 8 = 10

        8 🪣 are missing.

Question ❸: There are 10 🥄 in total.

        7 + 3 = 10

        3 + 7 = 10

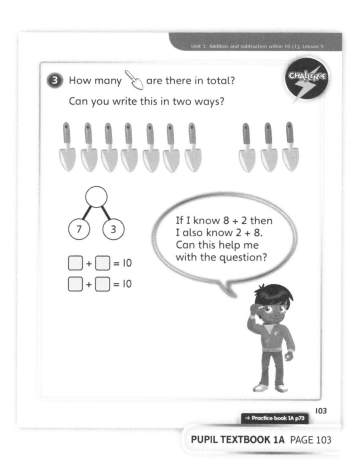

PUPIL TEXTBOOK 1A PAGE 103

Practice

WAYS OF WORKING Independent thinking

IN FOCUS
- Question ❺ involves using given number cards to complete three additions. This exercise could be made more practical by giving children access to real number cards.
- Question ❻ covers the misconception that there is a way of finding two facts for 5 + 5.

STRENGTHEN Strengthen children's understanding of the number bonds to 10 in question ❸ by asking: *What would you add to make another bond?* This question could also be modelled physically. Ask children to make bonds to 10 that match the question: the 5 and 10 towers will be left out. If children work systematically, they will also spot that the biggest number gets paired with the smallest number, and so on.

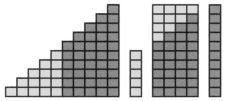

DEEPEN Deepen understanding in question ❻ by showing 5 + 5 = 5 + 5, and asking children to explain the calculation in relation to the pictures within the question. Guide them to understand that if there are five girls on one side of a see-saw and five boys on the other side, there will be ten children in total – even if the five boys and five girls swap sides.

ASSESSMENT CHECKPOINT In question ❺, check whether children have attempted to use 2 twice. It could be used in the first calculation, as 8 + 2 = 10, but is definitely needed in the second: 3 + 2 = 5.

ANSWERS Answers for the **Practice** part of the lesson appear in the separate **Practice and Reflect answer guide**.

Reflect

WAYS OF WORKING Pair work, Whole class

IN FOCUS This part of the lesson has been designed to gauge how confidently children swap the parts in the calculation to make 4 + 6 = 10.

DEEPEN If children are really confident with the commutative law, deepen their understanding by inviting them to write another calculation for 2 + 3 + 5 = 10 (a calculation with more than two parts).

ASSESSMENT CHECKPOINT Assess whether children are able to represent these addition facts using different resources, and to explain which represent each number bond.

ANSWERS Answers for the **Reflect** part of the lesson appear in the separate **Practice and Reflect answer guide**.

After the lesson ⏸

- How could children's grasp of the concept of commutativity be deepened and challenged?
- Were children able to explain how they knew addition was commutative, or did they struggle and assert they 'just know'?

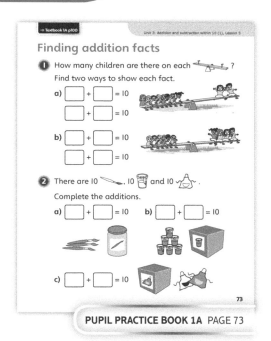

PUPIL PRACTICE BOOK 1A PAGE 73

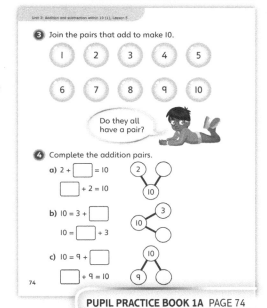

PUPIL PRACTICE BOOK 1A PAGE 74

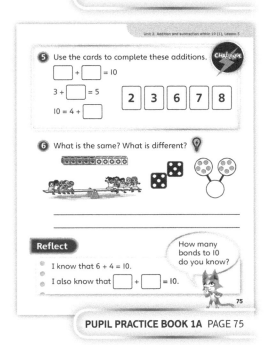

PUPIL PRACTICE BOOK 1A PAGE 75

Solving word problems – addition

Learning focus

In this lesson, children will find solutions to simple word and picture problems involving addition to 10.

Small steps

→ Previous step: Finding addition facts
→ **This step: Solving word problems – addition**
→ Next step: Subtraction – how many are left? (1)

NATIONAL CURRICULUM LINKS

Year 1 Number – Addition and Subtraction
- Solve one-step problems that involve addition and subtraction, using concrete objects and pictorial representations, and missing-number problems such as $7 = \_ - 9$.
- Represent and use number bonds and related subtraction facts within 20.

ASSESSING MASTERY

Children can find number stories in pictures and use addition to answer questions. Children can represent contexts using addition calculations, and explain the meanings of the parts of their calculations.

COMMON MISCONCEPTIONS

The number of objects in the pictures are not always represented in an ordered way, which may encourage children to go back to counting from zero to find the total. Draw links from previous lessons and model that once you have found how many objects are in one group, you can use that number to count on. Ask:
- *How many groups can you see?*

STRENGTHENING UNDERSTANDING

The contexts explored in this lesson show that number stories and number sentences describe the real world, in a similar way to that in which words and pictures do. Strengthen understanding by encouraging children to come up with their own context for one of the calculations. For example, instead of 6 jam tarts + 3 jam tarts, they could use 6 bears + 3 bears.

GOING DEEPER

Encourage children to explore this lesson in more depth by asking them to make up their own word problem, and to draw a picture that represents it, with the matching calculation alongside.

KEY LANGUAGE

In lesson: number stories, altogether, count, in total

Other language to be used by the teacher: parts, whole, addition calculation, greater than

STRUCTURES AND REPRESENTATIONS

Part-whole model, number line

RESOURCES

Mandatory: blank part-whole model, number line
Optional: classroom objects / PE equipment

Teaching Tools In the eTextbook of this lesson, you will find interactive links to a selection of teaching tools.

Before you teach

- Are children confident with the fundamental concept that two parts join together to make a whole, and recognise it on a part-whole model and in an addition calculation? If not, the real life contexts in this lesson may help children.
- What links could you make with other curriculum areas? Could curriculum links help children to compose their own word problems?

Discover

WAYS OF WORKING Pair work

ASK

- Question **1** a): *What do the 4 and the 4 mean?*
- Question **1** b): *Where on the picture can you see 1 person with 3 other people?*

IN FOCUS The picture contains lots of hidden number stories. Explain that you will be exploring them together throughout this lesson. Question **1** a) focuses attention on one part of the picture (people walking dogs) and elicits a number story from children. Question **1** b) focuses on a different part and a different story.

ANSWERS

Question **1** a): There are 8 in total.

Question **1** b): There is 1 person on one side of the see-saw, and 3 people on the other side: 1 + 3 = 4.

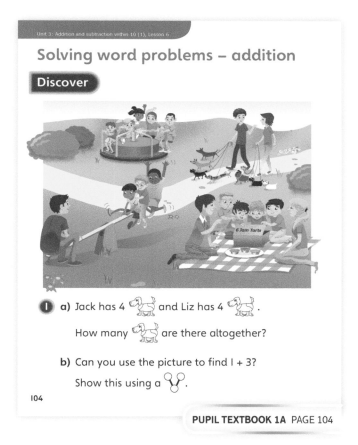

Solving word problems – addition

Discover

1 a) Jack has 4 🐕 and Liz has 4 🐕.
How many 🐕 are there altogether?

b) Can you use the picture to find 1 + 3?
Show this using a 🔵.

104

PUPIL TEXTBOOK 1A PAGE 104

Share

WAYS OF WORKING Whole class teacher led

ASK

- Question **1** a): *What does the number 4 show in this calculation?*
- Question **1** b): *What different thing does the number 4 show in this calculation?*
- *If you added 1 dog and 3 dogs, would that be the same as adding 1 ball and 3 balls?*

IN FOCUS Before Question **1** a), two different characters suggest different methods for solving the calculation. Look at what Dexter says. Ask: *Do you agree or disagree with Dexter? Counting would give us the right answer, but it would also take a long time.*

STRENGTHEN Strengthen children's understanding by discussing that the 4 in question **1** a) represents the number of dogs one person has (a part). The 4 in question **1** b) represents the number of people in total (whole). Encourage children to spot any other places in the picture where one number has different meanings.

Share

I can just count them.

I think adding is quicker.
I will use a 🔵 or a ⌗.

a) 4 + 4 = 8
There are 8 🐕 in total.

Use 1 ⬤ for each 🐕 or person.

b) 1 + 3 = 4
There are 4 people on the 🛝.

105

PUPIL TEXTBOOK 1A PAGE 105

Think together

WAYS OF WORKING Whole class teacher led (I do, We do, You do)

ASK

- Question ❶: *How many jam tarts can you see? How many jam tarts are hidden?*
- Question ❷: *You can see the whole picture, and all of the parts of the story. How many children are sitting? How many children are standing?*

IN FOCUS In question ❶, there are 3 jam tarts shown and 6 hidden in the box. Children may be tempted to start counting on from 3 on the number line, as that is the number they can see.

DEEPEN Deepen children's understanding of question ❶ by asking them to switch the numbers around. In the question, there are 6 tarts in the box and 3 tarts on the plate.

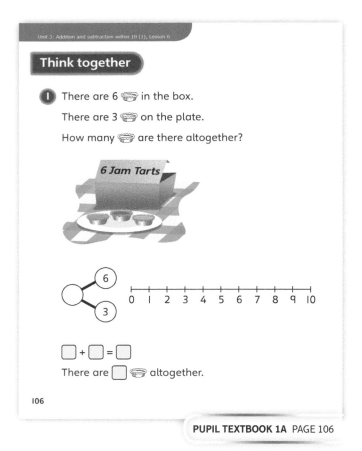

STRENGTHEN Strengthen children's understanding by asking them to work in pairs to complete question ❸, which prompts them to look again at the picture from the 'Discover' section. Ask children to tell their partners another number story they can see. The partner should articulate which number relates to which part of the story.

ASSESSMENT CHECKPOINT Assess how far children understand that calculations have meanings based on the contexts of the problems. Check that they grasp that changing contexts do not impact the answer.

ANSWERS

Question ❶ : 6 + 3 = 9
There are 9 🥧 altogether.

Question ❷ : 2 girls are on the 🎠.
3 boys are on the 🎠.
2 + 3 = 5
3 + 2 = 5
There are 5 children altogether.

Question ❸ : For example:
There are 2 adults and 4 children at the picnic.
2 + 4 = 6.
There are 6 people at the picnic altogether.

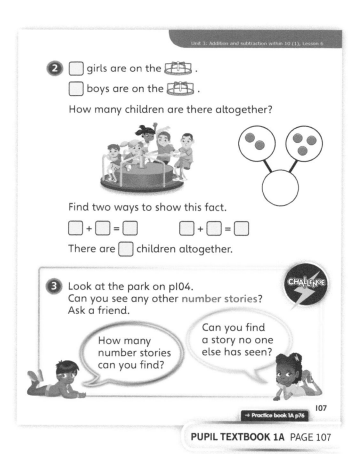

Practice

WAYS OF WORKING Independent thinking

IN FOCUS

- Question ① shows how there can be several number stories in one picture by splitting the children into two groups in two different ways.
- In question ②, the number of planes landing is not represented visually. Children could draw the 8 planes, or use concrete resources to represent them. They should be encouraged to count on or use their knowledge of number facts to work out the answer, rather than counting from 0.

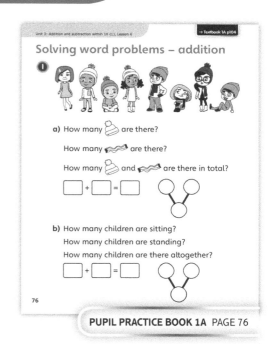

PUPIL PRACTICE BOOK 1A PAGE 76

STRENGTHEN Strengthen children's grasp of question ③ by suggesting they represent the 4 parts on the dartboards using cubes. (4 must be paired with 3, and 7 must be paired with 2.) Once there are two stacks of cubes, the greater whole can quickly be identified.

DEEPEN Question ③ is a *Challenge* question, and so will help to deepen children's understanding of parts and wholes. Encourage children to articulate that the whole formed on the left-hand dartboard is one of the parts on the right-hand dartboard.

ASSESSMENT CHECKPOINT When they are filling in the part-whole model in question ① a), assess whether children are able to explain which part is representing the hats, and which part is representing the scarves.

ANSWERS Answers for the **Practice** part of the lesson appear in the separate **Practice and Reflect answer guide**.

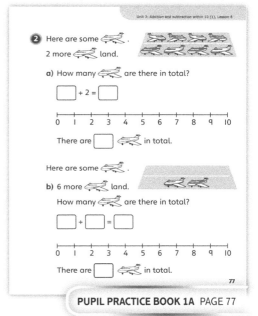

PUPIL PRACTICE BOOK 1A PAGE 77

Reflect

WAYS OF WORKING Pair work, Whole class

IN FOCUS Within the context given, children must write their own number story to match 4 + 5.

ASSESSMENT CHECKPOINT Listen for the children's language in explaining '= 9'. What do they say? They may say 'in total' or 'altogether' rather than 'equals'.

ANSWERS Answers for the **Reflect** part of the lesson appear in the separate **Practice and Reflect answer guide**.

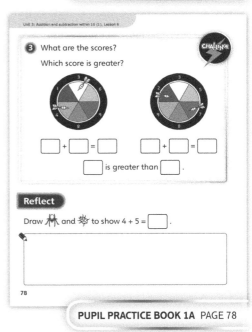

PUPIL PRACTICE BOOK 1A PAGE 78

After the lesson ⏸

- Are children fluent enough with their number bonds to 10 that they are using them in a variety of contexts, including contexts they have made up?
- Have any of the children shown an awareness of counting backwards, as well as counting on, when using the number line? This will be explored further in the next unit.

End of unit check

Don't forget the End of unit check proforma (page 108)!

WAYS OF WORKING Group work – adult led

IN FOCUS Question ❸ simply requires children to complete a number sentence. It will therefore allow you to identify those children who can work the question out mentally, and those who still need equipment or other support.

Think!

WAYS OF WORKING Pair work or small groups

IN FOCUS This question involves a lot of deep thinking. Any of the three choices could be the odd one out, as long as children's explanations are mathematically sound and appropriate (for instance, saying that two choices use the number 5, but the other does not, would not be acceptable).

When listening to explanations, encourage children to use the key vocabulary shown at the bottom of the **My journal** page.

Encourage children to think through or discuss the possible answers before writing their answer in **My journal**.

ANSWERS AND COMMENTARY Children who have mastered the concepts of this unit will be able to add and subtract using efficient methods, knowing when and how to use equipment to help them. They will be secure in their use of number bonds to 10 and be able to find different ways to make the same total. They will use the part-whole model and number line with confidence and be able to solve word problems involving addition or subtraction.

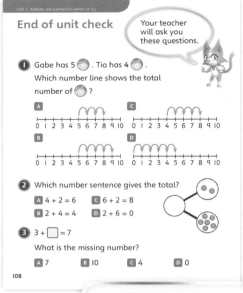

PUPIL TEXTBOOK 1A PAGE 108

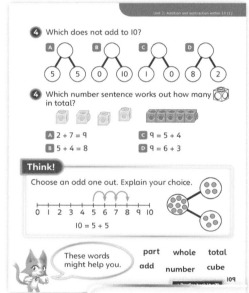

PUPIL TEXTBOOK 1A PAGE 109

Q	A	WRONG ANSWERS AND MISCONCEPTIONS	STRENGTHENING UNDERSTANDING
1	B	A suggests that children have some counting strategy difficulties; they may not be counting on, thinking instead that 5 + 4 = 5, 6, 7, 8.	Give children further daily counting support. Short, sharp sessions in which counters and number lines are used are very effective.
2	C	D indicates that children have not fully understood the part-whole model (they have assumed that because the whole is empty, the answer is 0).	Revise the structure of the part-whole model using apparatus: hoops and counters reinforce it well. A secure understanding of this model is important as a foundation for more complex work later on.
3	C	B suggests that children are confused by missing numbers and do not understand the function of the equals sign.	
4	C	B suggests that children have little understanding of place value; B may mean little to them, and they may have assumed that in C 1 + 0 = 10.	Give children number sentences to rearrange. For example, give them 2 + 3 = 5 and show them they could also write it as 3 + 2 = 5, 5 = 3 + 2, 5 = 2 + 3.
5	C	Not choosing C suggests that children are unfamiliar with number sentences in which the answer appears first.	

My journal

WAYS OF WORKING Independent thinking

ANSWERS AND COMMENTARY

Any of the three options could be the odd one out.

Possible explanations include:
- 10 = 5 + 5: I chose it because 5 + 3 = 8 and 4 + 4 = 8 are both ways of partitioning 8.
- 10 = 5 + 5: I chose it because the number line and part-whole model are both representations, not number sentences.
- 5 + 3 = 8: I chose it because 4 + 4 = 8 and 5 + 5 = 10 both show doubling.

Assess whether children use the correct vocabulary in their answers. Model exemplary answers to children. For example, if a child says, 'I choose 5 + 5 = 10 as the odd one out, because the other two both equal 8', say back to them, *Yes, the whole is 8 for both of them and the two parts make a total of 8, but in different ways.*

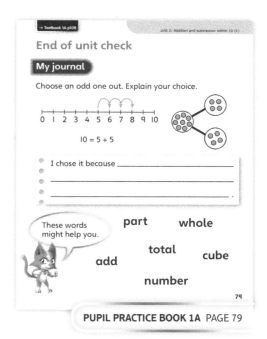

PUPIL PRACTICE BOOK 1A PAGE 79

Power check

WAYS OF WORKING Independent thinking

ASK
- *Do you think you could teach a friend something you have learned in this unit?*
- *Why did you choose the puzzled face?*

Power play

WAYS OF WORKING Pair work or small groups.

IN FOCUS Use the Power play to see if children can add pairs of 1-digit numbers mentally.

ANSWERS AND COMMENTARY If children can do the Power play, they are secure with single-digit addition strategies; watch to see if children need to use their fingers, or make markings on paper. If they cannot play the game, establish whether the problem is with basic counting or with the addition itself. Intervention activities to strengthen children's understanding will be necessary: counting games or adding games would work well; the use of equipment and structures such as the number line is imperative.

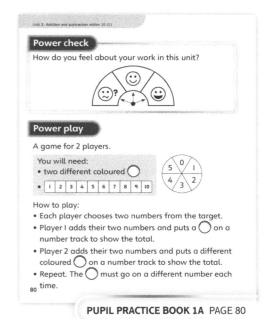

PUPIL PRACTICE BOOK 1A PAGE 80

After the unit ⏸

- What were children's strengths and weaknesses during the unit?
- How many children mastered the unit, and how many children need intervention?

Strengthen and *Deepen* activities for this unit can be found in the Power Maths online subscription.

Unit 4
Addition and subtraction within 10 ②

Mastery Expert tip! "Cubes or counters work well when taking away and counting what is left and a number line works well when counting backwards. Include lots of chanting forwards and backwards, including skip counting backwards, so children get used to hearing numbers going down as well as up."

Don't forget to watch the unit 4 video!

WHY THIS UNIT IS IMPORTANT

This unit focuses on subtraction within 10. Children will be introduced to the key language of subtraction and a range of scenarios in which subtraction takes place.

Within this unit, children are introduced to formal subtraction for the first time: they count how many are left, break apart a whole and find the difference. Children will model each of these situations using concrete and pictorial representations: taking away cubes, crossing out pictures and counting back on a number-line.

This unit builds on children's previous knowledge of number bonds to 10 and makes explicit links between subtraction facts and previously learnt addition facts. Children are asked to reason with subtraction facts and compare them to numbers using the < and > symbols.

WHERE THIS UNIT FITS

→ Unit 3: Addition and subtraction within 10 (1)
→ **Unit 4: Addition and subtraction within 10 (2)**
→ Unit 5: 2D and 3D shapes

This unit builds children's knowledge of number bonds within 10, their ability to use a number line to count forwards and backwards, and their understanding that two parts make a whole, in the context of subtraction. It looks at subtraction as the inverse of addition and teaches children to count backwards and work out a missing part, given the whole and the other part. Unit 5 will focus on the properties of 2D and 3D shapes.

Before they start this unit, it is expected that children:
- know how to count back from any number under 10
- understand the different components of a part-whole model and what each represents
- know what the symbols < and > mean.

ASSESSING MASTERY

Children who have mastered this unit will be able to correctly identify the parts and whole in subtraction calculations even when the = symbol is in different places. They will understand that subtraction, unlike addition, is not commutative. Children should be confident in using the part-whole model to represent subtraction and see 'numbers within the numbers'. When there is a subtraction fact where the two parts are the same, children will be able to explain how they still represent different things in context.

COMMON MISCONCEPTIONS	STRENGTHENING UNDERSTANDING	GOING DEEPER
Children may not understand that subtraction is not commutative and may switch numbers around in a subtraction number sentence.	Ask children to model subtraction number sentences using physical resources and explain what each part represents.	Show children a part-whole model and ask them to come up with as many different addition and subtraction number sentences as they can.
Children may incorrectly count back when using a number line so that the starting number is counted as one jump.	When jumping back on a number line, get children to physically jump backwards and count each time they do it.	Give children a series of addition and subtraction number sentences and ask them to compare them using < and >.

WAYS OF WORKING

Use these pages to introduce the unit focus to children. You can use the characters to remind children of the part-whole model and the language used for subtraction.

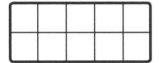

STRUCTURES AND REPRESENTATIONS

Part-whole model: This model helps children understand that two parts combine together to make a whole and that if you take one part away from the whole, you are left with the other.

Ten frame: The ten frame gives children a structure in which to put their starting number of objects. They can then remove or cross out the number being taken away and count what is left.

Number line: Number lines help children count backwards and keep track of how many they are counting back. They allow children to identify the starting point, the number counted on and the end point.

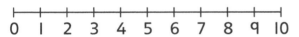

KEY LANGUAGE

There is some key language that children will need to know as part of the learning in this unit.

→ How many are left?
→ take away, taken away, subtract
→ subtraction, addition
→ count back, count backwards
→ difference
→ How many more? How many fewer?
→ more than, >, less than, <
→ missing part
→ number stories

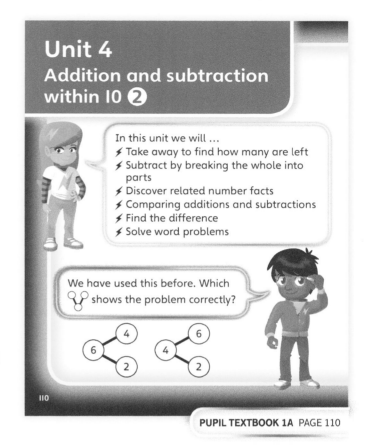

Unit 4
Addition and subtraction within 10 ❷

In this unit we will …
⚡ Take away to find how many are left
⚡ Subtract by breaking the whole into parts
⚡ Discover related number facts
⚡ Comparing additions and subtractions
⚡ Find the difference
⚡ Solve word problems

We have used this before. Which ⚬⚬ shows the problem correctly?

110

PUPIL TEXTBOOK 1A PAGE 110

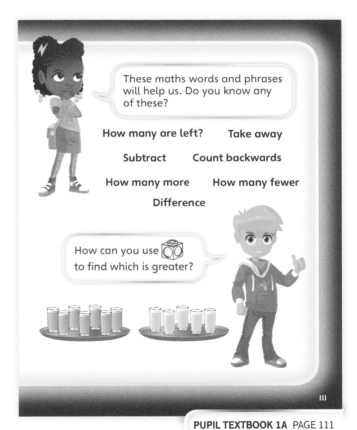

These maths words and phrases will help us. Do you know any of these?

How many are left?   Take away

Subtract   Count backwards

How many more   How many fewer

Difference

How can you use 🎲 to find which is greater?

III

PUPIL TEXTBOOK 1A PAGE 111

Subtraction – how many are left? ❶

Learning focus

In this lesson, children will work out simple 'how many left' subtractions within 10 by crossing out.

Small steps

→ Previous step: Solving word problems – addition
→ **This step: Subtraction – how many are left? (1)**
→ Next step: Subtraction – how many are left? (2)

NATIONAL CURRICULUM LINKS

Year 1 Number – Addition and Subtraction

- Represent and use number bonds and related subtraction facts within 20.
- Solve one-step problems that involve addition and subtraction, using concrete objects and pictorial representations, and missing number problems such as 7 = _ – 9.

ASSESSING MASTERY

Children can solve subtractions within 10 by crossing out or physically removing objects and counting how many are left. Children can use contexts to explain their answers and differentiate between the total number to begin with, the number taken away and the number left.

COMMON MISCONCEPTIONS

Children may get confused when using a pictorial representation with crossed out objects, as the total number of objects remains the same. Ask:

- *What does it mean if something is crossed out?*

Children may interpret the vocabulary 'How many left?' as 'How many have left and gone away', rather than 'How many remain, after some are taken away'. Ask:

- *Where does it show you how many are left behind?*

STRENGTHENING UNDERSTANDING

Strengthen understanding by using uninflated balloons, pictures of balloons or counters/cubes to model the concrete situation, and make memorable links between it and different representations. For example, children could hold onto inflated (but not tied) balloons in a line, and then release one so it whooshes around the room.

GOING DEEPER

Discuss with children that, if you remove two objects, you can count what remains or you can count back twice from the total amount. Encourage pairs to deepen understanding by using both methods for some given calculations.

KEY LANGUAGE

In lesson: how many are left?

Other language to be used by the teacher: take away, remain, in total, begin with

RESOURCES

Mandatory: cubes and/or counters

Optional: balloons/pictures of balloons

Teaching Tools In the eTextbook of this lesson, you will find interactive links to a selection of teaching tools.

Before you teach ⏸

- Are children secure with the contexts provided for subtraction?
- What physical resources could you provide to assist them in making the problems concrete?

Discover

WAYS OF WORKING Pair work

ASK

- Question ① a): *How many balloons did Amy have at the start? What has happened to one? Is Amy still holding it?*
- Question ① a): *How many flew away? How many balloons are left?*
- Question ① a): *Why do we not need to count the balloon that is floating away?*
- Question ① a): *How could you work this out if there were no pictures?*

IN FOCUS Question ① a) brings attention to the balloon floating away. The context should help children understand that the balloon is no longer there, and will no longer be counted when they are asked how many are left.

ANSWERS

Question ① a): There are 5 ◯ left.

Question ① b): There are 4 ◯ left.

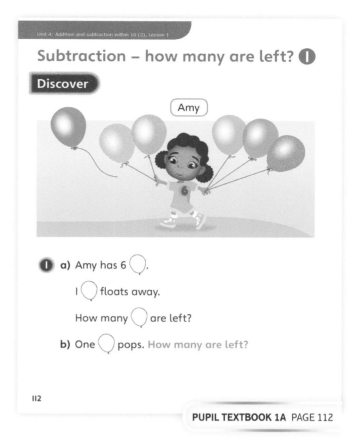

PUPIL TEXTBOOK 1A PAGE 112

Share

WAYS OF WORKING Whole class teacher led

ASK

- Question ① a): *What does each counter represent?*
- Question ① b): *What does crossing out represent?*

IN FOCUS Question ① a) prompts children to associate '1 floats away' with crossing out a balloon. Dexter suggests how to find the answer: by counting the ◯ left. Children can also refer to the number below the last balloon left.

STRENGTHEN In question ① b), ensure children can identify that the first balloon crossed out was from question ① a), and that one more has now popped. Ask children how many balloons have gone in total.

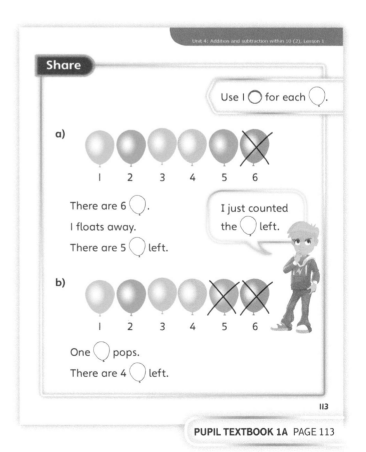

PUPIL TEXTBOOK 1A PAGE 113

Think together

Whole class teacher led (I do, We do, You do)

ASK

- Question ❶: *How many balloons are there in total?*
- Question ❶: *How do you know how many have popped?*

IN FOCUS Question ❸ scaffolds children in writing their own number sentences to match the pictures provided. (Note that they should not need to count each individual total, as they should see that it stays the same each time.)

STRENGTHEN Use cubes to represent the total number of balloons and the number taken away. Children could use different colours, or separate cubes laid out in different lines.

DEEPEN In question ❸, Ash prompts children to spot a pattern. Give children a set of blank scaffolds to fill in for each question and ask them to explain what happens to the number of balloons in total/that pop/that are left.

For even more depth, ask children to recreate the same pattern, but starting with taking away 4 balloons and then taking away one each time.

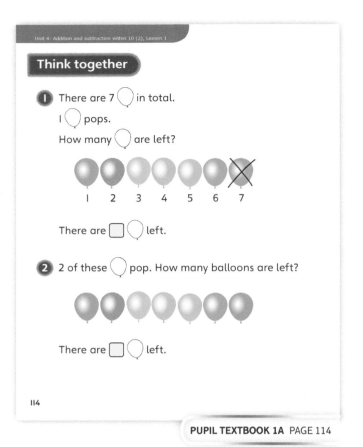

PUPIL TEXTBOOK 1A PAGE 114

ASSESSMENT CHECKPOINT In question ❸, assess whether children write the number of balloons underneath or count in their head. Check if they stop counting at the crossed-out balloons when working out how many are left.

ANSWERS

Question ❶: There are 6 ◯ left.

Question ❷: There are 5 ◯ left.

Question ❸ a): There are 5 ◯ in total. 1 ◯ pops.

There are 4 ◯ left.

Question ❸ b): There are 5 ◯ in total. 2 ◯ pop.

There are 3 ◯ left.

Question ❸ c): There are 5 ◯ in total. 3 ◯ pop.

There are 2 ◯ left.

Question ❸ d): There are 5 ◯ in total. 4 ◯ pop.

There is 1 ◯ left.

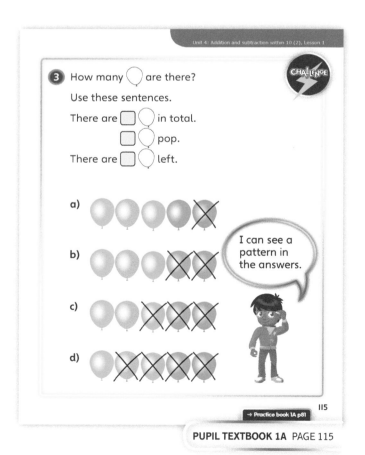

PUPIL TEXTBOOK 1A PAGE 115

Practice

WAYS OF WORKING Independent thinking

IN FOCUS In question **5**, Sparks suggests that children use counters to represent trucks. This will help them to make the connection between the abstract problem and concrete objects.

STRENGTHEN Suggest that children use counters or cubes to assist them in understanding the contexts and making their own sentences before question **5**, if they struggle to count using the pictures on the page.

DEEPEN In question **4**, children can work systematically from 10 birds in total and keep taking one away. Suggest that they try to find the same pattern as they did when doing the same thing with balloons.

ASSESSMENT CHECKPOINT Ascertain whether children, when crossing out objects, cross out systematically or pick any particular pictures. Encourage crossing out from the right, as this is consistent with counting backwards on a number line.

ANSWERS Answers for the **Practice** part of the lesson appear in the separate **Practice and Reflect answer guide**.

Reflect

WAYS OF WORKING Pair work, Whole class

IN FOCUS The **Reflect** question can prompt discussion about the numbers children have calculated in this lesson. Children can explain how they have worked out how many are left using the sentence prompt to help them.

ASSESSMENT CHECKPOINT Assess how children explain the way in which they work out how many are left. Do they use phrases such as 'count back', or 'take away'? Do they explain that they took away a number of objects and then counted the remaining ones from 0, or do they explain counting backwards from the total?

ANSWERS Answers for the **Reflect** part of the lesson appear in the separate **Practice and Reflect answer guide**.

After the lesson ⏸

- Were children comfortable with all of the different contexts for taking away and did they understand what the different numbers represented?
- Could children recognise and explain what approach they were taking to finding out how many were left?

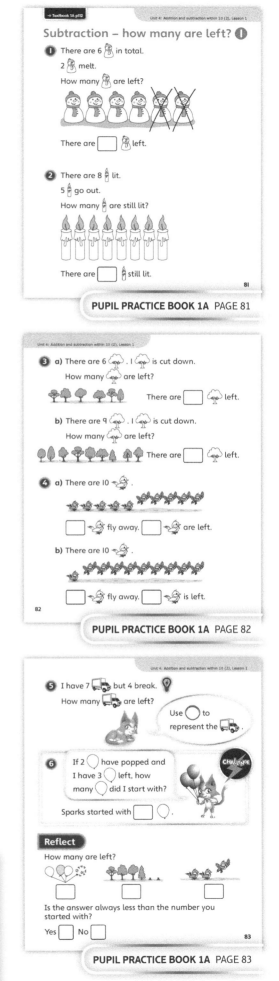

PUPIL PRACTICE BOOK 1A PAGE 81

PUPIL PRACTICE BOOK 1A PAGE 82

PUPIL PRACTICE BOOK 1A PAGE 83

Subtraction – how many are left? ②

Learning focus

In this lesson, children will work out simple 'how many left' subtractions within 10 by using part-whole models and ten frames.

Small steps

→ Previous step: Subtraction – how many are left? (1)
→ **This step: Subtraction – how many are left? (2)**
→ Next step: Subtraction – breaking apart (1)

NATIONAL CURRICULUM LINKS

Year 1 Number – Addition and Subtraction

- Represent and use number bonds and related subtraction facts within 20.
- Solve one-step problems that involve addition and subtraction, using concrete objects and pictorial representations, and missing number problems such as 7 = _ – 9.

ASSESSING MASTERY

Children can solve subtractions within 10 in different contexts. Children can represent subtraction using different models, such as a ten frame or part-whole model, and differentiate between the number left and the number taken away.

COMMON MISCONCEPTIONS

Children may incorrectly interpret ways of representing a total number on a ten frame, not recognising the number taken away and the number left. Guide children towards strategies such as using different-coloured cubes, keeping separate piles of cubes or crossing out. Ask:
- *Which part represents the total number to start with?*
- *Which part represents the number taken away?*
- *Which part represents the number that is left?*

STRENGTHENING UNDERSTANDING

Strengthen understanding by discussing the meaning of the – symbol and how it relates to taking away. Express this by conceptually joining the – symbol to the number that follows it, explaining that '– 2' means 'subtract 2'. This will help children to understand how the abstract symbol relates to the concrete context.

GOING DEEPER

In this lesson's subtractions, the whole is at the start of calculations; previously, it has been at the end. Encourage children to deepen understanding by spotting this difference and making the comparison.

KEY LANGUAGE

In lesson: in total, take away / **taken away**, **subtract**

Other language to be used by the teacher: remain, in total, begin with, – symbol

STRUCTURES AND REPRESENTATIONS

Ten frame

RESOURCES

Mandatory: blank ten frames, cubes and/or counters

Teaching Tools In the eTextbook of this lesson, you will find interactive links to a selection of teaching tools.

Before you teach

- Are there any remaining misconceptions from Lesson 1 about counting how many are left that need to be addressed?
- Are all children secure with how to use ten frames to represent subtraction problems?

Discover

WAYS OF WORKING Pair work

ASK

- Question ❶ a): *Looking at the picture, can you point to each of the children in the classroom?*
- Question ❶ a): *Do the adults count, if we are counting children?*
- Question ❶ a): *Can you point to each of the children leaving the classroom?*

IN FOCUS Question ❶ a) gives children the opportunity to explain how the different stages of the problem work: How many children there are in total to begin with, how many leave, and how many remain. Children should be able to explain the 'meaning' of the numbers and symbols in a subtraction calculation in terms of the real context and the stages of the calculation.

ANSWERS

Question ❶ a): 8 children are in the classroom. 2 children leave. 6 children are left in the classroom.

Question ❶ b): 2 children are left in the classroom now.

Subtraction – how many are left? ❷

Discover

❶ a) How many children are in the classroom?

How many children leave the classroom?

How many children are left in the classroom?

b) Four more children leave the classroom.

How many children are left in the classroom now?

116

PUPIL TEXTBOOK 1A PAGE 116

Share

WAYS OF WORKING Whole class teacher led

ASK

- Question ❶ a): *What do the different parts of the calculation represent? What does the 8 mean?*
- Question ❶ a): *What does the – symbol mean?*
- Question ❶ a): *What does the 2 mean?*
- Question ❶ a): *So, what does the – 2 mean?*
- Question ❶ a): *What does the 6 represent?*

IN FOCUS This part of the lesson prompts children to relate the problem to numbers in a subtraction and a ten frame. Draw attention to the – symbol. Ask children what they think this means and where it is represented on the ten frame.

STRENGTHEN Strengthen understanding by asking children to act out the problems. Start with 8 children standing, and then ask 2 to sit down. Discuss and clarify that you would not write 2 – 8 (that the calculation is not commutative) because the – 8 would mean you would take 8 away: in this problem, you need to take 2 away *from* 8. This can be repeated for question ❶ b).

Share

a) 8 children are in the classroom.

2 children leave the classroom.

$8 - 2 = 6$

☐ children are left in the classroom.

b) Four more children leave the classroom.

$6 - 4 = 2$

There are ☐ children left in the classroom.

117

PUPIL TEXTBOOK 1A PAGE 117

Think together

WAYS OF WORKING Whole class teacher led (I do, We do, You do)

ASK

- Question ❶ : *How does the picture show 3 children leaving?*
- Question ❶ : *Where in the subtraction do we write that 3 children leave?*
- Question ❷ : *What number should start the subtraction?*

IN FOCUS In this part of the lesson, children can strengthen their understanding that the different parts of a subtraction calculation have meaning, in the given context. In question ❸ , children become familiar with the empty circle being the field for an operation symbol, and the empty boxes being fields for missing numbers.

STRENGTHEN In question ❷ , ask children to explain what each part of the subtraction represents as they are writing the numbers. Ask: *Which part of the subtraction is the total? What symbol do you need to use to represent some being taken away? Which part of the subtraction shows what is left?*

PUPIL TEXTBOOK 1A PAGE 118

DEEPEN Deepen understanding in question ❸ by asking children to show the problem using a ten frame. Refer to what Ash says, and ask: *How is – 4 shown on the ten frame?*

ASSESSMENT CHECKPOINT Assess whether children put the – symbol before or after the number being taken away. There may be some confusion because when we say, for example, '4 children leave', we say the '4' first, followed by the word denoting subtraction.

ANSWERS

Question ❶: 9 – 3 = 6

There are 6 children left.

Question ❷: 7 – 4 = 3

There are 3 children left.

Question ❸: There are 10 ◯ in total.

4 ◯ are taken away.

10 – 4 = 6

There are 6 ◯ left.

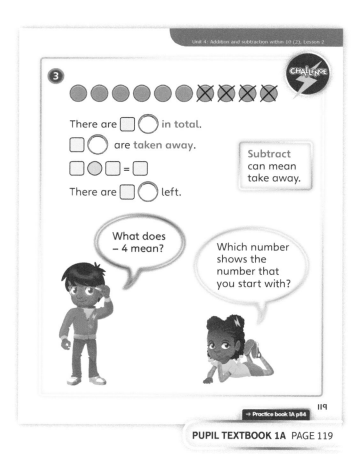

PUPIL TEXTBOOK 1A PAGE 119

Practice

WAYS OF WORKING Independent thinking

IN FOCUS In question **2**, children are given a completed ten frame and need to calculate subtractions by crossing out the correct number of counters. This provides an opportunity to relate these subtractions to their knowledge of number bonds to 10. In question **4**, prompt children to recognise that, in 8 – 4 = 4, the 4s have different meanings.

STRENGTHEN After question **3**, ask children to come up with their own sentences to match the pictures. For example: 'There were 8 apples. 3 were eaten. How many apples were left?'

DEEPEN Deepen understanding by encouraging children to come up with their own contexts to match the number sentences in question **5**.

ASSESSMENT CHECKPOINT Assess whether children recognise that the last number in a subtraction is the number that is left. Look for how children show the number sentence in questions **5** e) and **5** f). Do they lay the objects out in a line like a number line and write the corresponding numbers underneath, or do they draw them in a ten-frame structure?

ANSWERS Answers for the **Practice** part of the lesson appear in the separate **Practice and Reflect answer guide**.

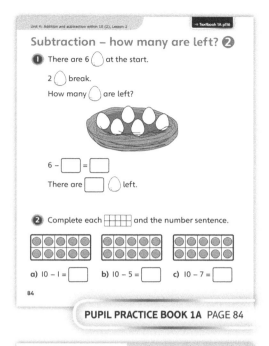

PUPIL PRACTICE BOOK 1A PAGE 84

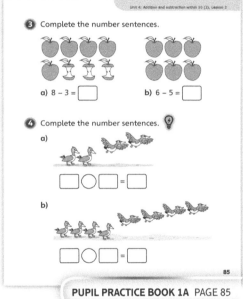

PUPIL PRACTICE BOOK 1A PAGE 85

Reflect

WAYS OF WORKING Pair work, Whole class

IN FOCUS This question asks children to describe a number fact in their own words (likely in a sentence). They could use cubes to help them represent it first, as Flo suggests.

ASSESSMENT CHECKPOINT Listen to children explaining the calculation. Do they use the phrases '5 in total' and 'take away 2'? Do they explain '– 2' by making the calculation concrete, saying 'cross two out' or 'take away two cubes'?

ANSWERS Answers for the **Reflect** part of the lesson appear in the separate **Practice and Reflect answer guide**.

After the lesson

- Did children understand the use of the – symbol, and what it meant in a subtraction?
- Were children able to understand subtractions in the pictures, concrete resources and different contexts?
- Did children use the language 'taken away' correctly, both in context and alongside the abstract subtractions?

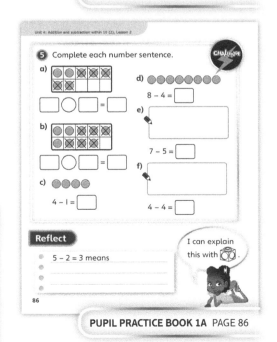

PUPIL PRACTICE BOOK 1A PAGE 86

Subtraction – breaking apart ❶

Learning focus

In this lesson, children will find two parts of a whole by breaking up a total. They will find one part by thinking about the whole and the other part.

Small steps

→ Previous step: Subtraction – how many are left? (2)
→ **This step: Subtraction – breaking apart (1)**
→ Next step: Subtraction – breaking apart (2)

NATIONAL CURRICULUM LINKS

Year 1 Number – Addition and Subtraction

• Represent and use number bonds and related subtraction facts within 20.

ASSESSING MASTERY

Children can understand how subtraction relates to breaking apart and to part-whole diagrams. Children can break a whole into two parts and can reason about one part and the whole in order to work out a missing part.

COMMON MISCONCEPTIONS

Children may have difficulty when asked to work out the total of two parts taken away from a whole, meaning they must count on from an original missing part. This can be confusing, as children must add in order to find out what number has been subtracted. Ask:

• *How many had been taken away before? If __ more are taken away, what is the total number being taken away now?*

STRENGTHENING UNDERSTANDING

In this lesson, the part-whole diagram is used to show how a whole is broken into parts, and some questions use the model in different orientations. Strengthen understanding by ensuring children understand which places on each model show parts.

GOING DEEPER

Deepen understanding by providing concrete examples of problems and using physical resources to represent objects in a problem. Put cubes or counters in a straight line, to emulate a number line. The number counted back can be collected and form a group, and the number left can become a different group. These can then be put into a blank part-whole model to represent the problem.

KEY LANGUAGE

In lesson: parts, take away / taken away, subtract

Other language to be used by the teacher: remain, in total, begin with, count back

STRUCTURES AND REPRESENTATIONS

Part-whole model, number line

RESOURCES

Mandatory: blank part-whole models, blank number lines, cubes and/or counters

Teaching Tools In the eTextbook of this lesson, you will find interactive links to a selection of teaching tools.

Before you teach

• If any children are unsure how to work out a missing part, how can this lesson be scaffolded to support them?
• Subtraction lessons use the same models as the addition lessons. How could you draw out previous learning about these models to support children's understanding?

Discover

Pair work

ASK

- Question 1 a): *How many cars are there in total?*
- Question 1 a): *How will you show that Ava washes 4?*

IN FOCUS Question 1 a) gives you the opportunity to guide children towards thinking of 4 as one part of 9 and 9 as the whole. In question 1 b), you can reinforce children's understanding that 2 *more* cars are washed – meaning *fewer* cars are dirty.

ANSWERS

Question 1 a): 5 🚗 are still dirty.

Question 1 b): There are 3 🚗 still dirty.

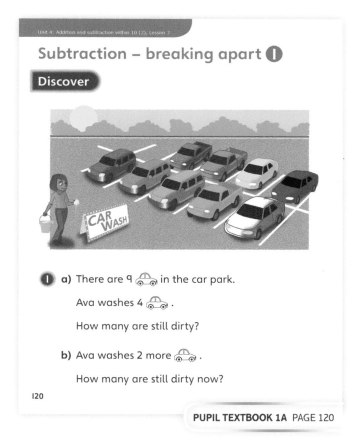

Subtraction – breaking apart 1

Discover

1 a) There are 9 🚗 in the car park.

   Ava washes 4 🚗 .

   How many are still dirty?

b) Ava washes 2 more 🚗 .

   How many are still dirty now?

120

PUPIL TEXTBOOK 1A PAGE 120

Share

Whole class teacher led

ASK

- Question 1 a): *How many cars are in each part?*
- Question 1 a): *What does each part represent?*
- Question 1 a): *Why are some cars circled?*

IN FOCUS In this part of the lesson, children relate the problem to a part-whole model. They have seen this model before when looking at subtractions – this time, however, the unknown is one of the parts and not the whole.

STRENGTHEN Strengthen understanding by encouraging children to use physical resources to show what each part represents.

DEEPEN In question 1 b), ask children to think of a number sentence to match this problem. Even though 2 *more* cars have been washed, addition should not be used. The subtractions they could mention are '9 – 6 = 3' and '5 – 2= 3'.

Share

a) There are 9 🚗 in the car park.

   Ava washes 4 🚗 .

   9 – 4 = 5

   5 🚗 are still dirty.

   5 6 7 8 9

Break the whole into parts.

9 / 4 5

I can check the answer by counting back.

b) Ava washes 2 more 🚗 .

   9 / 6 3

   There are 3 🚗 still dirty.

121

PUPIL TEXTBOOK 1A PAGE 121

Think together

Whole class teacher led (I do, We do, You do)

ASK

- Question ❶: *What does '– 5' represent?*
- Question ❶: *What do the two parts represent?*
- Question ❶: *What strategy will you use to find the parts?*

IN FOCUS In questions ❶ and ❷, the wholes of the part-whole models are filled in. Engage children's prior learning as they use the information from the problem to work out the missing parts. Question ❸ expands children's understanding of the model: it is blank and in a different orientation. Question ❸ b) makes both parts known, while the whole is unknown: children will need to add the two known parts, working backwards to find the whole. This provides an opportunity to discuss how addition can be used to assist and check subtractions.

STRENGTHEN Strengthen understanding by encouraging children to come up with matching calculations to the part-whole models in question ❸. If they are struggling, give children two options for calculations and ask them to work out which one is most appropriate. For example, in question ❸ a), show them '6 – 5 = 1' and '5 + 1 = 6'.

DEEPEN Challenge children to use the information given in a question to create their own problem about the other missing part. For example: In question ❶, they should start from their new knowledge that 3 cars are dirty and ask: *'How many cars have been washed?'* Highlight that children are using the same process as the question did.

ASSESSMENT CHECKPOINT Assess how accurately children fill in the part-whole models. In question ❸ b), do children understand that the information given is the two parts, and fill those in?

ANSWERS

Question ❶: 8 – 5 = 3

3 🚗 are still dirty.

Question ❷: 7 – 5 = 2

2 🚗 are still dirty.

Question ❸ a): Ava washed 1 🚗 .

Question ❸ b): There are 8 🚗 in total.

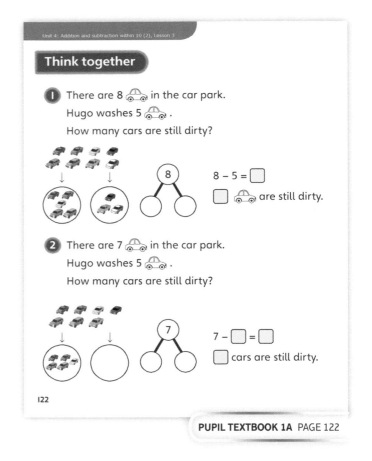

Practice

WAYS OF WORKING Independent thinking

IN FOCUS Question ② prompts children to devise a subtraction to find the number of apples. Children may want to count the number of apples to find the answer and fill the numbers in the number sentence afterwards. Question ⑤ b) provides the opportunity to discuss that 0 can be a correct answer. If children say 'zero', and wish to leave the answer box blank as their answer, show on a number line that 5 less than 5 lands on 0.

STRENGTHEN When children are completing a subtraction with an unknown part, ask them to show how they could work it out on the number line. They should be counting back from the total, and recognise that the number they jump back is the part that is known while the number on which they land is the missing part – for all contexts.

DEEPEN Deepen understanding by asking children to come up with their own contexts to match the part-whole models in question ③. Children will need to come up with contexts in which two groups make an overall total, such as bananas and apples making up a bowl of fruit.

ASSESSMENT CHECKPOINT Assess how children approach each new question. Do they have consistent strategies for working out the wholes and/or parts? Do they circle wholes/parts, or draw the calculations themselves? Do they rely on previous part-whole knowledge, and/or use resources to check?

ANSWERS Answers for the **Practice** part of the lesson appear in the separate **Practice and Reflect answer guide**.

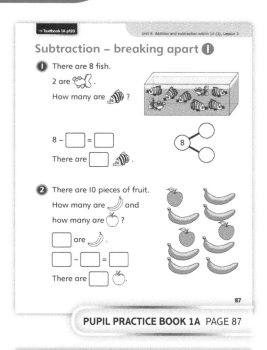

PUPIL PRACTICE BOOK 1A PAGE 87

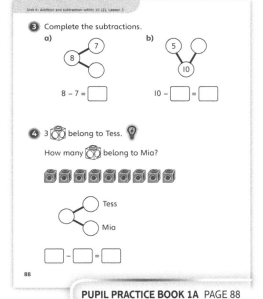

PUPIL PRACTICE BOOK 1A PAGE 88

Reflect

WAYS OF WORKING Pair work, Whole class

IN FOCUS The **Reflect** question highlights that a part-whole model can be represented in any orientation.

ASSESSMENT CHECKPOINT Assess whether children recognise that all of the models are the same (and that the missing part in each is 3). If they do, they will not need to calculate the subtraction each time.

ANSWERS Answers for the **Reflect** part of the lesson appear in the separate **Practice and Reflect answer guide**.

After the lesson ⏸

- Did all children understand that the – symbol can be used to find different parts of a whole?
- Were children able to relate a missing part in a part-whole model to counting back on a number line?
- Did the different contexts make sense to all children, and do you think their skills would remain secure in new contexts?

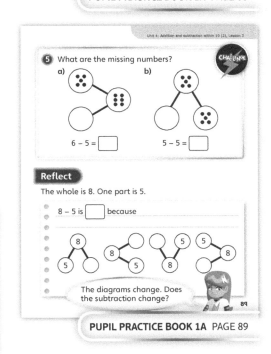

PUPIL PRACTICE BOOK 1A PAGE 89

Subtraction – breaking apart ❷

Learning focus

In this lesson, children will continue to find a missing part from the whole and the other part. Children will use a part-whole model and sentence scaffolds to help them to complete subtractions.

Small steps

→ Previous step: Subtraction – breaking apart (1)
→ **This step: Subtraction – breaking apart (2)**
→ Next step: Related facts – addition and subtraction (1)

NATIONAL CURRICULUM LINKS

Year 1 Number – Addition and Subtraction

• Represent and use number bonds and related subtraction facts within 20.

ASSESSING MASTERY

Children can correctly put a whole and a part from a subtraction into a part-whole model, recognising that the missing part forms a part of the whole that can be worked out using the remaining numbers. Children can start to link this process with subtraction calculations (whole – part = part).

COMMON MISCONCEPTIONS

When translating a subtraction in which a part is missing into a part-whole model, children may put both remaining numbers into the parts positions (as they have seen when learning about number bonds). Ask:
• *Does the subtraction tell you the whole? Where would the whole go on the part-whole model?*

STRENGTHENING UNDERSTANDING

Strengthen understanding by asking children to work in pairs, taking turns to show a number of cubes or counters to their partner and then hiding some (in their hand/under the table). The partner should then calculate the quantity missing. Use a container with defined sections for resources (such as a blank ten-frame or an egg box), so children can count the empty sections.

GOING DEEPER

Deepen understanding of subtractions by asking children to check them using addition. First, ask children to put the subtraction into a part-whole model. Ask: *Can you recognise which two numbers need to be added together to make the whole?* Provide blank calculations to help.

KEY LANGUAGE

In lesson: addition, take away / taken away, subtraction

Other language to be used by the teacher: remain, in total, begin with, count back

STRUCTURES AND REPRESENTATIONS

Part-whole model

RESOURCES

Mandatory: blank part-whole models, cubes and/or counters

Optional: blank ten-frames, empty egg boxes

Teaching Tools In the eTextbook of this lesson, you will find interactive links to a selection of teaching tools.

Before you teach

• Are all children secure with relating a part-whole model to a subtraction?
• Are children able to spot the mistake if a part and a whole are put into the wrong places in a part-whole model?

Discover

WAYS OF WORKING Pair work

ASK

- Question ❶ a): *How many counters can you see in total, in the first pair of hands?*
- Question ❶ a): *When some counters are being hidden, has the total number changed?*
- Question ❶ a): *Without looking in the hand, how can we work out how many counters are hidden?*

IN FOCUS This part of the lesson prompts children to work out a subtraction by thinking about how the parts relate to the whole. Ask children to look closely at the picture and to tell you what they see. Then read out the statements and ask children to point to the part of the picture that relates to each.

ANSWERS

Question ❶ a): There are 3 ◯ hidden in the 👊.

Question ❶ b): You can check by adding your answer to the number of counters visible in the second picture, and comparing this with the number of counters in the first picture. You could also use number bonds to 5, count back on a number line, use a part-whole model and/or perform the calculation using counters.

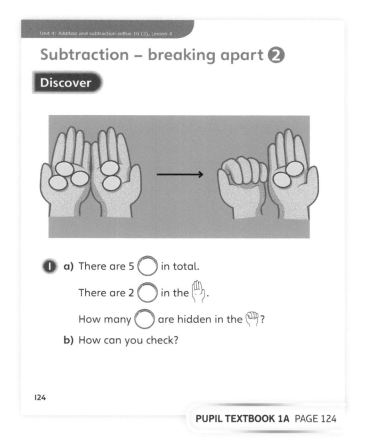

Subtraction – breaking apart ❷

Discover

❶ a) There are 5 ◯ in total.

There are 2 ◯ in the 🤚.

How many ◯ are hidden in the 👊?

b) How can you check?

124

PUPIL TEXTBOOK 1A PAGE 124

Share

WAYS OF WORKING Whole class teacher led

ASK

- In response to Astrid's comment: *Why don't you have to guess?*
- Question ❶ a): *How can you use counters to complete the missing part?*
- Question ❶ b): *Can you convince me you're right, using a diagram or counters?*
- Question ❶ b): *What representations can you use to help you?*

IN FOCUS This part of the lesson tests children's understanding of how addition facts and subtraction are related. Refer to what Flo says in part b) and relate this to number bonds.

DEEPEN To deepen understanding, ask children what would have changed if 3 counters had been hidden instead of 2. Encourage them to create their own part-whole models to show the missing part. Ask: *Do you get a different answer? Would a different addition be needed to check?*

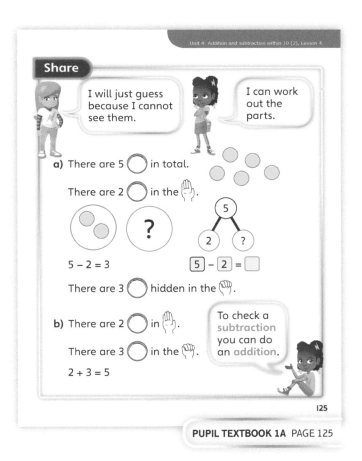

Share

I will just guess because I cannot see them.

I can work out the parts.

a) There are 5 ◯ in total.

There are 2 ◯ in the 🤚.

5 – 2 = 3

There are 3 ◯ hidden in the 👊.

5

2   ?

⑤ – ② = ☐

b) There are 2 ◯ in 🤚.

There are 3 ◯ in the 👊.

2 + 3 = 5

To check a subtraction you can do an addition.

125

PUPIL TEXTBOOK 1A PAGE 125

Think together

Think together

WAYS OF WORKING Whole class teacher led (I do, We do, You do)

ASK

- Question **1**: *What do 5 and 4 represent? Which is a part and which is a whole?*
- Questions **1** and **2**: *How can the pictures help you work out what is missing?*
- Question **3**: *Can you show how many cakes are hidden using a different resource?*

IN FOCUS There is a blank part-whole model next to a partly filled-in subtraction in question **3**. Use this as a prompt to encourage children to draw the cakes, to help them represent the problem.

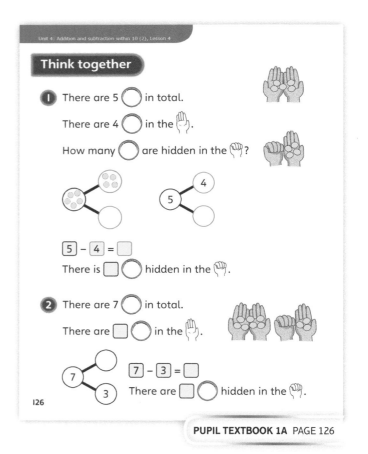

PUPIL TEXTBOOK 1A PAGE 126

STRENGTHEN Strengthen understanding by making the context of question **3** concrete: ask children to act out the problem using different resources. Ask them to say the sentences, substituting 'cake' for the resource they have chosen (for example, 'There are 4 cubes hidden under the table.').

DEEPEN Ask children to create their own addition to check how many cakes are hidden. Encourage them to label each part of their addition with 'cakes hidden under cloth', 'cakes I can see' and 'total number of cakes'.

ASSESSMENT CHECKPOINT For questions **1** and **2**, ensure children understand that it does not matter in which part section of the part-whole diagram the known part is written. In question **3**, assess whether children draw and then cross out or circle cakes when solving the subtraction problem, as they have seen done in previous lessons.

ANSWERS

Question **1**: 5 − 4 = 1

There is 1 ⃝ hidden in the ✊.

Question **2**: 7 − 3 = 4

There are 4 ⃝ hidden in the ✊.

Question **3**: 6 − 2 = 4

There are 4 🧁 hidden under the cloth.

PUPIL TEXTBOOK 1A PAGE 127

Practice

WAYS OF WORKING Independent thinking

IN FOCUS In question **5**, children use multiple-choice selections to complete subtractions. Before children do any calculations for question **5** a), take this opportunity to ask: *Do you think the answer will be less than the whole and/or the other part?* If so, ask: *Do you think the answer could reasonably be 7?* If children are unsure, ask them to choose and try out a number, checking their calculations with resources.

STRENGTHEN In question **3**, ask if children have seen these types of number bonds anywhere else. Suggest that they represent the problems using cubes, and comment on what is the same about the two towers.

DEEPEN After question **5**, encourage children to create their own subtractions in which one of the multiple-choice cards (1, 3 or 7) is the subtracted part. They will have to think about how addition relates to subtraction in order to do this. For example, if they want 6 to be their missing part, they could add 3 to get a whole of 9 (9 − 3 = ?).

ASSESSMENT CHECKPOINT In question **4**, assess whether children are correctly putting the whole and part into the part-whole model. Are they representing the unknown with a question mark or any other symbol before working it out, or do they put the correct missing part straight in?

ANSWERS Answers for the **Practice** part of the lesson appear in the separate **Practice and Reflect answer guide**.

Reflect

WAYS OF WORKING Pair work

IN FOCUS The **Reflect** question targets the misconception of mixing up the whole and a part in subtractions. The second part-whole model is also orientated so the parts are on top, which may have led to the error in the subtraction.

ASSESSMENT CHECKPOINT Assess whether children are able to identify the mistakes and articulate what has happened. Ask them to write the correct subtractions to match the part-whole models when they have explained which parts have been mixed up.

ANSWERS Answers for the **Reflect** part of the lesson appear in the separate **Practice and Reflect answer guide**.

After the lesson ⏸

- Were there sufficient opportunities within this lesson for children to experiment with resources and their own contexts to make subtractions?
- Have children mastered calculating subtractions and using corresponding part-whole models?
- Were children able to identify and articulate when mistakes with part-whole models have been made, and correct them?

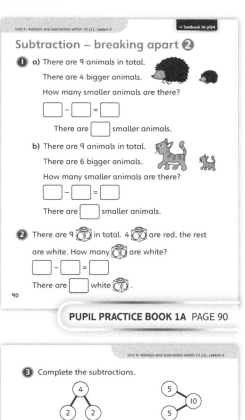

PUPIL PRACTICE BOOK 1A PAGE 90

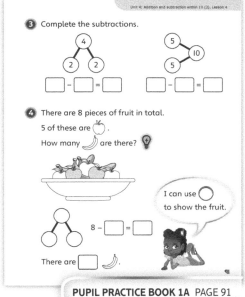

PUPIL PRACTICE BOOK 1A PAGE 91

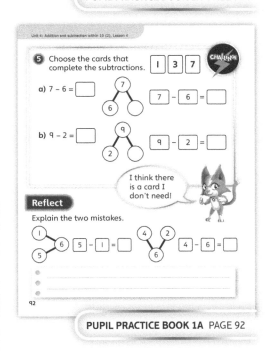

PUPIL PRACTICE BOOK 1A PAGE 92

Related facts – addition and subtraction ❶

Learning focus

In this lesson, children will find both additions and subtractions from one part-whole model.

Small steps

→ Previous step: Subtraction – breaking apart (2)
→ **This step: Related facts – addition and subtraction (1)**
→ Next step: Related facts – addition and subtraction (2)

NATIONAL CURRICULUM LINKS

Year 1 Number – Addition and Subtraction

• Represent and use number bonds and related subtraction facts within 20.

ASSESSING MASTERY

Children can recognise which numbers represent the whole and which represent parts, and can translate them correctly into a part-whole model. Children can swap the parts in additions (a + b = c and b + a = c) and translate this into subtractions, understanding that taking away one part will give the other (c – b = a and c – a = b).

COMMON MISCONCEPTIONS

Children may assume that subtraction is commutative, and think that parts can be swapped around (as in an addition). Display an incorrect subtraction such as 3 – 5 = 2 and ask:
• *If you have only 3, can you take 5 away?*

Use cubes to demonstrate that, if you start with 3, you cannot take away more than 3.

Children may, similarly, think a part and the whole can be swapped around. Display an incorrect subtraction such as 3 – 2 = 5 and ask:
• *Is 3 the whole? Which numbers are the parts?*

Use cubes to demonstrate that, if you start with 3 and take something away, you cannot make 5.

STRENGTHENING UNDERSTANDING

Strengthen understanding by using different-coloured cubes to represent different parts, and placing them in a blank part-whole model. All the cubes can then be counted to find the whole. (This highlights that the whole is made up of two parts joining.)

GOING DEEPER

Deepen understanding by discussing different ways of writing the same calculations, with the = sign in different places. When working on additions, start with '__ = __ + __' and ask children if the answer changes when you move the = sign and the whole. This can be repeated for subtractions.

KEY LANGUAGE

In lesson: add, **number sentence**, take away / taken away, subtract

Other language to be used by the teacher: remain, in total, begin with, count back

STRUCTURES AND REPRESENTATIONS

Part-whole model

RESOURCES

Mandatory: blank part-whole models, cubes and/or counters

Optional: different-coloured cubes

 Teaching Tools In the eTextbook of this lesson, you will find interactive links to a selection of teaching tools.

Before you teach ❚❚

• Were all children able to identify and explain the mistakes in the part-whole models from the **Reflect** section in the previous lesson?
• Are children secure with commutativity in addition? If not, how could you develop this understanding during the lesson?

Discover

WAYS OF WORKING Pair work

ASK

- In response to the picture: *How many different types of object can you see?*
- Question ❶ a): *Which two groups of objects are you looking at?*
- Question ❶ a): *How will you find the total?*

IN FOCUS Question ❶ a) requires children to isolate target groups from a wider range. Ask children to describe what they see. Refine their answer from 'lots of sports equipment' to 'some balls, some cones and some hoops'. Help them to understand the nature of different parts in what they see.

ANSWERS

Question ❶ a): There are 5 ⬤.

There are 3 ⬤.

There are 8 balls in total. You could check by performing the commutative addition (5 + 3 / 3 + 5), or by counting on a number line, using a part-whole model and/or using counters or cubes to perform the addition.

Question ❶ b): There are 7 balls in total now. This can be found by taking 1 away from 3 and performing the addition 5 + 2 = 7 or 2 + 5 = 7. (Alternatively, children may take 1 away from the whole to calculate 8 – 1 = 7. Ensure they do understand that 1 is being taken from a part of this whole.)

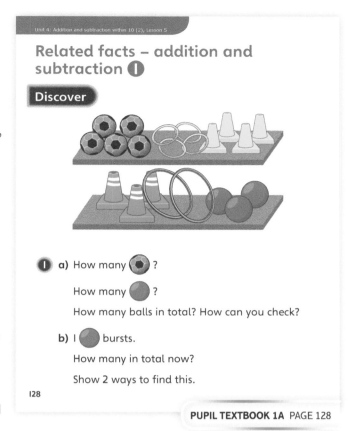

Related facts – addition and subtraction ❶

Discover

❶ a) How many ⬤ ?

How many ⬤ ?

How many balls in total? How can you check?

b) 1 ⬤ bursts.

How many in total now?

Show 2 ways to find this.

128

PUPIL TEXTBOOK 1A PAGE 128

Share

WAYS OF WORKING Whole class teacher led

ASK

- Question ❶ a): *What is different about the two additions?*
- Question ❶ a): *Does it matter which one you do?*
- Question ❶ b): *Why are we adding 2? How many blue balls did we have before, and what happened?*

IN FOCUS This part of the lesson gives you an opportunity to focus on the commutativity of addition. Ask children if it matters into which part section in a part-whole model each number goes. Refer to what Sparks says: it does not matter in which order the parts in an addition go. Ask children to predict if the same thing will happen in part b).

DEEPEN After question ❶ b), refer children back to their answer to ❶ a) and put the number 8 into the whole section of a part-whole model. Ask children how many balls popped, and put that into a part section. Enter how many balls are left into the other part section. Ask children to create a subtraction to match this model: 8 – 1 = 7.

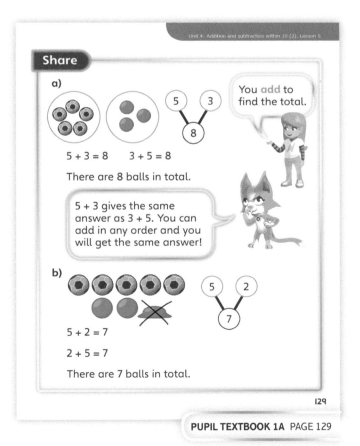

PUPIL TEXTBOOK 1A PAGE 129

Think together

Whole class teacher led (I do, We do, You do)

ASK

- Question ❶: *What are you trying to find in these subtractions?*
- Question ❶: *When subtracting, with which number do we start?*

IN FOCUS These questions require children to understand what they are working out when writing subtractions, and what the different numbers mean. This can be difficult to understand in an abstract context. (If children are struggling in question ❶, suggest that they cover one group of cones with their hand to make it clear what the unknown is.)

STRENGTHEN In question ❸, ask children to make a physical model using different-coloured cubes to show correctly what the sentences are telling them (3 cubes of one colour, 1 of another). Prompt them to attempt to construct the incorrect part-whole model using their cubes and then to correct it: they should articulate that the whole and the part have been mixed up. Discuss what Ash is asking about – 4. Ask: *What situations that require – 4 have you seen? Would the 4 be in the correct place in the part-whole model if you were taking away 4?*

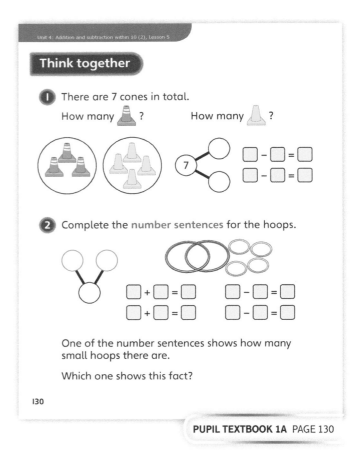

PUPIL TEXTBOOK 1A PAGE 130

DEEPEN Ask children to describe what different pieces of information the calculations in question ❷ can tell them (the number of big hoops, the number of small hoops and the number of hoops in total). Do they spot a pattern? Are there always some numbers that go together? The parts are always next to each other, on either side of the = sign, and the whole is at the start or the end of the calculation.

ASSESSMENT CHECKPOINT When they are completing question ❶, assess whether children recognise easily what each number in the subtraction means. When they have completed the subtractions, ask children what each answer tells them (7 – 4 = 3 green cones; 7 – 3 = 4 yellow cones).

ANSWERS

Question ❶: 7 – 3 = 4; 7 – 4 = 3

Question ❷: 2 + 4 = 6; 4 + 2 = 6

   6 – 4 = 2; 6 – 2 = 4

   The number sentence 6 – 2 = 4 shows how many small hoops there are.

Question ❸: There is 1 tennis ball.

   The mistakes made are that 1 (a part) and 4 (the whole) have been mixed up in the part-whole diagram, and that 3 (a part) and 4 (the whole) have been mixed up in the calculation.

PUPIL TEXTBOOK 1A PAGE 131

Practice

WAYS OF WORKING Independent thinking

IN FOCUS Question **2** requires children to find the three numbers for the calculations by counting the number of objects in each group and the total number of objects. Children first need to place these numbers correctly into the part-whole model, before completing the number facts. In the facts, the position of the whole varies. (If children struggle to position the whole correctly, point out that it should be entered in the darker boxes.)

Question **5** assesses whether children understand what numbers in calculations mean in context.

STRENGTHEN In question **4**, children write out two calculations twice each, as the parts are equal (3 + 3 = 6 / 6 – 3 = 3). Ask them to articulate what the different parts represent, even when they are the same. They could use highlighters to highlight the 'left side' one colour and the 'right side' another colour.

DEEPEN Deepen understanding in question **5** by asking children to discuss where the different types of numbers (parts and wholes) are in the three calculations. Ask: *Do you spot a pattern? Are there always some types of numbers that go together?* (In these calculations, the parts are always next to each other, before the = symbol, and the whole is at the end of the calculation.) Ask children to rearrange the calculations by moving the = symbol and the whole, and the parts if possible, in ways that mean the calculations remain correct.

ASSESSMENT CHECKPOINT In question **1**, ask children to explain what each part of each addition and subtraction means. Ask: *Which number shows the number of frogs on the lily pad? Which number shows the number of frogs swimming?* Assess whether children are able to articulate what each calculation is trying to find.

ANSWERS Answers for the **Practice** part of the lesson appear in the separate **Practice and Reflect answer guide**.

Reflect

WAYS OF WORKING Pair work

IN FOCUS This section focuses on the very common error of putting numbers from a context incorrectly into calculations, and understanding that parts in additions are commutative whereas those in subtractions are not. It provides no visual help or pictorial aids and requires children to look at the numbers only.

ASSESSMENT CHECKPOINT Assess whether children can identify the 3 correct calculations in their head or if they are reliant on resources to help them work out the answers. Gauge if they can articulate that you cannot take a bigger number away from a smaller number (and so spot that 5 – 9 = 4 is wrong) based purely on the position of the whole in the calculation.

ANSWERS Answers for the **Reflect** part of the lesson appear in the separate **Practice and Reflect answer guide**.

After the lesson ⏸

- Were children able to construct correct additions and subtractions from different contexts?
- Were children secure with commutativity in additions, and did they understand that it is not appropriate in subtractions?
- Were there any arrangements of calculations children found particularly difficult?

PUPIL PRACTICE BOOK 1A PAGE 93

PUPIL PRACTICE BOOK 1A PAGE 94

PUPIL PRACTICE BOOK 1A PAGE 95

Related facts – addition and subtraction ②

Learning focus

In this lesson, children will find four addition and four subtraction facts from the same context. They will see the = symbol in different parts of number sentences and be able to explain the meaning of each part of the number sentences.

Small steps

→ Previous step: Related facts – addition and subtraction (1)
→ **This step: Related facts – addition and subtraction (2)**
→ Next step: Subtraction – counting back

NATIONAL CURRICULUM LINKS

Year 1 Number – Addition and Subtraction

• Represent and use number bonds and related subtraction facts within 20.

ASSESSING MASTERY

Children can derive different facts from a context, understanding how to translate them into number sentences, and create number sentences to show a specific fact. Children can identify what each part in the number sentence means and switch numbers around to show the same fact.

COMMON MISCONCEPTIONS

Children may think that the = symbol means 'write the answer here', rather than 'is equal to'. Ask:
• *What does the = symbol mean?*

STRENGTHENING UNDERSTANDING

Strengthen understanding by using printed +, – and = symbols and number cards, or magnetic numbers. Children can then physically move the numbers in a calculation around, or test out combinations of which they are unsure before writing them down. Children could also move numbers around pre-printed scaffolds, if you would prefer them to clarify what type of number sentences they are making.

GOING DEEPER

Once children are confident with deriving different number sentences from one context, deepen understanding by looking at the patterns they have made and coming up with generalised number sentences. For example:

part + part = whole   whole = part + <u>part</u>   <u>part</u> = whole – part

part + <u>part</u> = whole   whole – <u>part</u> = part   part = whole – <u>part</u>

whole = <u>part</u> + part   whole – part = <u>part</u>

KEY LANGUAGE

In lesson: take away, taken away, subtract, part, whole

Other language to be used by the teacher: remain, in total, begin with, count back

STRUCTURES AND REPRESENTATIONS

Part-whole model

RESOURCES

Mandatory: blank part-whole models, cubes and/or counters

Optional: printed +, – and = symbols, number cards or magnetic numbers, pre-printed number-sentence scaffolds

Teaching Tools   In the eTextbook of this lesson, you will find interactive links to a selection of teaching tools.

Before you teach

• If children have previously seen number sentences with the = symbol only at the end, how will you first introduce its use in a different place?
• What resources could you use to help children to derive different number facts from a context?

Discover

Pair work

ASK

• Question **1** a): *How does the picture relate to the facts you are given?*
• Question **1** a): *What do the 6 and 2 represent?*
• Question **1** b): *What number will represent the whole?*

IN FOCUS Question **1** a) prompts children to calculate how many rings Leon scores. This is a starting point for question **1** b), which asks in how many different ways this fact can be shown. This process builds on previous learning of building a fact family. It can also lead to a discussion of the = symbol and and where it should appear in a number sentence.

ANSWERS

Question **1** a): Leon scores 4 rings.

Question **1** b): $6 - 2 = 4$; $4 = 6 - 2$; $6 - 4 = 2$; $2 = 6 - 4$;
$4 + 2 = 6$; $6 = 4 + 2$; $2 + 4 = 6$; $6 = 2 + 4$

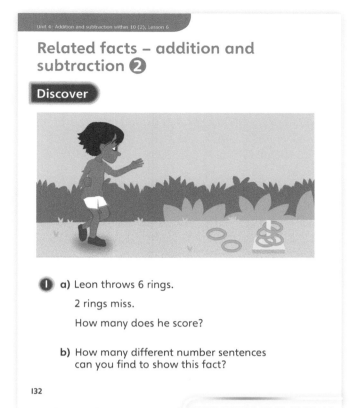

Unit 4: Addition and subtraction within 10 (2), Lesson 6

Related facts – addition and subtraction ❷

Discover

1 a) Leon throws 6 rings.

2 rings miss.

How many does he score?

b) How many different number sentences can you find to show this fact?

132

PUPIL TEXTBOOK 1A PAGE 132

Share

Whole class teacher led

ASK

• Question **1** b): *What do the numbers in the number sentences mean?*
• Question **1** b): *What is different about these calculations? Look at the position of the = symbol.*
• Question **1** b): *Do all the number sentences still work?*

IN FOCUS Question **1** a) gives an opportunity to embed understanding of parts, a whole and the structure of a part-whole model. Suggest that, when looking at the part-whole model and number sentence, children assign each of the numbers the label 'part' or 'whole' and ascertain whether the part-whole model has been drawn correctly.

DEEPEN When looking at question **1** a), ask children which of the numbers in the number sentence could be switched around to give the same fact. Discuss why $2 - 6 = 4$, for example, does not work.

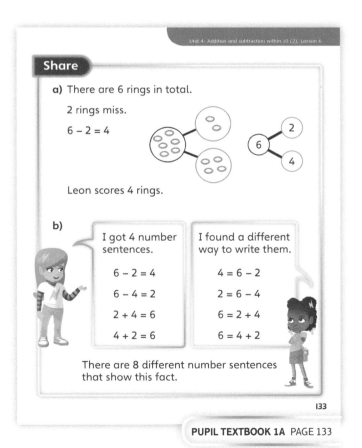

Unit 4: Addition and subtraction within 10 (2), Lesson 6

Share

a) There are 6 rings in total.

2 rings miss.

$6 - 2 = 4$

Leon scores 4 rings.

b)

I got 4 number sentences.

$6 - 2 = 4$
$6 - 4 = 2$
$2 + 4 = 6$
$4 + 2 = 6$

I found a different way to write them.

$4 = 6 - 2$
$2 = 6 - 4$
$6 = 2 + 4$
$6 = 4 + 2$

There are 8 different number sentences that show this fact.

133

PUPIL TEXTBOOK 1A PAGE 133

Think together

Whole class teacher led (I do, We do, You do)

ASK

- Question ①: *Where on the part-whole model can we see how many rings miss?*
- Question ③: *Where on the picture will you find the different parts?*

IN FOCUS In question ①, one number sentence is scaffolded so children see that the missing part can be at the start or end of the number sentence. In question ③, the number-sentence scaffolds are gradually removed so children have to think about where to place each number and then each symbol.

STRENGTHEN In question ③, children could strengthen their understanding by using counters to model the number fact, using different colours or groups to represent hoops that scored and hoops that missed. Then, if children are unsure what each number sentence is asking them to find, you can cover up the appropriate group and ask what is missing.

DEEPEN Talk about what types of number sentence can be worked out from one context. Ask: *Are there more addition or more subtraction facts?* Draw children to the conclusion that there are equal numbers of addition and subtraction facts because each is the inverse of the other. Discuss how number sentences can also be varied depending on where the = symbol is. Isolate a 'whole – part' calculation and show that the '= missing part' can go either side, but the calculation does not change.

ASSESSMENT CHECKPOINT Assess whether children are able to explain what they are trying to find, and are correctly putting numbers into the number sentences. In question ③, ensure that children recognise that the final, entirely missing facts should be subtraction number sentences, rather than rewritten addition sentences.

ANSWERS

Question ①: $7 - 4 = 3$

$\qquad$ $3 = 7 - 4$

$\qquad$ 3 rings miss.

Question ②: $5 + 1 = 6$

$\qquad$ $1 + 5 = 6$

$\qquad$ $6 - 5 = 1$

$\qquad$ $6 - 1 = 5$

Question ③: $9 = 4 + 5$ $\qquad$ $4 + 5 = 9$

$\qquad$ $9 = 5 + 4$ $\qquad$ $5 + 4 = 9$

$\qquad$ $5 = 9 - 4$ $\qquad$ $9 - 4 = 5$

$\qquad$ $4 = 9 - 5$ $\qquad$ $9 - 5 = 4$

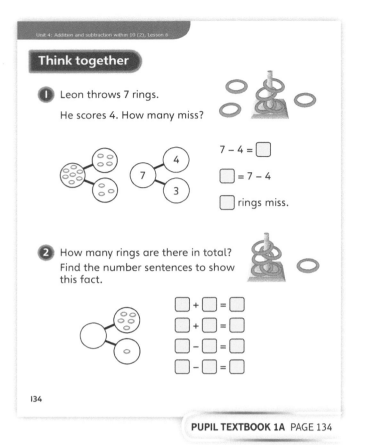

PUPIL TEXTBOOK 1A PAGE 134

PUPIL TEXTBOOK 1A PAGE 135

Practice

WAYS OF WORKING Independent thinking

IN FOCUS In question **2**, the possible subtraction facts are found with the = symbol in different places. In question **3**, the number sentences have been grouped by having the same answer, not by having the same operation (as in question **2**).

STRENGTHEN Show children a number sentence in which the two parts are the same: for example 5 + 5 = 10. Ask children how many number sentences they can make from this fact. Children may think they can make only 4, but show them that each part can still represent something different and so 8 facts can still be made. For example, in a context of 5 skittles standing and 5 knocked over, the two 5s represent different things: changing the parts around in the number sentences changes the meaning of what you are trying to find out.

DEEPEN If children are confident filling in different blank number sentence scaffolds from a context, encourage them to write the blank scaffolds themselves, representing missing numbers as squares and missing symbols as circles. Ask: *Are you able to write the eight different scaffolds you have seen during this lesson?* (Essentially, they have to come up with only 4 blank scaffolds, and duplicate each one.) Encourage children to fill in their scaffolds afterwards.

ASSESSMENT CHECKPOINT Assess whether children, when putting numbers into the number sentences, put the symbols in first to help them. Ensure that, if children generally start by putting the whole next to the = symbol, they understand that this will not work in subtractions.

ANSWERS Answers for the **Practice** part of the lesson appear in the separate **Practice and Reflect answer guide**.

Reflect

WAYS OF WORKING Pair work

IN FOCUS The **Reflect** question prompts children to explain and reword what they have learned this lesson, with no visual prompts or cues and no scaffolds to help them.

ASSESSMENT CHECKPOINT Assess whether children are able to generate 3 other subtractions from this fact or just one other, with the = symbol at the end, and whether they understand how addition facts are linked to the subtraction. Look for any children who still rely on drawing a part-whole model to help them think through what each number is.

ANSWERS Answers for the **Reflect** part of the lesson appear in the separate **Practice and Reflect answer guide**.

After the lesson ⏸

- Were all children clear about the role of the = symbol, and what it means in any part of a number sentence?
- Were children able to relate addition and subtraction facts, and understand which numbers could be switched around to retain the same facts?
- Did children have to calculate at any point in the lesson to check their work, or did they trust their ability to arrange and rearrange number sentences correctly?

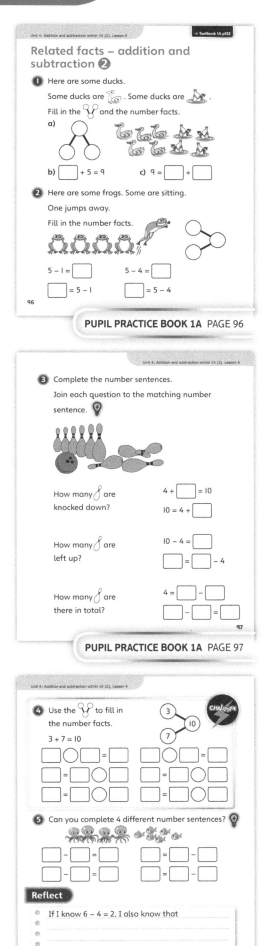

PUPIL PRACTICE BOOK 1A PAGE 96

PUPIL PRACTICE BOOK 1A PAGE 97

PUPIL PRACTICE BOOK 1A PAGE 98

Subtraction – counting back

Learning focus

In this lesson, children will calculate subtraction number sentences using a number line to count back from the bigger number.

Small steps

→ Previous step: Related facts – addition and subtraction (2)
→ **This step: Subtraction – counting back**
→ Next step: Subtraction – finding the difference

NATIONAL CURRICULUM LINKS

Year 1 Number – Addition and Subtraction

- Solve one-step problems that involve addition and subtraction, using concrete objects and pictorial representations, and missing number problems such as $7 = \_ - 9$.
- Read, write and interpret mathematical statements involving addition (+), subtraction (−) and equals (=) signs.
- Add and subtract one-digit and two-digit numbers to 20, including zero.

ASSESSING MASTERY

Children can work out a subtraction number sentence by counting how many steps back on a number line they need to jump to arrive at the answer, recognising that the number of steps is one of the numbers in the subtraction. Children can use the language 'less than' and relate the − symbol to counting backwards.

COMMON MISCONCEPTIONS

When working out a subtraction on a number line, children may not understand that the part taken away in the number sentence is the number of *jumps* they make. For a subtraction such as 9 − 6, children may circle both 9 and 6 and count the spaces between the two numbers instead of jumping 6 back and circling 3. Ask:

What does '− 6' mean? How many do we need to count back? On what number do we land? Is this our answer?

STRENGTHENING UNDERSTANDING

Strengthen understanding of counting back by using a hopscotch grid outside or a giant number line in the classroom. Children can stand by their starting number and then physically jump backwards the correct number of times to see where they land.

GOING DEEPER

Once children are confident about going backwards to find the answer to a subtraction number sentence, deepen understanding by asking them to use their knowledge of additions to check the calculation. Ask children to count forward the same number of steps to check whether the same starting point is reached. If they can, ask them to give the addition number sentence that matches what they are doing.

KEY LANGUAGE

In lesson: count backwards, less than, subtract, take away

Other language to be used by the teacher: starting number

STRUCTURES AND REPRESENTATIONS

Number line

RESOURCES

Mandatory: blank number lines, cubes and/or counters

Optional: hopscotch grid, giant number line

Teaching Tools In the eTextbook of this lesson, you will find interactive links to a selection of teaching tools.

Before you teach

- Are all children secure with using a number line when counting forwards?
- Are all children secure with the term 'less than'?

Discover

WAYS OF WORKING Pair work

ASK

- Question ① a): *Where has Maya started on the number line?*
- Question ① a): *Is she jumping forward or backwards?*
- Question ① a): *When she has jumped, what is a strategy to keep track of what her starting number was? Circle it.*

IN FOCUS These questions use a pictorial representation of a number line: ask children to identify on what Maya is jumping in the picture. They also require children to understand that the term 'more' does not necessarily suggest addition: When saying 'Maya jumps two *more* times', ask children in which direction she will be jumping. Point out that it is the number of steps Maya is jumping *backwards* that is getting bigger, not the number on the number line.

ANSWERS

Question ① a): Maya lands on 6.

Question ① b): Maya lands on 4.

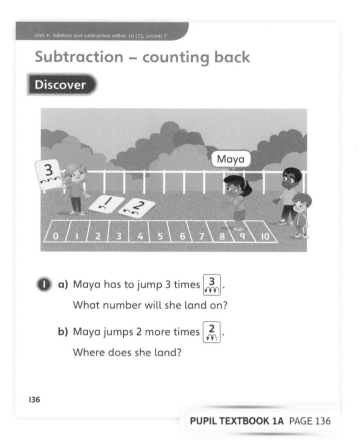

Subtraction – counting back

Discover

① a) Maya has to jump 3 times ⌐3⌐.
   What number will she land on?

b) Maya jumps 2 more times ⌐2⌐.
   Where does she land?

136

PUPIL TEXTBOOK 1A PAGE 136

Share

WAYS OF WORKING Whole class teacher led

ASK

- Question ① a): *Look at how Dexter has counted back. Has he started at the right number? Has Maya started at the right number?*
- Question ① a): *Do we need to find 3 on the number line?*
- Question ① b): *When Maya jumps back 2 more times, what was her starting point?*

IN FOCUS These questions allow you to ensure children understand they should not start their backwards count with their starting number, and that 3 in this context is the number of jumps back Maya makes and isn't the 3 already showing on the number line.

DEEPEN Ask children how many jumps back Maya has done *in total*, from 9 to 4. They could use their own number lines to help them count how many jumps backwards they have to make. Some children may spot that the 5 total jumps back are made from the parts 3 and 2, and they will be able to write the subtraction number sentence 9 – 5 = 4 to match all of the jumps back.

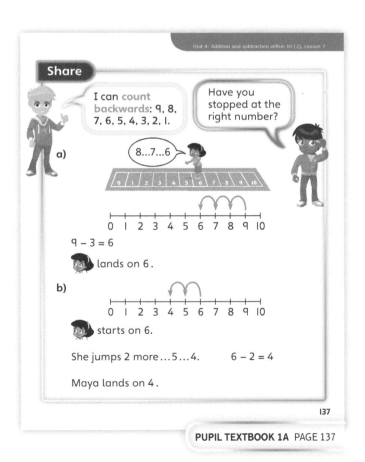

Share

I can **count** backwards: 9, 8, 7, 6, 5, 4, 3, 2, 1.

Have you stopped at the right number?

a) 8...7...6

0 1 2 3 4 5 6 7 8 9 10

9 – 3 = 6

lands on 6.

b)

0 1 2 3 4 5 6 7 8 9 10

starts on 6.

She jumps 2 more...5...4.   6 – 2 = 4

Maya lands on 4.

137

PUPIL TEXTBOOK 1A PAGE 137

Think together

WAYS OF WORKING Whole class teacher led (I do, We do, You do)

ASK

- Question **1**: *Where does the number sentence show 'I less'?*
- Question **1**: *What does this look like on the number line?*
- Question **2**: *Which numbers are missing on Maya's number line?*
- Question **3**: *Where is 0 in each of these number lines?*

IN FOCUS In questions **1** and **2**, the term 'less than' is used. (Ensure children understand that this term represents the jumps backwards on the number line.) In question **3**, all of the number sentences have the same answer: '0'. This provides an opportunity for you to guide children towards the understanding that any number taken away from itself will be 0, referring to what Ash says about seeing a pattern.

STRENGTHEN Strengthen children's understanding by asking them to consider patterns in what they see. Ask: *When counting backwards on a number line, is the number reached always less than the starting number? Does that mean that the starting number is always more than the number reached?* Ask children to explain, using the numbers and examples they have just seen.

DEEPEN Ask children to show the pattern in question **3** using a different resource. For example, 3 cubes take away 3 cubes gives 0 cubes. Ask children to come up with more examples of number sentences with the answer 0. Encourage them to express what generalised pattern they are seeing in a sentence.

ASSESSMENT CHECKPOINT Assess whether children recognise that the answers to the subtraction number sentences and the 'less than' statements are the same. Consider whether they need to calculate each one individually, or can see that both ask the same question with different words.

ANSWERS

Question **1**: 6 − 1 = 5; 1 less than 6 is 5.

Question **2**: 5 − 2 = 3; 2 less than 5 is 3.

Question **3**: 3 − 3 = 0
2 − 2 = 0
1 − 1 = 0

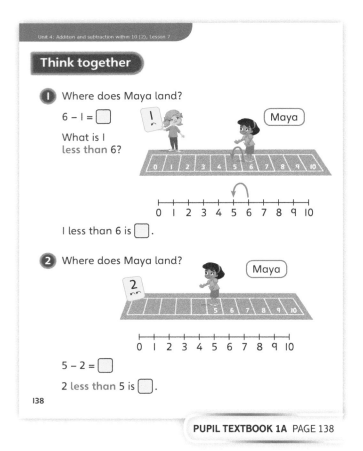

PUPIL TEXTBOOK 1A PAGE 138

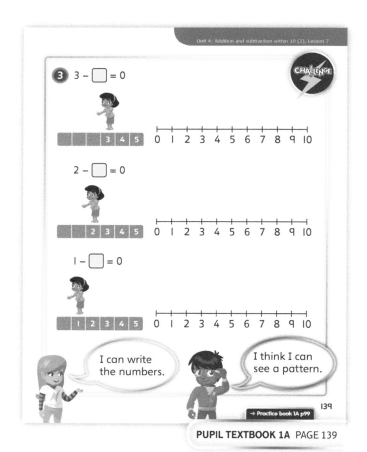

PUPIL TEXTBOOK 1A PAGE 139

Practice

WAYS OF WORKING Independent thinking

IN FOCUS In question ❷, children need to match each number sentence to the correct number line, relating what is being taken away to the number of jumps. In questions ❶ and ❸, children need to count back onto spaces presented differently from a regular number line.

STRENGTHEN In question ❺, children have to generate different subtraction number sentences with the same answer. Strengthen children's grasp of the question by suggesting they work systematically to find all the different subtractions, starting from the answer and counting up to find a starting point greater than it.

DEEPEN Ask children to complete the question ❺ activity for different target numbers under 10. Encourage them to spot a pattern between the target number and the number of number sentences that can be generated for it (with the maximum starting number being 10): there will always be one more number sentence than the target number, because the operation – 0 should be included.

ASSESSMENT CHECKPOINT Assess whether children, when counting back, make the mistake of starting counting from their starting number. When they count back out loud, ensure children say out loud the numbers on which they land on a number line, not the number of jumps: if they are counting back 2 from 7, for example, they should say, 'Six, five'. They also need to recognise when to stop the count.

ANSWERS Answers for the **Practice** part of the lesson appear in the separate **Practice and Reflect answer guide**.

Reflect

WAYS OF WORKING Pair work

IN FOCUS The **Reflect** question allows children to explain and reword different subtraction strategies, such as using part-whole models, counting what is left, breaking apart a whole and finding the difference on a number line.

ASSESSMENT CHECKPOINT Assess whether children can explain each method. Listen to assess whether there is a method children prefer, and if they use the term 'less than' in their explanations.

ANSWERS Answers for the **Reflect** part of the lesson appear in the separate **Practice and Reflect answer guide**.

After the lesson ⏸

- Did children understand what the different parts of subtraction number sentences represent on a number line? For example, did they understand that the part being taken away represents the number of jumps?
- Could children work out a question worded 'less than' using the counting back method on a number line?
- Were children confident using 0 in number sentences: counting back to 0 and counting back 0 jumps?

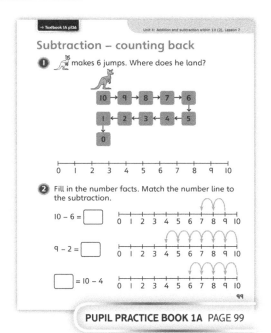

PUPIL PRACTICE BOOK 1A PAGE 99

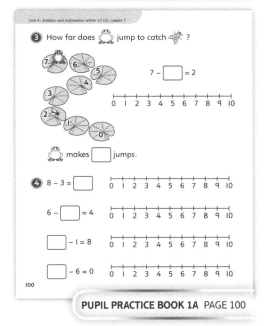

PUPIL PRACTICE BOOK 1A PAGE 100

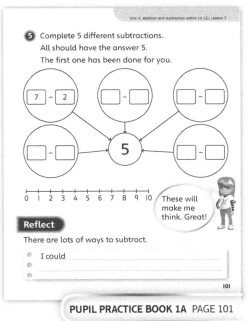

PUPIL PRACTICE BOOK 1A PAGE 101

Subtraction – finding the difference

Learning focus

In this lesson, children will answer questions worded 'how many more' and 'how many fewer'. They will compare quantities of objects to find the difference and represent this on a number line.

Small steps

→ Previous step: Subtraction – counting back
→ **This step: Subtraction – finding the difference**
→ Next step: Solving word problems – subtraction

NATIONAL CURRICULUM LINKS

Year 1 Number – Addition and Subtraction

- Solve one-step problems that involve addition and subtraction, using concrete objects and pictorial representations, and missing number problems such as $7 = \_ - 9$.
- Read, write and interpret mathematical statements involving addition (+), subtraction (–) and equals (=) signs.
- Add and subtract one-digit and two-digit numbers to 20, including zero.

ASSESSING MASTERY

Children can compare different quantities of objects in terms of *how many* more or fewer there are. Children can understand that the difference is the same when comparing two groups in terms of more and fewer, and express this correctly in a sentence (for example, 'there are 2 more in the first group' and 'there are 2 fewer in the second group').

COMMON MISCONCEPTIONS

Children may line up groups of objects inaccurately when comparing them, meaning that objects from one group do not correspond with those from the other. Demonstrate how to line up the objects consistently, and explain that anything left over (anything that can't be matched) is the difference between the groups. Ask:
- *How are you going to line up the objects? Which objects are the ones left over? Which group has more? Which group has fewer?*

STRENGTHENING UNDERSTANDING

Strengthen understanding by asking two unequal groups of children to sit in rows on the carpet, with the smaller group spread out to take up the same amount of space. Then ask children to pair up with someone from the other group. Explain that the children with no partners make up the *difference* between these two groups: there are *more* children in one group and *fewer* in the other.

GOING DEEPER

Use classroom stationery objects to deepen understanding by asking children to go on a comparison hunt. Choose a number for comparison, and ask them to find out how many more or fewer pens, pencils, rubbers, sharpeners etc. there are in the room. Provide blank sentence scaffolds and number sentences to help children record their thinking.

KEY LANGUAGE

In lesson: how many more, how many fewer, compare, difference, count on, count back

Other language to be used by the teacher: comparison model

STRUCTURES AND REPRESENTATIONS

Number line

RESOURCES

Mandatory: blank number lines, cubes and/or counters

Optional: classroom stationery objects, blank sentence scaffolds and number sentences

Teaching Tools In the eTextbook of this lesson, you will find interactive links to a selection of teaching tools.

Before you teach

- Are all children secure with counting on or backwards from different starting points?
- How familiar are children with the words 'more' and 'fewer'?
- How could you link 'finding more' and 'finding fewer' to subtraction facts?

Discover

WAYS OF WORKING Pair work

ASK

- In response to the picture: *How many children are in the first row? How many are there in the second row?*
- *What does 'how many more' / 'how many fewer' mean?*
- After question ① b): *Why are both answers the same?*

IN FOCUS Question ① requires children to understand the concept of more and fewer. Children may count how many children are in each row of the picture, and then not know what to do with those numbers, or mistakenly say there are '8 more' because 8 is more than 6.

ANSWERS

Question ① a): There are 2 more children in the back row.

Question ① b): There are 2 fewer children in the front row.

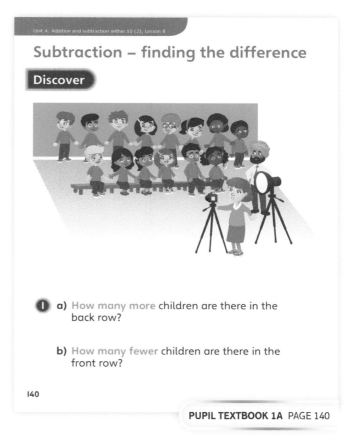

Subtraction – finding the difference

Discover

① a) How many more children are there in the back row?

b) How many fewer children are there in the front row?

140

PUPIL TEXTBOOK 1A PAGE 140

Share

WAYS OF WORKING Whole class teacher led

ASK

- *What do the counters represent?*
- *Why are the counters in two rows?*
- *How does the grid help us?*
- *Why are the arrows going in different directions on the number lines?*

IN FOCUS This section uses two key terms that you have the opportunity to discuss. Look at what Astrid says and discuss what 'compare' means (lining up both groups of objects to see how far they match). Discuss the word 'difference', and that it explains how many more or fewer things there are when you compare them. Highlight what Sparks says: counting on or back will still find the difference.

DEEPEN Ask children to arrange counters as shown, and then to rearrange them so that there is no difference between the rows. Ask children to explain how this would look in the picture in the **Discover** section: for example, 'The boy on the end could come and sit on the bench.'

Share

I need to line up the ◯ so that I can **compare** and find the **difference**.

You can **count on** or count back to find the difference.

If I know how many more then do I know how many fewer?

a)
0 1 2 3 4 5 6 7 8 9 10
There are 2 more children in the back row.

b)
0 1 2 3 4 5 6 7 8 9 10
There are 2 fewer children in the front row.

141

PUPIL TEXTBOOK 1A PAGE 141

Think together

WAYS OF WORKING Whole class teacher led (I do, We do, You do)

ASK

- Question ❶: *How are you going to show the children in rows using the grid?*
- Question ❶: *Where are you going to start on the number line?*
- Question ❶: *Where is 'how many more' shown on the number line?*
- Question ❶: *What subtraction fact matches what you have shown on the number line?*

IN FOCUS In this part of the lesson, comparing rows of objects is linked to a subtraction fact and a number line. Referring to what Dexter and Ash say in relation to question ❸ gives you the opportunity to ask children to check previous examples and discuss whether the pattern is always the same.

STRENGTHEN In question ❶, guide children to an understanding that the number of children in the longer row should be their starting point on the number line, and can be circled. The number in the shorter row is the one to which they need to jump back. The number of jumps needed is the difference between the two groups.

DEEPEN In questions ❶ and ❷, deepen children's understanding by asking them to pose another question for the same context. For example, in question ❶, guide them to ask, 'How many fewer children are there in the back row?' Ensure they do not simply substitute the word 'more' for 'fewer' (or 'fewer' for 'more') without changing the row to which they are referring.

ASSESSMENT CHECKPOINT Assess whether children recognise that the difference between two points on the number line is the number of jumps back. Ensure that they understand that the number that is more in one row is the same as the number that is fewer in the other row.

ANSWERS

Question ❶: 7 – 4 = 3
There are 3 more children in the front row.

Question ❷: 9 – 4 = 5
There are 5 fewer children in the front row.

Question ❸ a): 7 – 3 = 4
There are 4 more children in the back row.

Question ❸ b): 7 – 3 = 4
There are 4 fewer children in the front row.

Unit 4: Addition and subtraction within 10 (2), Lesson 8

Think together

❶ How many more children are there in the front row?

0 1 2 3 4 5 6 7 8 9 10

☐ – ☐ = ☐

There are ☐ more children in the front row.

❷ How many fewer children are there in the front row?

0 1 2 3 4 5 6 7 8 9 10

☐ – ☐ = ☐

There are ☐ fewer children in the front row.

142

PUPIL TEXTBOOK 1A PAGE 142

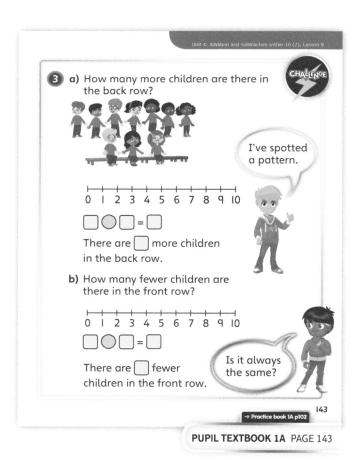

❸ a) How many more children are there in the back row?

CHALLENGE

0 1 2 3 4 5 6 7 8 9 10

☐ ◯ ☐ = ☐

There are ☐ more children in the back row.

I've spotted a pattern.

b) How many fewer children are there in the front row?

0 1 2 3 4 5 6 7 8 9 10

☐ ◯ ☐ = ☐

There are ☐ fewer children in the front row.

Is it always the same?

143

→ Practice book 1A p102

PUPIL TEXTBOOK 1A PAGE 143

Practice

WAYS OF WORKING Independent thinking

IN FOCUS In question **3**, Ash's question challenges children's thinking that there can only be one solution. Ensure that children understand that 'the difference' can mean there is one more or one fewer. Encourage children to make or draw the original tower and then adapt it either way. Question **4** provides no pictorial representations to support thinking. (Children could draw the problem or represent it on a number line to help them work it out.)

STRENGTHEN Strengthen understanding in question **3** by asking children to write some number sentences to match the context and guide their drawing. For example, '1 more than 5 is 6' / '5 + 1 = 6', or '1 less than 5 is 4' / '5 − 1 = 4'.

DEEPEN Ask children to come up with their own sentences to match the number cards given in question **4**. As 0 is included, they could use learning from the previous lesson to come up with a range of sentences that all have '0' as their answer: for example, '9 less than 9 is 0'.

ASSESSMENT CHECKPOINT Assess whether children, if representing any of the questions using physical resources, understand the need to put them in neat rows or a grid. Ensure children do not try to make lines the same length no matter the number of objects. Assess whether children are using the terms 'difference', 'more' and 'fewer' correctly when comparing groups.

ANSWERS Answers for the **Practice** part of the lesson appear in the separate **Practice and Reflect answer guide**.

Reflect

WAYS OF WORKING Pair work

IN FOCUS In the **Reflect** question, children need to count each group accurately to know that the difference is 0. When 2 more birds arrive, they should grasp that the number of birds on the two branches has to stay equal so the difference remains the same (0).

ASSESSMENT CHECKPOINT Assess whether children assume that there are more birds on one branch because of the way they look, rather than counting accurately. Ensure children can understand 0 being a 'difference' between two groups, and that they can articulate that it means both numbers must be the same.

ANSWERS Answers for the **Reflect** part of the lesson appear in the separate **Practice and Reflect answer guide**.

After the lesson

- Did children understand that the word 'difference' can mean 'more than' or 'fewer than'?
- Did children understand the importance of matching up objects in different groups in order to compare them accurately?
- Were children able to represent difference on a number line and in a subtraction fact?

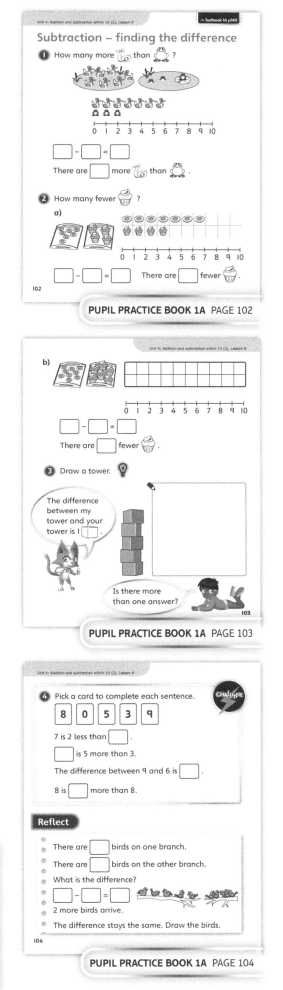

PUPIL PRACTICE BOOK 1A PAGE 102

PUPIL PRACTICE BOOK 1A PAGE 103

PUPIL PRACTICE BOOK 1A PAGE 104

Solving word problems – subtraction

Learning focus

In this lesson, children will solve subtraction word problems using a range of strategies. They will make up their own subtraction problem from a given context.

Small steps

→ Previous step: Subtraction – finding the difference
→ **This step: Solving word problems – subtraction**
→ Next step: Comparing additions and subtractions (1)

NATIONAL CURRICULUM LINKS

Year 1 Number – Addition and Subtraction

- Solve one-step problems that involve addition and subtraction, using concrete objects and pictorial representations, and missing number problems such as $7 = \_ - 9$.
- Read, write and interpret mathematical statements involving addition (+), subtraction (−) and equals (=) signs.
- Add and subtract one-digit and two-digit numbers to 20, including zero.

ASSESSING MASTERY

Children can find maths stories and solve problems using calculations that represent each story, recognising that there are different kinds of subtraction problem: 'take away', 'break apart' and 'find the difference'. Children can use a part-whole model, number line or ten frame to solve a subtraction problem, making deliberate choices about which method is most appropriate and whether or not this involves a physical resource.

COMMON MISCONCEPTIONS

When making up their own subtraction stories, children may become confused by the context and make up addition stories instead. They may also have difficulty relating subtraction stories to 'finding the difference', as nothing is physically removed (such as ice creams being eaten or birds flying away). Ask:

- *Look at the numbers in your story. What is the whole? What is the one part that you know? What is the part you are trying to find out?*

STRENGTHENING UNDERSTANDING

Strengthen understanding by providing objects from the stories and asking children to act like detectives, uncovering and demonstrating the maths buried in the various contexts. Children should explain the meaning of the different parts of a subtraction in each context, and connect the different subtractions with earlier learning.

GOING DEEPER

Deepen understanding by asking children to represent a given subtraction fact, such as $9 - 3 = 6$, in a blank part-whole model, ten frame and number line. Provide subtraction stories such as, 'There were 9 cakes and 3 got eaten. How many are left?' and 'There are 9 children standing in one row and 6 in another row, what is the difference between them?'. Children should discuss which model is appropriate for which question and why.

KEY LANGUAGE

In lesson: whole, part, missing part, difference, subtract, take away

Other language to be used by the teacher: compare, more, fewer

STRUCTURES AND REPRESENTATIONS

Number line, part-whole model, ten frame

RESOURCES

Mandatory: blank number lines, blank part-whole models, blank ten frames, cubes and/or counters

Teaching Tools In the eTextbook of this lesson, you will find interactive links to a selection of teaching tools.

Before you teach

- Do children struggle with a particular subtraction method? How could you address this?
- In the previous lesson, were children confident knowing that 'finding the difference' is the same as subtraction?

Discover

WAYS OF WORKING Pair work

ASK

- Question ❶ a): *What is 7 in the picture?*
- Question ❶ a): *What does – 3 mean?*

IN FOCUS The picture leads children to make up their own subtraction story. They first have to find what the 7 and the 3 could represent in the picture.

ANSWERS

Question ❶ a): There are 7 🍦 in total. 3 of them have melted.

Question ❶ b): 7 – 3 = 4

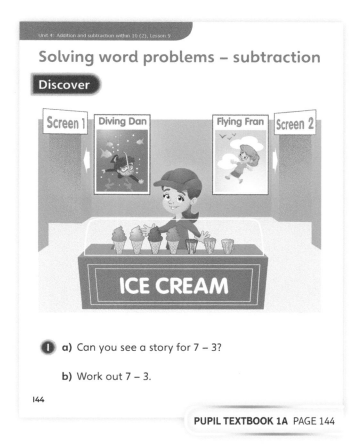

Share

WAYS OF WORKING Whole class teacher led

ASK

- Question ❶ a): *Why is this a subtraction question?*
- Question ❶ a): *What representations did you use?*
- Question ❶ b): *How could you check your answer?*

IN FOCUS Children should recognise that they are looking for a whole of 7 and a part of 3. Question ❶ b) uses a number line to demonstrate how to solve the calculation.

DEEPEN Ask children to come up with a different subtraction question based on the ice creams ('How many fewer melted ice creams are there than remaining ice creams', for example), and to decide which model(s) would help them work out the answer. To deepen understanding still further, ask, 'What if one more ice cream melted?' Again, ask children to show the answer on their model.

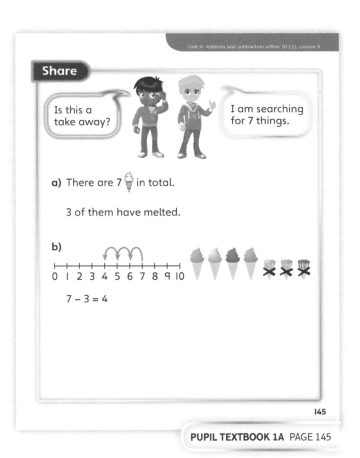

Think together

Whole class teacher led (I do, We do, You do)

ASK

- Question **1**: *Are the two parts the same? What do they represent?*
- Question **2**: *Is this a take away or a comparison question?*
- Question **3**: *What could your subtraction story be? What sort of subtraction story will you make up – take away or find the difference?*

IN FOCUS Questions **1** and **2** revise existing skills, but question **3** prompts children to choose elements of the pictures to create their own subtraction stories. Children could use the melted ice cream model from the **Discover** and **Share** sections or the comparison model from question **2** or use something new (for example, calculating how many people had ice creams).

STRENGTHEN In question **3**, if children are coming up with take-away stories only, refer to what Dexter says about finding a difference; then ask children to pick a context in which to find the difference, and provide them with a scaffold if necessary. Ask children to model their stories using counters and/or a number line – if they choose a part-whole model to show a comparison question, they may be confused.

DEEPEN When children have successfully thought of one take-away or comparison question and represented it, ask them to use the same context to frame another type of question. For example, if children have proposed, 'There are 8 ice creams in total and 5 have melted. How many are left?', guide them towards a phrasing such as, 'What is the difference between the number of ice creams remaining and the number that has melted?'

ASSESSMENT CHECKPOINT Ensure that children are making up subtraction stories rather than addition stories (for example, 'There are 7 people in one row and 3 in the other. How many people are there in total?'). Assess whether children are secure with what information they need to provide in each story in order to make a calculation possible (and not phrasing a question as, for example, 'There are 8 ice creams and some melt. How many are left?').

ANSWERS

Question **1**: 10 – 5 = 5
5 people are not wearing 🕶.

Question **2**: 6 – 4 = 2
There are 2 more people in the line for Screen 1.

Question **3**: Answers may include but are not limited to:
- There are 8 ice creams and 5 melt. How many are left?
- There are 7 people in the first line and 3 in the second line. How many more people are there in the first line?
- What is the difference between the number of red and yellow counters?
- Start on 10 and jump back 4. What number do you land on?

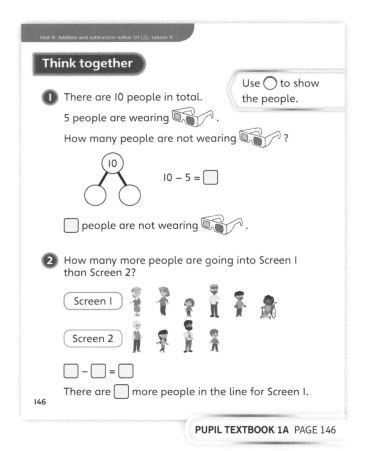

PUPIL TEXTBOOK 1A PAGE 146

PUPIL TEXTBOOK 1A PAGE 147

Practice

WAYS OF WORKING Independent thinking

IN FOCUS In question **2**, children match calculations with questions, which embeds understanding of what each number represents in a subtraction fact. In question **3**, children fill in the blanks for two subtraction stories and then compare them using the term 'more'. In question **4**, children have to work out which group contains more before they can complete the sentence 'How many more ___ than ___?'.

STRENGTHEN In question **4**, encourage children to draw the different groups of stars in rows to compare them. This may help them to answer the question and fill in the blanks correctly (and can form the basis for using bar models later).

DEEPEN Ask children to use the scaffold from question **4** and example objects of their own to make up their own questions. They will have to create two groups of objects with a difference, as well as working out how to structure the facts into a sentence that makes sense.

ASSESSMENT CHECKPOINT Assess whether children understand, in question **2**, that the questions are asking them to work out how many snowmen *need* carrots/hats, not how many *have* them. In question **4**, notice whether children work out the calculation 5 – 3 = 2 before completing the sentence scaffold that appears before it, and whether they develop strategies for keeping track of which number represents which part (i.e. a drawing underneath each number).

ANSWERS Answers for the **Practice** part of the lesson appear in the separate **Practice and Reflect answer guide**.

Reflect

WAYS OF WORKING Pair work

IN FOCUS Asking children to write their own subtraction story is a good indicative tool to assess their understanding of what each number may mean in context. Ask children to draw or represent their problem with resources and/or models.

ASSESSMENT CHECKPOINT Assess whether children correctly take away 2 objects from 10 in their stories, and notice what contexts they use. It is important that they understand 8 and 2 should be parts of 10 as a whole, or that 2 is the difference between 8 and 10.

ANSWERS Answers for the **Reflect** part of the lesson appear in the separate **Practice and Reflect answer guide**.

After the lesson ⏸

- Did children struggle with any particular contexts?
- Were children able to come up with an accurate subtraction context independently, or did they need prompting and scaffolding?
- Were children able to relate each of their subtraction stories to the correct subtraction facts?

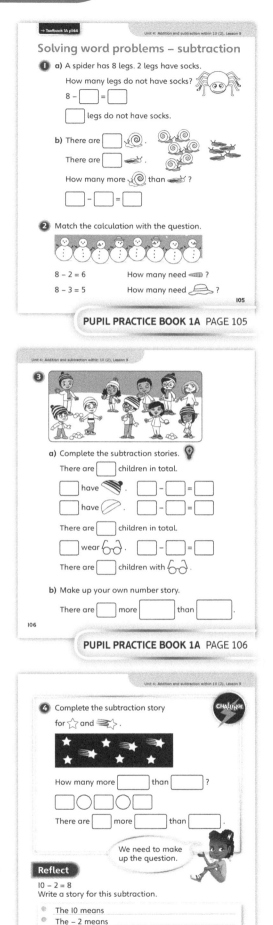

PUPIL PRACTICE BOOK 1A PAGE 105

PUPIL PRACTICE BOOK 1A PAGE 106

PUPIL PRACTICE BOOK 1A PAGE 107

175

Comparing additions and subtractions ❶

Learning focus

In this lesson, children will solve addition and subtraction problems together in context. They will compare numbers, using the < and > symbols to answer questions.

Small steps

→ Previous step: Solving word problems – subtraction
→ **This step: Comparing additions and subtractions (1)**
→ Next step: Comparing additions and subtractions (2)

NATIONAL CURRICULUM LINKS

Year 1 Number – Addition and Subtraction

- Solve one-step problems that involve addition and subtraction, using concrete objects and pictorial representations, and missing number problems such as 7 = _ – 9.
- Read, write and interpret mathematical statements involving addition (+), subtraction (–) and equals (=) signs.

ASSESSING MASTERY

Children can solve multi-step addition and subtraction problems within 10, and compare numbers within a context, to answer questions. Children can use the < and > symbols correctly and use different models to represent a problem, relating them back to the original context.

COMMON MISCONCEPTIONS

Children may struggle to interpret the numbers in multi-step calculations and become confused or overwhelmed by the amount of information. Ask:
- *What is the question asking you to work out?*

STRENGTHENING UNDERSTANDING

The problems in this lesson have two steps: 1) Work out the answer to a calculation; 2) Compare that answer with a given total. Strengthen understanding by modelling one of the steps and letting children complete the other.

GOING DEEPER

Once children have come up with number facts such as 9 > 8, deepen understanding by asking them to rewrite the fact using a context from the problem and the language 'more than' and 'less than'. For example: 'Nine children is more than eight seats.' If appropriate, prompt them to add a final explanatory sentence, for example: 'They need one more seat.'

KEY LANGUAGE

In lesson: more than, less than, add, subtract, take away, compare

Other language to be used by the teacher: more, fewer, not enough

STRUCTURES AND REPRESENTATIONS

Ten frame, part-whole model, number line

RESOURCES

Mandatory: blank ten frames, blank part-whole models, blank number lines, cubes and/or counters

Teaching Tools In the eTextbook of this lesson, you will find interactive links to a selection of teaching tools.

Before you teach ⏸

- Are children confident coming up with number sentences based on contexts?
- How could you scaffold any struggling children's approaches to the problem?
- Are all children secure with what the symbols < and > mean?

Discover

ASK

- Question ① a): *How many people are waiting to go on the ride?*
- Question ① a): *How can you tell how many seats there are?*
- Question ① a): *Can everybody have a seat?*

IN FOCUS Question ① a) requires a yes/no answer, not a number, but requires most of the thinking needed to calculate ① b). Children may count the seats or rely on the text in the picture ('Maximum 8 people'), but need to count the people waiting.

ANSWERS

Question ① a): No, not everyone can go on the ride together.

Question ① b): There is 1 person left.

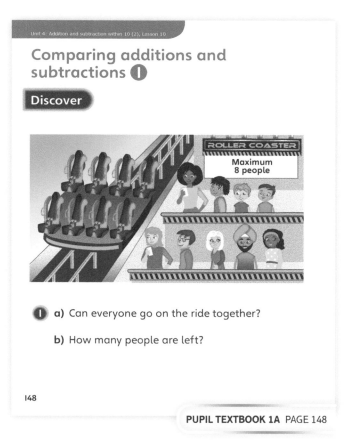

Comparing additions and subtractions ①

Discover

① a) Can everyone go on the ride together?

b) How many people are left?

148

PUPIL TEXTBOOK 1A PAGE 148

Share

ASK

- Question ① a): *What does each number mean in the calculation?*
- Question ① a): *Why do you need to know if 9 is greater or smaller than 8?*
- After question ① b): *Can you see both the addition and the subtraction?*

IN FOCUS This part of the lesson prompts children to use resources and/or models to add the two rows of people together before comparing them to the number of seats. It then suggests performing a take-away subtraction to find that there is one person left.

DEEPEN Look at what Dexter is asking in question ① b), and ask children what he means by there being 'a better way'. What other way(s) would they choose to calculate this?

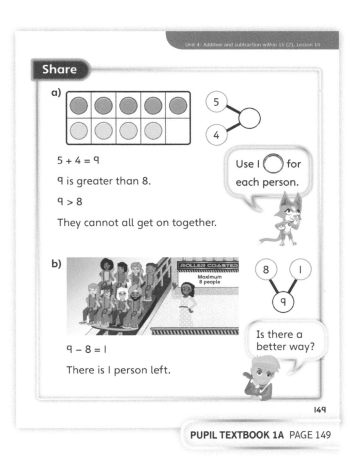

Share

a)

$5 + 4 = 9$

9 is greater than 8.

$9 > 8$

They cannot all get on together.

Use I ◯ for each person.

b)

$9 - 8 = 1$

There is I person left.

Is there a better way?

149

PUPIL TEXTBOOK 1A PAGE 149

Think together

WAYS OF WORKING Whole class teacher led (I do, We do, You do)

ASK

- *What information does each picture tell you?*
- *What information does each question tell you?*

IN FOCUS Questions ❶ and ❷ have been segmented and scaffolded to guide children towards finding the answer and linking it back to the context. The maximum number of seats is different in question ❷, so children can not rely on their previous knowledge to help them.

STRENGTHEN Strengthen understanding by asking children to act out the problems. Use chairs as seats on the ride and have children stand in lines, as in the pictures. When people decide to leave, children can move away from the main group. The questions can then be solved as the remaining children attempt to sit on the seats.

DEEPEN Ask children to look at the problem from another angle and come up with opposing statements and number facts that use the term 'less than' or the < symbol. For example, after writing, '8 is greater than 6. 8 > 6', ask them to write '6 is less than 8. 6 < 8'. Children could also come up with different finishing statements: 'There are not enough seats.' / 'There are too many people.'

ASSESSMENT CHECKPOINT When children fill in the sentence scaffolds comparing numbers, assess whether they understand what two numbers they are comparing. Listen to see if, when reading aloud, children add on words to give the numbers context: for example, '8 *seats* is greater than 6 *children*'.

ANSWERS

Question ❶ a): $9 - 3 = 6$

Question ❶ b): 8 is greater than 6. / 6 is less than 8.
$8 > 6 / 6 < 8$
They can all go on the ride together.

Question ❷: There are 6 people in total.
$6 - 0 = 6$
They can all go on the ride together.

Question ❸: $6 - 1 = 5 < 8$
They can all go on the ride.

Think together

❶ There are 9 people waiting for the ride.

3 people leave.

a) How many people are left waiting for the ride?

☐ – ☐ = ☐   0 1 2 3 4 5 6 7 8 9 10

b) Can they all go on the ride together?

☐ is _____ than ☐.

☐◯☐

They _____ all go on the ride together.

❷ How many people are there in total?

Can they all go on the ride together?

☐◯☐ = ☐

They _____ all go on the ride together.

150

PUPIL TEXTBOOK 1A PAGE 150

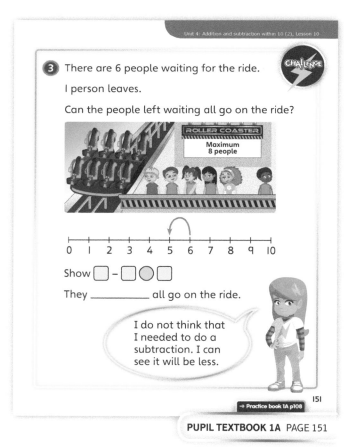

❸ There are 6 people waiting for the ride.

I person leaves.

Can the people left waiting all go on the ride?

CHALLENGE

Maximum 8 people

0 1 2 3 4 5 6 7 8 9 10

Show ☐ – ☐◯☐

They _____ all go on the ride.

I do not think that I needed to do a subtraction. I can see it will be less.

→ Practice book 1A p108

151

PUPIL TEXTBOOK 1A PAGE 151

Practice

WAYS OF WORKING Independent thinking

IN FOCUS In question **1**, children are asked about children that are not represented pictorially. They then need to compare the number of bikes and children, and answer a yes/no question about whether each child can have a bike. The remaining questions require children to calculate an addition or subtraction fact before it can be compared with a number.

STRENGTHEN If children struggle with question **1**, they could draw stick people next to the bikes. In question **4**, ask children to note down which numbers are < 5 (1, 2, 3, 4) and which are > 5 (6, 7, 8, 9) in each bubble; then, once they have worked out the number facts, the link required will be clearer.

DEEPEN Ask children to choose a comparative number fact from question **5** (for example, 4 + 3 < 6) and to write their own word problem to match it. They could use the context from the **Discover**, **Share** and **Think together** sections: two rows of people waiting for a ride with 6 seats.

ASSESSMENT CHECKPOINT In questions **2**–**5**, assess whether children need to cross out the number fact and replace it with the single digit before comparing them with the given numbers. Can children immediately recognise when the two sides are equal, as they recognise the number bonds?

ANSWERS Answers for the **Practice** part of the lesson appear in the separate **Practice and Reflect answer guide**.

Reflect

WAYS OF WORKING Pair work

IN FOCUS In the **Reflect** question, children secure their understanding by completing the number sentences with the correct comparative symbols.

ASSESSMENT CHECKPOINT Assess whether children replace the calculations with their single-digit answers before comparing them with the given numbers and deciding which symbol to use, or if they are able to hold the information in their heads.

ANSWERS Answers for the **Reflect** part of the lesson appear in the separate **Practice and Reflect answer guide**.

After the lesson ⏸

- Were children able to work out these multi-step problems in story contexts, both abstractly and using concrete resources?
- When the calculations were abstract, what strategies (or resources) did children use to help them arrive at the right answers?

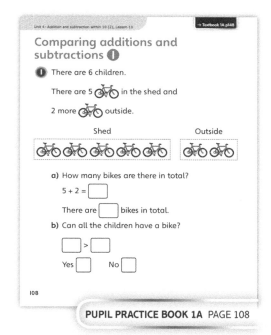

PUPIL PRACTICE BOOK 1A PAGE 108

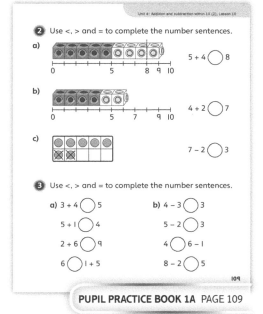

PUPIL PRACTICE BOOK 1A PAGE 109

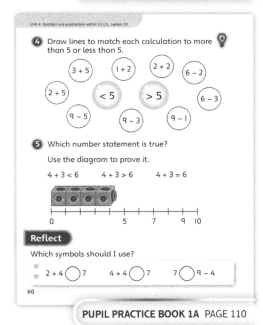

PUPIL PRACTICE BOOK 1A PAGE 110

Comparing additions and subtractions ②

Learning focus

In this lesson, children will compare two addition facts to work out which answer is more (or less) than the other. They will compare these facts using < and > symbols

Small steps

→ Previous step: Comparing additions and subtractions (1)
→ **This step: Comparing additions and subtractions (2)**
→ Next step: Solving word problems – addition and subtraction

NATIONAL CURRICULUM LINKS

Year 1 Number – Addition and Subtraction

- Solve one-step problems that involve addition and subtraction, using concrete objects and pictorial representations, and missing number problems such as $7 = \_ - 9$.
- Read, write and interpret mathematical statements involving addition (+), subtraction (–) and equals (=) signs.

ASSESSING MASTERY

Children can compare two calculations rather than a calculation and a number, understanding the need to work out both number facts before comparing them. Children can apply previous knowledge of comparing numbers with the < and > symbols when comparing two facts and use the = symbol correctly, even when the numbers in the facts are not the same.

COMMON MISCONCEPTIONS

Children may not understand why the = symbol can be used when two facts contain different numbers (but have the same total): for example, $5 + 2 = 6 + 1$. Ask: *What do you need to do first?*

When comparing, for example, $7 - 6$ and $2 + 3$, children may assert that $7 - 6$ is more because both the numbers are higher. Ask:
- *If the numbers are more / less, does that mean the number fact will be more / less?*
- *Are the symbols in the number facts the same? What does this mean?*

STRENGTHENING UNDERSTANDING

Strengthen understanding by using different-coloured cubes to show the parts of a calculation. Putting the two stacks of cubes together in this way looks like the comparison model children have encountered previously, and can lead them to use the < and > symbols correctly.

GOING DEEPER

Once children are confident with filling in blank spaces with <, > or = correctly, deepen understanding by asking them to complete scaffolds in which <, > or = has already been given. Tell children they can use any numbers up to 10 to make any or all of these statements true. For example:

$$\_ + \_ > \_ + \_ \qquad\qquad \_ - \_ < \_ - \_ \qquad\qquad \_ - \_ > \_ + \_$$

KEY LANGUAGE

In lesson: more than, greater than, less than, fewer than, equal

Other language to be used by the teacher: add, subtract, take away, compare

STRUCTURES AND REPRESENTATIONS

Number line

RESOURCES

Mandatory: blank number lines, cubes and/or counters

Optional: different-coloured cubes, </> number-sentence scaffolds

Teaching Tools In the eTextbook of this lesson, you will find interactive links to a selection of teaching tools.

Before you teach

- Are all children confident with comparing a number and a calculation?
- Are all children able to move between calculating addition and subtraction facts with ease?

Discover

Pair work

ASK

- Question ❶: *How do you know which waiter has the most drinks? What did you do to work that out?*
- Question ❶: *Which number fact is each waiter showing?*
- Question ❶: *When you are comparing which waiter has the most, which two numbers are you comparing?*

IN FOCUS In this part of the lesson, children are prompted to compare two wholes made up of different parts.

ANSWERS

Question ❶: Emily has 7 ⬚. Nate has 6 ⬚.

Emily has the most ⬚.

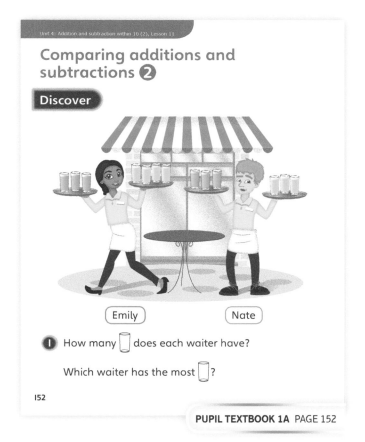

PUPIL TEXTBOOK 1A PAGE 152

Share

Whole class teacher led

ASK

- Question ❶: *What does each number mean in the calculation?*
- Question ❶: *Why do you need to know if 7 is greater or smaller than 6?*
- Question ❶: *Can you see the addition and the subtraction?*

IN FOCUS Children are prompted to use resources and/or models to work out the total number of drinks carried by each waiter. However, Flo suggests ignoring the trays that have 3 drinks on them, and simply considering the number of drinks on the other tray.

DEEPEN Ask children to rewrite the number facts using the 'less than' symbol. For example, they could first change 7 > 6 to 6 < 7 and therefore 3 + 3 < 3 + 4.

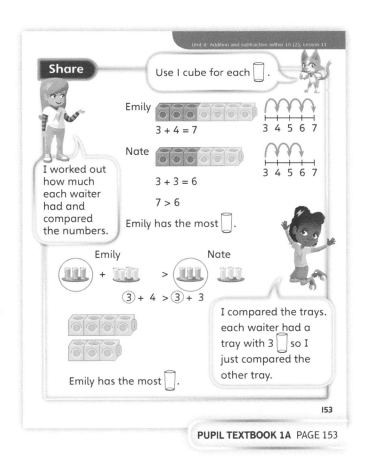

PUPIL TEXTBOOK 1A PAGE 153

Think together

WAYS OF WORKING Whole class teacher led (I do, We do, You do)

ASK

- *What information does each question tell you?*
- *What information does each pair of pictures tell you?*

IN FOCUS Questions ❶ and ❷ continue to compare calculations. In question ❸, children compare quantities in two different ways, by comparing the whole numbers and the number facts that use different operations. (Children may have difficulty seeing that an addition fact can be equal to a subtraction fact, so suggest that they work out the individual totals first; then link them back to the original calculations.)

STRENGTHEN In question ❶, children could label each calculation with the waiter's name in order to strengthen understanding. 'Emily has more than Nate' could turn into 'Emily > Nate' and lead to '9 > 8' and then '4 + 5 > 3 + 5'. In question 3, arrows can be drawn between the different number facts to show which answer forms which part of the next calculation.

DEEPEN In question ❷, ask children, 'What if one more drink from each tray fell over?' Encourage children to recognise that the number of drinks on the left will still be more, as one has been taken away from *each* tray. Reinforce this by asking, 'What if one more drink was put on each tray?'

ASSESSMENT CHECKPOINT Assess whether children understand they have to work out the total of each side separately before performing comparisons. Look at how they respond to questions, to see whether they instinctively know which waiter has more drinks based on the pictures alone (for example, Emily *looks* like she is holding more drinks in question ❶, without them needing counting). If this is happening, ensure children perform the calculations to prove or check what they already believe.

ANSWERS

Question ❶: 4 + 5 = 9
  3 + 5 = 8
  4 + 5 > 3 + 5 / 3 + 5 < 4 + 5

  Emily has more 🥛.

Question ❷: 5 − 1 > 6 − 3

  There are more 🥛

Question ❸: 4 + 3 = 7; 9 − 2 = 7
  7 = 7
  4 + 3 = 9 − 2

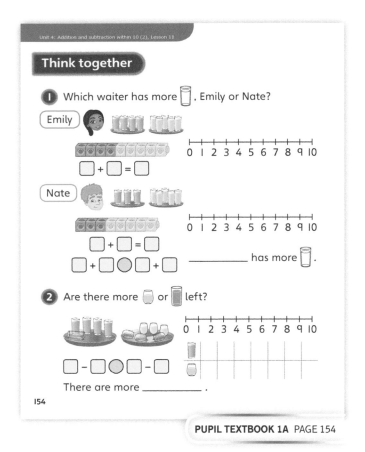

PUPIL TEXTBOOK 1A PAGE 154

PUPIL TEXTBOOK 1A PAGE 155

Practice

WAYS OF WORKING Independent thinking

IN FOCUS All of the **Practice** questions require children to work out both sides of the calculation before comparing them. In question ❶, there is a multiple-choice answer to guide children through comparing two amounts and working out which is more. In question ❷, children have to rewrite both calculations and put in the correct symbols to compare both facts. Questions ❸ and ❹ require children only to put in the correct symbol to compare both calculations.

STRENGTHEN In question ❹, no pictorial representations have been used. Suggest that children draw the different sides of the calculation to compare them. They could draw different-coloured cubes being added together, and cross out cubes to show subtraction.

DEEPEN There are multiple possibilities to complete question ❺. Ask children to work systematically to fill them in in different ways. For example, in '5 – 2 > __ + __', a total of 0, 1 or 2 would work on the other side. To deepen understanding, encourage children to find all the different addition calculations to make those totals.

ASSESSMENT CHECKPOINT Assess whether children, if using drawings or resources to represent each calculation, line them up neatly for easy comparison or align them randomly and need to count to find the right total.

ANSWERS Answers for the **Practice** part of the lesson appear in the separate **Practice and Reflect answer guide**.

Reflect

WAYS OF WORKING Pair work

IN FOCUS In this **Reflect** question, the numbers 2, 3, 4 and 5 have been given to fill in the number sentence scaffolds. In the addition scaffold, children can put in the numbers in any order. They can then work out the total of each side and add the correct comparative symbol. Once they become more familiar with the numbers they are using, they can consider how to construct their subtraction calculation more carefully.

ASSESSMENT CHECKPOINT Assess whether children recognise that there are more constraints when trying to make two different subtraction facts, as the bigger number has to come first on each side.

ANSWERS Answers for the **Reflect** part of the lesson appear in the separate **Practice and Reflect answer guide**.

After the lesson ⏸

- Did the original context in the lesson help children understand the concept, and did this need to be referenced throughout the lesson?
- Did children start to use the < and > symbols based on instinct?
- Were children able to compare addition and subtraction calculations with ease, or was this a point of confusion?

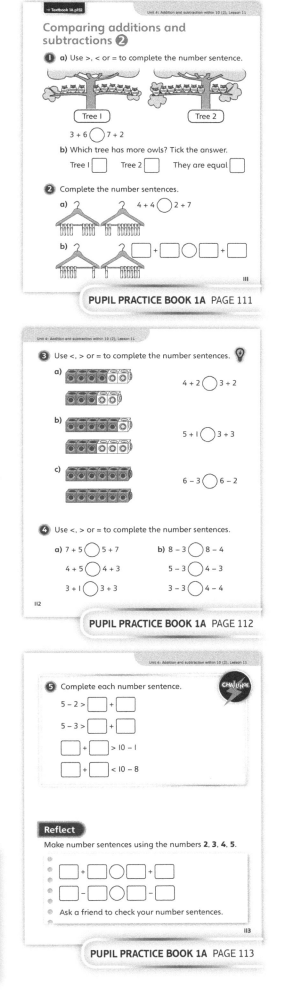

PUPIL PRACTICE BOOK 1A PAGE 111

PUPIL PRACTICE BOOK 1A PAGE 112

PUPIL PRACTICE BOOK 1A PAGE 113

183

Solving word problems – addition and subtraction

Learning focus

In this lesson, children will answer a range of addition, subtraction and 'finding the difference' questions. They will make up their own word problems based on a pictorial prompt.

Small steps

→ Previous step: Comparing additions and subtractions (2)
→ **This step: Solving word problems – addition and subtraction**
→ Next step: Naming 3D shapes (1)

NATIONAL CURRICULUM LINKS

Year 1 Number – Addition and Subtraction

- Solve one-step problems that involve addition and subtraction, using concrete objects and pictorial representations, and missing number problems such as $7 = \_ - 9$.
- Read, write and interpret mathematical statements involving addition (+), subtraction (−) and equals (=) signs.
- Add and subtract one-digit and two-digit numbers to 20, including zero.

ASSESSING MASTERY

Children can read different contexts and problems, identifying the numbers with which they need to work (including the whole, parts and the whole or part that is unknown) and what operations should be used. Children can work with a bar model, recognising what part of the problem each part of the bar model represents.

COMMON MISCONCEPTIONS

Children may have difficulty interpreting the words in a problem that suggest which operation they need to use. Ask:
- *What parts of the problem do you know? What is the problem asking you to find out?*

STRENGTHENING UNDERSTANDING

Strengthen understanding for those who struggle to see what calculation to do based on a context by making a display of common words or phrases that come up in addition and subtraction word problems. For example, write words such as 'total' and 'altogether' next to an addition symbol, and phrases such as 'how many left' and 'how many more' next to a subtraction symbol.

GOING DEEPER

Ask children to use cubes to solve a problem, and then deepen understanding by asking them to represent the cubes as a bar model. (This can be done by making cube sticks to represent different parts of the problem and drawing around them.) Children should then label the parts of the bar model with the numbers they represent. If this is too abstract, children could draw around each individual cube to create a pictogram of the problem.

KEY LANGUAGE

In lesson: add, total, altogether, subtract, take away, how many left, how many more

Other language to be used by the teacher: difference, compare, bar model, representation

STRUCTURES AND REPRESENTATIONS

Number line, part-whole model

RESOURCES

Mandatory: blank number lines, blank part-whole models, cubes and/or counters

Optional: craft paper and marker pens

Teaching Tools In the eTextbook of this lesson, you will find interactive links to a selection of teaching tools.

Before you teach

- Are all children familiar with the language surrounding addition and subtraction?
- How could you introduce using a bar model alongside concrete resources?
- How could you scaffold children's ideas, if they are struggling to see which operation needs to be used in a given context?

Discover

WAYS OF WORKING Pair work

ASK

- Question ① a): *What numbers do you need in order to work out how many there were in total?*
- Question ① b): *If 2 are eaten, are they being added or taken away?*
- Question ① b): *From what number are they being taken away?*

IN FOCUS Children must first identify each component in the picture (how many doughnuts there are in the basket and how many there are in each of the packets) before identifying the operation needed to solve the problem.

ANSWERS

Question ① a): There are 7 🍩 in total.

Question ① b): There are 5 🍩 left.

Share

WAYS OF WORKING Whole class teacher led

ASK

- Question ① a): *How has Astrid used cubes to help?*
- Question ① a): *Why does Flo say to put the cubes together? What is she trying to do?*
- Question ① b): *Why are two cubes and two doughnuts crossed out?*
- After question ① b): *Why are the arrows on the number lines going in different directions?*

IN FOCUS In this part of the lesson, children are prompted to use physical resources to help them work out the problem. For the addition problem, cubes are put together. For the subtraction problem, cubes are then crossed out. Both questions have also been worked out on number lines. Draw attention to the direction the arrows are going in each question.

DEEPEN Ask children to put the numbers from each problem into a part-whole model. Ensure they are clear in what they are trying to find out in each case: in question ① a), the whole is unknown; in ① b), a part is unknown.

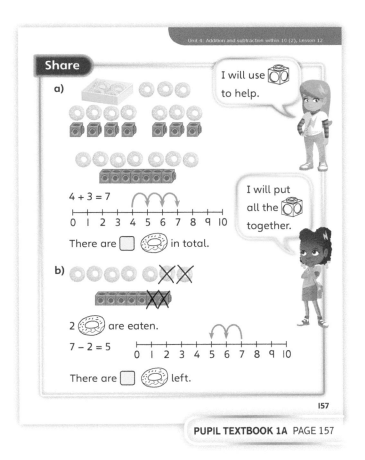

Think together

Think together

WAYS OF WORKING Whole class teacher led (I do, We do, You do)

ASK

- Question ❶: *What does each bar represent? Would it represent the same number if it were individual cubes?*
- Question ❷: *Does 8 represent the whole or the part?*
- Question ❷: *How do you represent 5 being eaten? What operation is that?*
- Question ❸: *How can you use cubes to show this problem and what do you do with them?*

IN FOCUS In question ❶, a simple bar model is introduced alongside the cube representation. Highlight the differences between the bars and the cubes: there are no individual cubes shown in the bars, but the sizes of the cube sticks and bars are the same. It is important to point out that the bar representing 5 is bigger than the bar representing 4.

STRENGTHEN In question ❸, encourage children to use cubes to represent the problem. You could suggest they put the cubes together and draw around them to create a simple bar model like those in question ❶: the numbers are the same, but the context is different. Ask children to look at the cube sticks / bars, and to explain how they could know which bar represents which number without labels. Ask: *Which bar is bigger and which is smaller?*

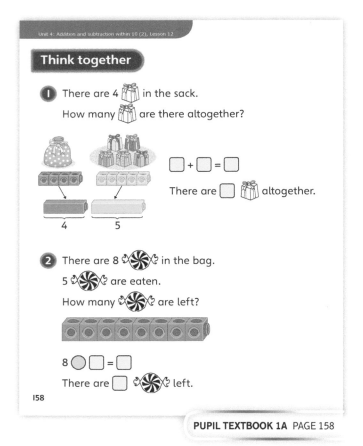

PUPIL TEXTBOOK 1A PAGE 158

DEEPEN In question ❷, ask children to draw around a stick of 8 cubes, to represent how many sweets there are. Ask them where the 3 is, and what that would look like on this bar. (They could create sticks of 5 and 3 cubes to help them.) This will start children thinking about how bars could represent subtraction.

ASSESSMENT CHECKPOINT In question ❸, read what Dexter says about counting the cubes carefully and listen for whether children start counting from 6, 4 or from 0. Assess whether they are aware that the most efficient method is to count on from 6, or whether they count on from 4 because that is the first number mentioned in the question. Children may alternatively be able to recognise this as a number bond to 10 and not need to calculate at all.

ANSWERS

Question ❶: 4 + 5 = 9

There are 9 🎁 altogether.

Question ❷: 8 − 5 = 3

There are 3 🍬 left.

Question ❸: 4 + 6 = 10

There are 10 🍩 in total.

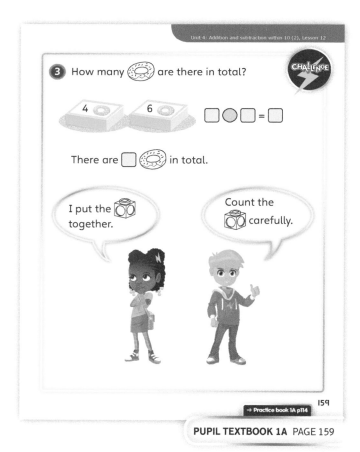

PUPIL TEXTBOOK 1A PAGE 159

Practice

WAYS OF WORKING Independent thinking

IN FOCUS Question **2** a) describes 3 cubes and then 5 cubes being put in a cup. In part b), 6 cubes are removed but the pictorial representation of the cubes remains as 3 and 5: children must cross off 6 cubes from the whole (split into its original parts). Children will have to cross out cubes from both parts and so understand that these two parts have become a whole. Question **3** includes another simple bar model alongside representations of cubes that must be matched to incomplete calculations. Children will need to look at the numbers *and* the operations to make their matches.

STRENGTHEN In question **2** b), strengthen understanding by suggesting that children physically make sticks of 3 and 5 cubes from which to take away 6. One of the sticks will be completely broken up and only 2 cubes from one of the groups will be left.

DEEPEN In question **4**, different numbers have been represented using different shapes. Deepen understanding by challenging children to use the same shapes, representing the same numbers, to create their own calculations. Children may find it helps to write the calculations using the numbers first. If children feel secure, they could also assign other numbers to new different shapes, and create more number facts.

ASSESSMENT CHECKPOINT In question **3**, detect whether children leave making a match to the bar model until last, by process of elimination, or if they are able to work out that it must mean 3 + 2 (either by proportion or as the other cube sticks are too large). In question **4**, assess what strategies children use to work out what shape represents what number. They may recognise that their best starting point is that two matching squares must mean the parts are the same, and that only equal numbers can make 10. Alternatively, they may find this problem too abstract and need further scaffolding.

ANSWERS Answers for the **Practice** part of the lesson appear in the separate **Practice and Reflect answer guide**.

Reflect

WAYS OF WORKING Pair work

IN FOCUS Within the context given, children must write their own maths question to match the picture.

ASSESSMENT CHECKPOINT Assess whether children are able to explain what their number sentence is trying to find out, and what each number means with regards to the picture. Check that they can also construct a correct calculation to match their question.

ANSWERS Answers for the **Reflect** part of the lesson appear in the separate **Practice and Reflect answer guide**.

After the lesson ⏸

- Were children able to recognise the correct operations for the different contexts given?
- What sort of word problems were children able to create independently? What does this tell you about their understanding?

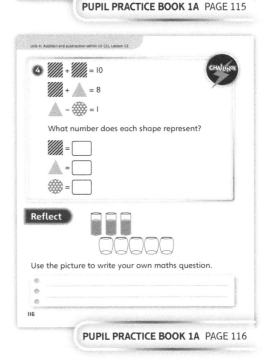

PUPIL PRACTICE BOOK 1A PAGE 114

PUPIL PRACTICE BOOK 1A PAGE 115

PUPIL PRACTICE BOOK 1A PAGE 116

End of unit check

> **Don't forget the End of unit check proforma (page 160)!**

WAYS OF WORKING Group work – adult led for Q **1**–**5**

IN FOCUS

- Question **3** requires children to correctly interpret the part-whole model understand number sentences with the = sign in different places.
- Question **4** requires greater understanding of subtraction through the context of 'more than'.
- Question **5** requires children to compare two calculations to be made. They should work out 8 – 2 and then ascertain which number could not be used to complete the subtraction fact.

Think!

WAYS OF WORKING Pair work or small groups

IN FOCUS

- This question highlights the misconception that subtraction is commutative: the numbers in all the facts match the part-whole model but one of them has the whole and one of the parts in the wrong order, and is therefore incorrect. An extra layer of thought is required as the number sentences have the = sign in different places.
- Draw children's attention to the words at the bottom of the **My journal** page and encourage them to match them to the part-whole model and facts.
- Encourage children to think through or discuss the meaning of the – 6 in 3 – 6 = 3 before writing their answer in **My journal**. It means 'take away six': children should see that this does not match the part-whole model. as 6 is the whole.

ANSWERS AND COMMENTARY To show mastery, children can come up with their own number story to match the part-whole model where the parts are the same. In their story, the parts will represent separate and distinct objects but have the same value e.g. 3 birds on the branch, 3 flying away/ 3 children standing, 3 children sitting.

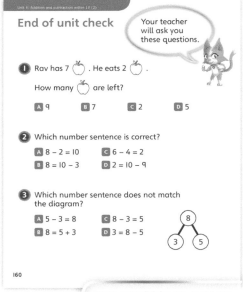

PUPIL TEXTBOOK 1A PAGE 160

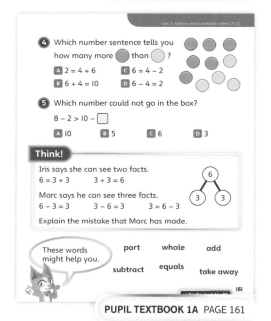

PUPIL TEXTBOOK 1A PAGE 161

Q	A	WRONG ANSWERS AND MISCONCEPTIONS	STRENGTHENING UNDERSTANDING
1	D	A indicates that the child has added 7 and 2 instead of subtracting.	Children may misinterpret these questions as addition, since they are more familiar with this operation. Use concrete resources such as cubes to model taking away from a whole amount, or stacks of cubes to compare and find the difference.
2	C	A suggests that the child has recognised all the numbers needed for a number bond to 10 and not looked at the operation.	
3	A	D indicates lack of fluency, as it suggests that the child thinks it must be wrong because the part comes first in the number sentence.	
4	D	B suggests that the child has assumed that the word 'more' means this is an addition question.	
5	D	B or C suggests that the child does not have a solid understanding of the > symbol.	

My journal

Independent thinking

ANSWERS AND COMMENTARY

The mistake is 3 – 6 = 3 because this calculation is incorrect and does not match the part-whole model.

When first looking at Marc's statements, some children may immediately point at 3 = 6 – 3 as being incorrect because of the position of the = sign. Encourage children to work out each statement and articulate which numbers are the parts and which is the whole. Can children represent each number sentence using cubes to help them articulate which one is correct? If children struggle to explain, show them the subtraction generalisations 'whole – part = part' and 'part = whole – part' and ask which statement does not match.

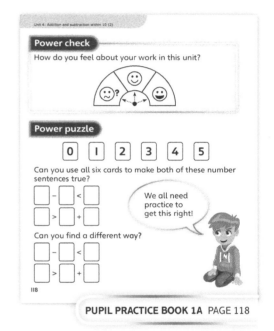

PUPIL PRACTICE BOOK 1A PAGE 117

Power check

WAYS OF WORKING Independent thinking

ASK

- *Why do you feel like that about subtraction?*
- *What helps you work out subtraction questions?*

Power puzzle

WAYS OF WORKING Pair work or small groups

IN FOCUS This Power puzzle incorporates multiple elements of understanding from this unit and requires children to work strategically. Can children use trial and error, gradually refining their answer to fit? Using real number cards will reinforce the restriction that each number can only be used once.

ANSWERS AND COMMENTARY Check whether children read the statements using 'is more than' or 'is less than'. For the scaffold [ ] – [ ] < [ ], show children that their answer to the first part must actually be smaller than the number they are comparing it to. If children can correctly fill in the Power puzzle, they have demonstrated good understanding of multiple operations and symbols. Ask them if they can find as many different ways as possible to make each statement true.

PUPIL PRACTICE BOOK 1A PAGE 118

After the unit ⏸

- Were children more confident calculating addition than subtraction number sentences?
- Could children spot the deliberate mistakes? Could children identify if they make the same mistakes in their own work?

Strengthen and *Deepen* activities for this unit can be found in the Power Maths online subscription.

Unit 5
2D and 3D shapes

Mastery Expert tip! "Providing children with 2D and 3D shapes that they could handle and explore not only helped to strengthen understanding but also enabled them to think carefully about how to describe the features of different shapes and identify similarities and differences."

Don't forget to watch the unit 5 video!

WHY THIS UNIT IS IMPORTANT

This unit introduces children to 2D and 3D shapes and their properties. Children will learn to name the different shapes and identify the features that determine how they are classified. By exploring the similarities and differences, children will make the distinction between 2D and 3D shapes.

Throughout the unit, shapes are presented with different orientations. This helps children focus on the specific mathematical properties of the shapes and secures their understanding of classifying 2D and 3D shapes. They will also learn to identify individual shapes within composite shapes (where several shapes are joined together) and explore the relationship between 2D and 3D shapes.

Children will then begin to explore sequences using shapes, and to identify patterns. Children will apply these skills when exploring patterns and sequences in number in future units.

WHERE THIS UNIT FITS

→ Unit 4: Addition and subtraction within 10 (2)
→ **Unit 5: 2D and 3D shapes**
→ Unit 6: Numbers to 20

This unit builds on the work that children have done sorting objects. It draws on their skills of identifying similarities and differences and making direct comparisons, and develops their skill of identifying patterns and sequences in shapes. Unit 6 will focus on numbers to 20.

Before they start this unit, it is expected that children:
• know the names of basic 2D and 3D shapes
• understand that shapes are classified based on specific properties
• know that shapes can be sorted by different criteria.

ASSESSING MASTERY

Children who have mastered this unit will be able to identify and describe the key properties of 2D and 3D shapes, using the correct mathematical terminology. They will be able to ignore non-significant differences such as colour, size and orientation in order to classify shapes.

As their shape recognition becomes more secure, they will be able to identify, describe and continue repeating patterns made of shapes.

COMMON MISCONCEPTIONS	STRENGTHENING UNDERSTANDING	GOING DEEPER
Children may apply the names of 2D shapes to 3D shapes or vice versa.	Give children concrete representations of the shapes and encourage them to talk about their similarities and differences. Provide children with labels to match with the shapes.	Ask children to find what different shapes have in common. They could explore combining 2D or 3D shapes to create a different shape.
Children may fail to recognise a shape when its orientation changes and may focus on superficial differences such as colour or size.	Ask children to sort a variety of different shapes by different characteristics. As they do so, discuss the names of the shapes and how we know what the shapes are called.	Ask children to identify shapes that are only partially revealed or by touch alone. Ask children to justify their decisions.

Unit 5: 2D and 3D shapes

WAYS OF WORKING

These pages will help you identify children's prior knowledge of the names and properties of 2D and 3D shapes. Focus on the vocabulary introduced by Flo: ask children what each term means and assess the accuracy and confidence of their answers.

STRUCTURES AND REPRESENTATIONS

It is important that children have a range of 2D and 3D shapes to manipulate and explore. These should include: cube, cuboid, sphere, cylinder, pyramid, cone, circle, triangle, square, rectangle.

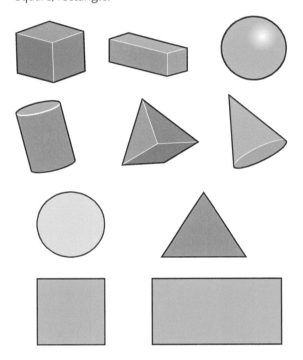

KEY LANGUAGE

It is important that children describe shapes using the correct mathematical terminology.

→ 2D, 3D

→ cube, cuboid, sphere, cylinder, pyramid, cone

→ circle, triangle, square, rectangle

→ side, edge, face, corner

→ pattern, repeat

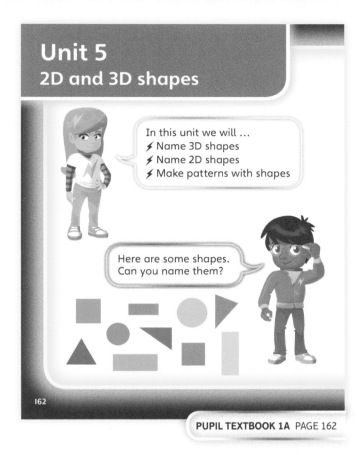

PUPIL TEXTBOOK 1A PAGE 162

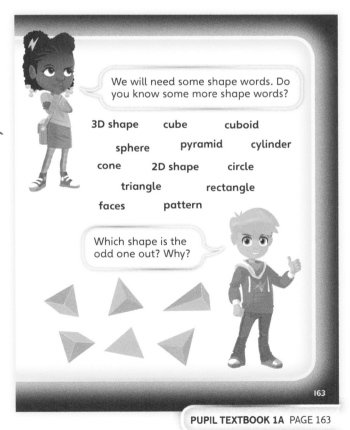

PUPIL TEXTBOOK 1A PAGE 163

191

Naming 3D shapes ①

Learning focus

In this lesson, children will learn to name and identify 3D shapes. They will compare shapes, identifying their similarities and differences.

Small steps

→ Previous step: Solving word problems – addition and subtraction
→ **This step: Naming 3D shapes (1)**
→ Next step: Naming 3D shapes (2)

NATIONAL CURRICULUM LINKS

Year 1 Geometry – Properties of Shape

Recognise and name common 2D and 3D shapes, including: 3D shapes [for example, cuboids (including cubes), pyramids and spheres].

ASSESSING MASTERY

Children can identify the common properties of the same type of 3D shape even when they are visually different (for example, different size, colour, orientation or dimensions). Children can use the correct terminology for the properties in order to justify their reasoning.

COMMON MISCONCEPTIONS

Children may misname 3D shapes as 2D shapes. They may fail to name a shape correctly when presented with an unfamiliar orientation. They may name a shape as a familiar object, for example as a 'ball', 'dice' or 'box'. To challenge this misconception, ask:
• *What type of shape is a dice?* Reinforce your question by showing children a multi-sided dice.

STRENGTHENING UNDERSTANDING

To strengthen understanding, show children a selection of concrete 3D shapes and everyday items that correspond to those shapes. Ask children to pair up or sort the shapes using sorting hoops. Ask: *How are these shapes the same or different?* Ask children to rotate the shapes into different orientations. Ask: *Has the shape changed?*

GOING DEEPER

Show children a cube, cuboid and cylinder made out of modelling material. Tell children these can all be grouped together. Ask: *What do the shapes have in common? What will happen to the end face of each shape if I cut them in half?* Children can predict what will happen and then find out by trying. The end face does not change shape or size and is the same for all three shapes: this defines a prism. Ask: *Would this be true for any of the other shapes? Why?*

KEY LANGUAGE

In lesson: 3D, cube, cuboid, sphere, pyramid, cylinder, shape, pair, same, different

Other language to be used by the teacher: similarities, differences, properties, face, edge

STRUCTURES AND REPRESENTATIONS

Pictorial representations of cube, cuboid, sphere, cylinder, pyramid, cone

RESOURCES

Mandatory: concrete 3D shapes including a cube, cuboid, sphere, cylinder and pyramid

Optional: modelling material to model 3D shapes, sorting hoops, an opaque bag, everyday items relating to the 3D shapes (for example, a golf ball, a cereal box, an empty sweet tube and dice)

Teaching Tools In the eTextbook of this lesson, you will find interactive links to a selection of teaching tools.

Before you teach

• What resources will you need to support children's understanding of 3D shapes?
• How could you display key terminology for children to refer to?
• What experience of 3D shapes do children have?

Discover

WAYS OF WORKING Pair work

ASK

- *Why have you grouped those shapes together?*
- *How are they the same or different?*
- *How do you know which shapes are cubes?*
- *Can you pair them differently?*

IN FOCUS Question ① a) highlights that shapes are alike based on certain properties and that size or colour do not distinguish alike shapes. Determine if children are using the correct terminology and names. Are children basing their decisions on key properties? What do they already know? What misconceptions do they have?

ANSWERS

Question ① a):

cube   cuboid   sphere   pyramid

Question ① b): The cylinder does not have a pair.

PUPIL TEXTBOOK 1A PAGE 164

Share

WAYS OF WORKING Whole class teacher led

IN FOCUS Question ① a): Astrid's statement reinforces that some properties are or are not important when naming 3D shapes. You could follow this up in class by comparing concrete 3D shapes.

ASK

- *What properties did you look at in order to pair your shapes?*
- *What properties did you ignore?*
- *Did you find any shapes difficult to pair?*
- *Could you have paired them differently?*
- *Are cubes and cuboids the same?* (Cubes are a special type of cuboid. A cuboid is made up of six rectangles placed at right angles to one another. A cuboid that has six square faces is given the special name 'cube'.)

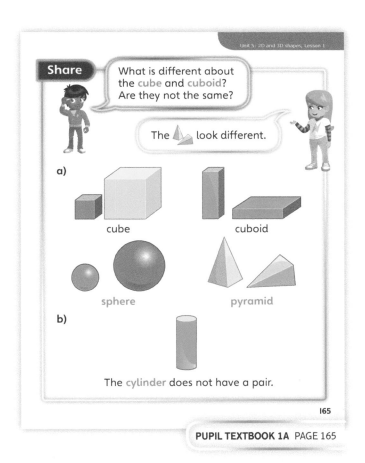

PUPIL TEXTBOOK 1A PAGE 165

Think together

WAYS OF WORKING Whole class teacher led (I do, We do, You do)

ASK

- Question ❶: *How do you know that the other shapes are not cubes?*
- *What do the cubes, pyramids or spheres all have in common?*
- Question ❷ b): *What makes the sphere different from the ovoid?*
- Question ❸: *How do you know what the shapes are called?*

IN FOCUS Question ❸ prompts children to look beyond the aesthetic properties of an object and focus on the properties of the shapes. It distinguishes between the name of the object and the more abstract name of the shape. It prompts children to realise that 3D shapes can be found in their everyday environment.

STRENGTHEN Having concrete 3D shapes for children to hold and manipulate can help them to identify the shapes in the pictures. Encourage children to rotate them so that they match the orientations in the pictures. Ask: *Does turning the shape change the shape?*

DEEPEN Ask children to find two different types of shapes that have similarities and to explain how they are similar. Ask: *How many different ways could you group the shapes?*

ASSESSMENT CHECKPOINT Question ❶ and ❷ a) can help you determine whether children can see beyond the orientation and colour of the shape.

Children's responses to question ❸ will determine whether they can focus on the properties of shape. Ask children to describe the properties of the shapes that they identify. Are they counting and describing faces? Can they describe the differences between different shapes?

ANSWERS

❶: The yellow, purple and red shapes are cubes.

❷ a): There are 2 pyramids.

❷ b): 3 of the shapes are not spheres.

❸:

sphere   cylinder   cuboid   cube

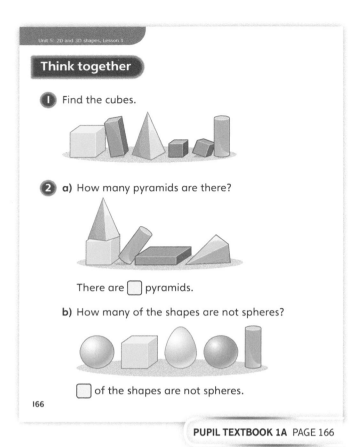

PUPIL TEXTBOOK 1A PAGE 166

PUPIL TEXTBOOK 1A PAGE 167

Practice

WAYS OF WORKING Pair work

IN FOCUS Question ❸ looks at everyday objects, encouraging children to focus on the properties of shapes in order to identify them. One object is a compound shape, which is a shape consisting of two or more basic shapes (in this case, a sphere and a cylinder).

STRENGTHEN Have some of the objects pictured in question ❸ for children to hold, such as the dice and the golf ball. This will enable them to make comparisons between the concrete shapes and the pictorial representations.

DEEPEN Put shapes in an opaque bag so that the shapes cannot be seen. Ask a child to put their hand into the bag and hold a shape without taking it out. Can they identify it by touch alone? Ask: *How do you know what it is?* They could then describe the shape they are holding for another child to identify.

ASSESSMENT CHECKPOINT Questions ❶ and ❷ assess whether children can identify the shapes, regardless of size and orientation.

Question ❸ determines whether children can focus solely on the properties of the shapes in order to identify the shapes.

Question ❹ prompts children to draw on their knowledge in order to identify incomplete shapes.

ANSWERS Answers for the **Practice** part of the lesson appear in the separate **Practice and Reflect answer guide**.

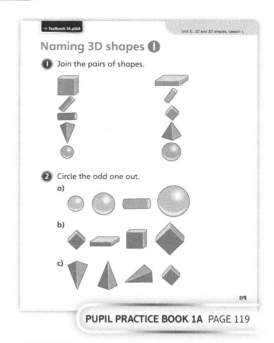

PUPIL PRACTICE BOOK 1A PAGE 119

PUPIL PRACTICE BOOK 1A PAGE 120

Reflect

WAYS OF WORKING Independent thinking

IN FOCUS The **Reflect** part of the lesson prompts children to relate the properties of 3D shapes to their everyday experiences. They need to think of the objects by their properties of shape, ignoring other features such as the object's name, size, colour, pattern and purpose.

Refer to what Ash is asking. Can children use their broader experiences to suggest where pyramids are found?

ASSESSMENT CHECKPOINT Assess whether children are able to identify objects that are the same shapes as those pictured. Check whether they can think of an example for all four shapes (or all five shapes if you include Ash's question).

ANSWERS Answers for the **Reflect** part of the lesson appear in the separate **Practice and Reflect answer guide**.

After the lesson ⏸

- Were children confident in identifying the 3D shapes, regardless of their colour, size and orientation?
- Were children able to stop relying on the concrete 3D shapes or did some children still need concrete 3D shapes to support their reasoning?
- Were children starting to use mathematical terminology in order to describe 3D shapes and their properties?

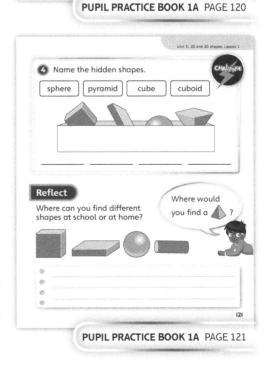

PUPIL PRACTICE BOOK 1A PAGE 121

Naming 3D shapes ②

Learning focus

In this lesson, children will build on their ability to name and describe 3D shapes in more challenging arrangements. They will also be introduced to the cone.

Small steps

→ Previous step: Naming 3D shapes (1)
→ **This step: Naming 3D shapes (2)**
→ Next step: Naming 2D shapes (1)

NATIONAL CURRICULUM LINKS

Year 1 Geometry – Properties of Shape

Recognise and name common 2D and 3D shapes, including: 3D shapes [for example, cuboids (including cubes), pyramids and spheres].

ASSESSING MASTERY

Children can use correct terminology to describe the properties of a range of 3D shapes. Children can make careful comparisons and identify both differences and similarities between different 3D shapes.

COMMON MISCONCEPTIONS

Children may believe that a curved surface is a face, such as on a sphere or cone. Remind them that a face has to be flat. Challenge this misconception by asking:
• *How many faces? How many curved surfaces? What is the difference between a face and a curved surface?*

Children may see cubes as a separate shape to a cuboid. Challenge this misconception by asking:
• *How many cuboids are there altogether?*

STRENGTHENING UNDERSTANDING

The use of concrete 3D shapes can help children to identify pictorial representations of the same shapes. As you work through each learning section, encourage children to match the arrangements in the pictures with the concrete 3D shapes and ask them to identify which shapes they have used. You can offer further support by labelling the concrete 3D shapes in the classroom, then cover the labels as children become more confident.

GOING DEEPER

Ask children to find similarities between two different shapes. Ask: *What are the similarities between a cone and a pyramid? How are a cylinder and a cuboid alike?*

KEY LANGUAGE

In lesson: 3D, cube, cuboid, sphere, cylinder, pyramid, **cone**, shape, how many, same

Other language to be used by the teacher: similarities, differences, properties, edges, faces, square, triangular, circular, curved, curved surface, flat

STRUCTURES AND REPRESENTATIONS

Pictorial representations of cube, cuboid, sphere, cylinder, pyramid, cone

RESOURCES

Mandatory: concrete 3D shapes including a cube, cuboid, sphere, cylinder, pyramid and cone

Optional: 3D shape name labels, everyday items relating to the 3D shapes (for example, a golf ball, a cereal box, an empty sweet tube and dice)

Teaching Tools In the eTextbook of this lesson, you will find interactive links to a selection of teaching tools.

Before you teach

• How confident are children in identifying and naming the shapes from Lesson 1?
• How will you support children who find it difficult to identify shapes when they are connected to other shapes?
• How will you question and support children in order to develop the use of correct mathematical vocabulary when they describe the properties of shapes?

Discover

WAYS OF WORKING Pair work

ASK

- *Which shapes can you see?*
- *How many of each shape can you see?*
- *What are the similarities and differences between Gita and Finn's rockets?*
- *Question ❶ b): Can you name and describe each shape?*

IN FOCUS Question ❶ a) requires children to recognise similarities and differences between the two rockets by identifying and describing shapes in different orientations.

ANSWERS

Question ❶ a): Gita's rocket has broken.

Question ❶ b): The sphere and the cone were not used.

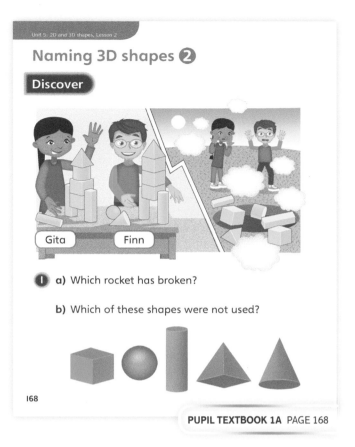

Naming 3D shapes ❷

Discover

❶ a) Which rocket has broken?

b) Which of these shapes were not used?

168

PUPIL TEXTBOOK 1A PAGE 168

Share

WAYS OF WORKING Whole class teacher led

ASK

- *Can you create Gita or Finn's rocket for yourself using shapes?*
- *How do you know that Gita's rocket is the rocket that broke?*
- *Why do you think that the sphere and the cone were not used?*
- *Which shapes are easy or difficult to tell apart?*

IN FOCUS Question ❶ a) models the sequence of shapes used to create the rockets, supporting children in separating the rockets out into the individual component shapes.

The pictures of the sphere and the cone in question ❶ b) provide scaffolding for children's reasoning and provide the proof for the answer.

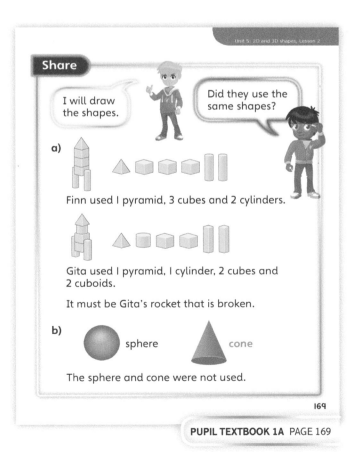

Share

I will draw the shapes.

Did they use the same shapes?

a)

Finn used 1 pyramid, 3 cubes and 2 cylinders.

Gita used 1 pyramid, 1 cylinder, 2 cubes and 2 cuboids.

It must be Gita's rocket that is broken.

b) sphere cone

The sphere and cone were not used.

169

PUPIL TEXTBOOK 1A PAGE 169

Think together

Whole class teacher led (I do, We do, You do)

ASK
- *How could you make it easier to identify the shapes?*
- *What are the similarities between the different shapes?*
- *What properties of the shapes do you look at first?*
- *What is it about the pictures that makes identifying the shapes easier?*

IN FOCUS Question **3** prompts discussion about cubes being a type of cuboid. It encourages children to identify the properties that they have in common. Can children identify that squares are a type of rectangle?

STRENGTHEN Allow children access to concrete 3D shapes. They can use these shapes to replicate the pictures in this part of the lesson, then dismantle the compound shapes they have created to sort and identify the individual shapes that they used.

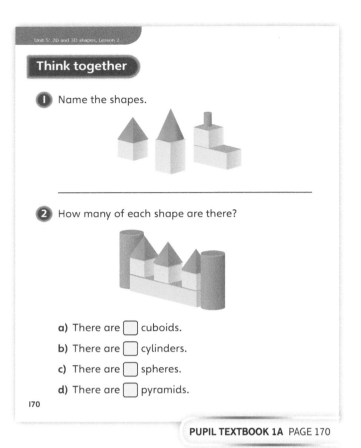

PUPIL TEXTBOOK 1A PAGE 170

DEEPEN Can children identify that all cuboids have six rectangular faces, that some cuboids have only square faces, that some cuboids have only oblong faces and that some cuboids have a mixture of square and oblong faces? To deepen understanding, refer to Ash and Flo's questions. Ask: *What can you say is true of all cuboids? What can you say is true for some but not all cuboids?*

ASSESSMENT CHECKPOINT Assess whether children can recognise cubes as cuboids and identify their common properties.

ANSWERS

Question **1**: Cube and pyramid; cuboid and cone; cuboid, cube and cylinder.

Question **2** a): There are 4 cuboids.

Question **2** b): There are 2 cylinders.

Question **2** c): There are 0 spheres.

Question **2** d): There are 3 pyramids.

Question **3**: There are 4 cuboids.

PUPIL TEXTBOOK 1A PAGE 171

Practice

IN FOCUS Question **3** requires children to identify the individual shapes within compound shapes, requiring careful observation and application of knowledge.

STRENGTHEN Have concrete 3D shapes so that children can replicate the pictures in this part of the lesson and identify the shapes that they use. Labelling the shapes can provide further support if they still struggle to recall the names of the shapes.

DEEPEN Describe a shape, one property at a time. After describing each property, ask: *Which shape do you think it could be?* How many properties do you need to describe before children can identify exactly which shape it is? Children could then question you about a shape that you are thinking about, in order to identify the shape in your mind.

ASSESSMENT CHECKPOINT Assess whether children can recognise cubes as cuboids. Prompt them to count and describe the faces of the shapes.

Questions **4** and **5** will help you determine whether children are able to focus on the properties of the shapes and ignore the context and aesthetic properties of the shapes.

ANSWERS Answers for the **Practice** part of the lesson appear in the separate **Practice and Reflect answer guide**.

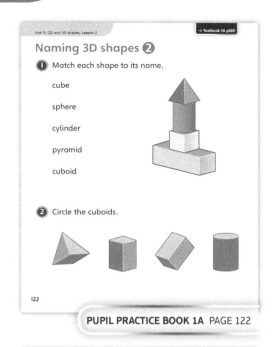

PUPIL PRACTICE BOOK 1A PAGE 122

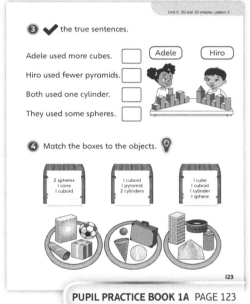

PUPIL PRACTICE BOOK 1A PAGE 123

Reflect

IN FOCUS The **Reflect** part of the lesson requires children to use correct mathematical terminology and to recall what they have learnt without visual prompts.

ASSESSMENT CHECKPOINT Assess whether children use the correct terminology and can correctly spell the names of the shapes. Refer to Ash's question. Check whether children can find an example of each shape in the classroom and label them.

ANSWERS Answers for the **Reflect** part of the lesson appear in the separate **Practice and Reflect answer guide**.

After the lesson ⏸

- Were children able to identify 3D shapes in their environment?
- How carefully were children considering the properties of the 3D shapes when they compared them, particularly with cubes and other cuboids?
- Were children using the correct terminology to name and describe different 3D shapes?

PUPIL PRACTICE BOOK 1A PAGE 124

Naming 2D shapes ①

Learning focus

In this lesson, children will learn to identify and name the 2D shapes: circle, triangle, rectangle and square.

Small steps

→ Previous step: Naming 3D shapes (2)
→ **This step: Naming 2D shapes (1)**
→ Next step: Naming 2D shapes (2)

NATIONAL CURRICULUM LINKS

Year 1 Geometry – Properties of Shape

Recognise and name common 2D and 3D shapes, including: 2D shapes [for example, rectangles (including squares), circles and triangles].

ASSESSING MASTERY

Children can identify, name and describe a circle, square, rectangle and triangle, regardless of the shapes' colour, orientation and size. Children can identify non-examples of the shapes and explain why they do not meet the criteria of specific shapes.

COMMON MISCONCEPTIONS

Children may fail to identify shapes correctly when the shapes are rotated. Hold up a square and ask: *Can you name this shape?* Then rotate the square by 45 degrees and ask: *Can you name the shape?* Do children call it a diamond?

Children may only recognise equilateral triangles and fail to recognise other types of triangles as triangles. Ensure that representations of all three types of triangle are available. Children do not need to know the name of the shapes at this stage, they just need to recognise them all as triangles.

STRENGTHENING UNDERSTANDING

Have a variety of concrete 2D shapes available for children to handle. Ask children to create pictures with them and encourage them to name the shapes that they use.

GOING DEEPER

Encourage children to explore the 2D concrete shapes more deeply by themselves. Ask: *Can you use two or four triangles to create a rectangle? Can you fold a rectangle or square to make a triangle? What different triangles can you make?*

KEY LANGUAGE

In lesson: 2D, circles, triangles, shape, square, rectangle, sphere, corners

Other language to be used by teacher: sides, curved, straight

STRUCTURES AND REPRESENTATIONS

Pictorial representations of 2D shapes of different sizes, including: squares, rectangles, triangles, circles and parallelograms

RESOURCES

Mandatory: a selection of concrete 2D representations of squares, rectangles, triangles, circles and parallelograms

Optional: sorting hoops

Teaching Tools In the eTextbook of this lesson, you will find interactive links to a selection of teaching tools.

Before you teach

- How will you explain the difference between 2D and 3D shapes?
- How will you encourage children to use correct mathematical vocabulary to describe the 2D shapes?
- How will you draw on children's knowledge from the previous lessons on 3D shapes?

Discover

WAYS OF WORKING Pair work

ASK

- *How do you know whether the shapes in the picture are triangles or circles?*
- *How is the blue blob similar to a circle?*
- *Did any of the shapes surprise you? Why?*

IN FOCUS Question 1 b) requires children to find shapes that are not triangles. Children need to be secure with the properties of a triangle in order to find shapes that do not meet that criteria. The irregular pentagon has a similar appearance to a triangle, so ensure that children look closely at the number of sides and corners on this shape.

ANSWERS Question 1 a): There are 5 circles and triangles (2 circles and 3 triangles).

Question 1 b): 9 of the shapes are not triangles.

PUPIL TEXTBOOK 1A PAGE 172

Share

WAYS OF WORKING Whole class teacher led

ASK

- Question 1 a): *Does it matter if the shapes in each row are different colours or sizes? Why?*
- *What is different about the triangles?*
- *Do these shapes remind you of any 3D shapes? Why?*
- *What makes a triangle a triangle?*

IN FOCUS Question 1 a) explores the concept that a square is a type of rectangle (a regular rectangle).

Question 1 b) sorts the shapes into two discrete sets: 'triangles' and 'not triangles'. It shows how shapes can be grouped by 'yes' or 'no' criteria. Discuss with children how such a variety of shapes ended up in one set, just because they do not have three straight sides and three corners.

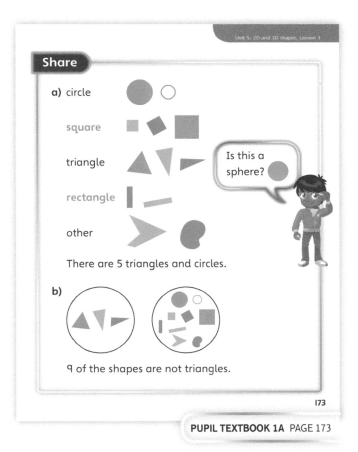

PUPIL TEXTBOOK 1A PAGE 173

Think together

WAYS OF WORKING Whole class teacher led (I do, We do, You do)

ASK

- *How do you know whether a shape is a square, a triangle or a rectangle?*
- Questions **1** and **2**: *Which shapes did you rule out first?*
- Questions **1** and **2**: *Were there any shapes that you had to think more carefully about?*

IN FOCUS Question **3** challenges children's thinking about what makes a rectangle. The criteria 'four straight sides' and 'four corners' are no longer sufficient. Ask children to describe how the corners of the rectangles and parallelogram differ.

STRENGTHEN Have a selection of concrete 2D shapes available for children to handle. Encourage them to touch the sides and corners as they count them and to physically sort the shapes, perhaps using sorting hoops.

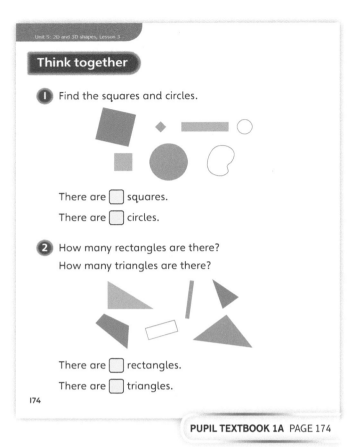

PUPIL TEXTBOOK 1A PAGE 174

DEEPEN Ask children what the shapes in question **3** have in common (for example, the colour, number of sides or number of corners). Can they think of another type of shape that matches those features (for example, a square)? Do they think that the parallelogram would still be the odd one out if they added that other shape to the picture? Why?

ASSESSMENT CHECKPOINT Assess whether children are confident in identifying examples and non-examples of a given shape. Check whether they can describe the features of squares, rectangles and triangles to justify their answers.

ANSWERS

Question **1** : There are 3 squares. There are 2 circles.

Question **2** : There are 2 rectangles. There are 3 triangles.

Question **3** : The third shape (the parallelogram) is the odd one out because it is not a rectangle.

PUPIL TEXTBOOK 1A PAGE 175

Practice

WAYS OF WORKING Pair work

IN FOCUS Question ④ introduces the idea that 2D shapes can be created by combining other 2D shapes. There are two possible answers to this question: a 1×6 arrangement or a 2×3 arrangement. This question encourages children to think creatively. If children do not find the two possibilities in their pair, ask: *Is that the only way of doing it?*

STRENGTHEN Have a selection of concrete 2D shapes for children to handle. If necessary, help children to label the concrete 2D shapes and talk about their properties. Can children compare the concrete shapes with the pictorial representations in the questions?

DEEPEN Extend question ④ by asking: *What other 2D shapes can you make from different 2D shapes? Can you create a rectangle by using two triangles? Can you use circles to create other shapes? Why?* While exploring this, children may create shapes that they do not recognise. Reassure them that, even though they do not recognise these shapes, they are still shapes.

ASSESSMENT CHECKPOINT Assess whether children can identify and describe a circle, rectangle, triangle and square. Question ② should help you check that children can identify non-examples of a shape and explain why.

Question ⑤ should allow you to assess whether children can identify individual 2D shapes when they are part of a compound shape.

ANSWERS Answers for the **Practice** part of the lesson appear in the separate **Practice and Reflect answer guide**.

Reflect

WAYS OF WORKING Independent thinking

IN FOCUS The **Reflect** part of the lesson asks children to identify 2D shapes that are partly obscured. Children need to draw on their knowledge and experience of 2D shapes in order to identify them. To expand their thinking, ask children to describe how they can be sure that the shape is a triangle or a rectangle. This will challenge them to be flexible and creative in their thinking.

ASSESSMENT CHECKPOINT Assess whether children are using the correct mathematical terminology to name and describe 2D shapes.

ANSWERS Answers for the **Reflect** part of the lesson appear in the separate **Practice and Reflect answer guide**.

After the lesson ⏸

- Did the use of concrete 2D shapes enable children to understand the pictorial representations?
- Were children able to make links between 2D shapes and 3D shapes?
- Were you able to challenge children's thinking and encourage them to provide justifications when identifying shapes?

PUPIL PRACTICE BOOK 1A PAGE 125

PUPIL PRACTICE BOOK 1A PAGE 126

PUPIL PRACTICE BOOK 1A PAGE 127

Naming 2D shapes ②

Learning focus

In this lesson, children will link their learning from previous lessons in Unit 5, understanding the relationship between 2D and 3D shapes.

Small steps

→ Previous step: Naming 2D shapes (1)
→ **This step: Naming 2D shapes (2)**
→ Next step: Making patterns with shapes

NATIONAL CURRICULUM LINKS

Year 1 Geometry – Properties of Shape

Recognise and name common 2D and 3D shapes, including: 2D shapes [for example, rectangles (including squares), circles and triangles].

ASSESSING MASTERY

Children can identify and name the faces of 3D shapes. They can envisage how 3D shapes can be used to create 2D shapes and identify which 3D shapes can be used to create 2D shapes.

COMMON MISCONCEPTIONS

Children may still be confused about naming 2D and 3D shapes, for example by calling a cube a square. They may believe that a face is the same as a curved surface. Ask:
- *How many faces are there on a sphere?*
- *How many curved surfaces are there on a sphere?*
- *What is the difference between a face and a curved surface?*
- *What 3D shapes can you remember?*
- *What 2D shapes can you remember?*

STRENGTHENING UNDERSTANDING

Have a selection of concrete 3D shapes available and invite children to explore making 2D shapes by printing using paint and concrete 3D shapes. Have a display of vocabulary relating to 2D and 3D shapes (for example, face, edge, side, curved surface) for children to refer to.

GOING DEEPER

Ask children to predict what shapes can be printed using the faces and curved surfaces of the cone, cylinder, hemisphere and sphere. Ask them to justify their predictions and then test these predictions using paint and the concrete 3D shapes.

KEY LANGUAGE

In lesson: 2D, 3D, cube, cone, cuboid, cylinder, sphere, pyramid, **faces**, triangle, square, circle, rectangle, overlap, different

Other language to be used by the teacher: sides, edges, corners

STRUCTURES AND REPRESENTATIONS

Pictorial representations of cube, cone, cuboid, cylinder, sphere, pyramid, hemisphere, triangle, square, circle and rectangle

RESOURCES

Mandatory: concrete 3D representations of cube, cone, cuboid, cylinder, sphere, pyramid, cone and hemisphere

Optional: dry-wipe markers, paint and paper for shape-printing, sorting hoops, 3D shape name labels, display of vocabulary relating to 2D and 3D shapes (for example, face, edge, side, curved surface)

Teaching Tools In the eTextbook of this lesson, you will find interactive links to a selection of teaching tools.

Before you teach

- How secure are children in distinguishing between and naming 2D and 3D shapes?
- Are children able to describe the properties of 2D and 3D shapes?
- How will you use concrete 2D and 3D shapes to strengthen children's understanding?

Discover

WAYS OF WORKING Pair work

ASK

- Question **1** a): *How do you know which shapes Irene used?*
- Question **1** a): *Which faces did Irene not use?*

IN FOCUS Question **1** a) encourages children to make links between 2D and 3D shapes. It helps them to isolate a specific property of a shape and look carefully at their similarities and differences.

ANSWERS Question **1** a): Irene used the cube for the square head. She used the cone and the cuboid for the body.

Question **1** b): Irene printed the purple leg first because the green leg overlaps it.

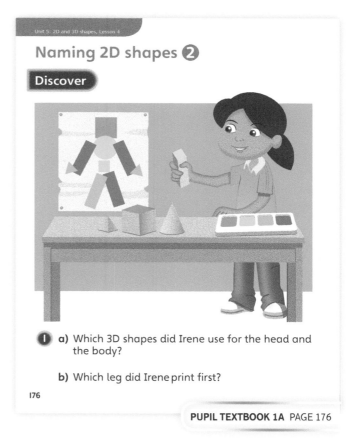

PUPIL TEXTBOOK 1A PAGE 176

Share

WAYS OF WORKING Whole class teacher led

ASK

- Refer to what Dexter and Flo say by asking: *Could Irene have used another shape to make the head?*
- Refer to what Flo says about cuboids having square faces by asking: *Is this true?*
- Question **1** b): *What do you think the first shape Irene printed was?*

IN FOCUS Question **1** b) asks children to think about the order in which the picture is printed. This encourages them to use positional language and provide justification for their answers. They may generate more than one possibility. This can prompt discussion that, sometimes in mathematics, there may not be a definitive answer and that answers should be supported with reasoning and justification.

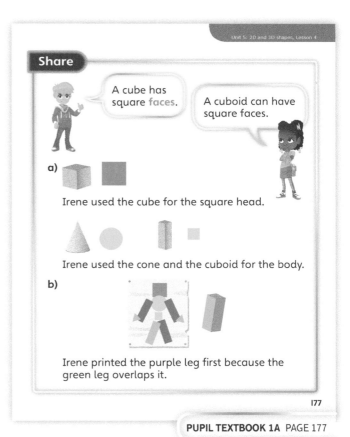

PUPIL TEXTBOOK 1A PAGE 177

Think together

WAYS OF WORKING Whole class teacher led (I do, We do, You do)

ASK

• *What shapes can you use to print a square?*
• *Can you use a cube or pyramid to print a rectangle?*
• *How many different 2D shapes could you make with a cube or a pyramid?*
• *How does this knowledge help you to describe 3D shapes?*

IN FOCUS Question ❸ challenges the misconception that a curved surface is a circle, which often comes from knowing that a circle has one curved side. Discuss the fact that a flat circular face is needed to print a circle. Some children may see that the curved surface of the cone can be rolled.

STRENGTHEN Have a selection of cuboids and pyramids available for children to handle. In question ❶, children can explore printing or drawing round each face to determine what rectangles these shapes can produce. In question ❷, children can tick each face with a dry wipe marker as they count them to help them keep track of which faces they have counted.

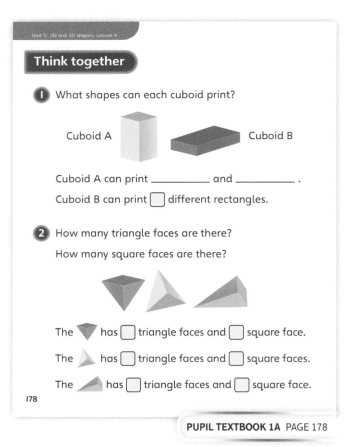

Think together

❶ What shapes can each cuboid print?

Cuboid A   Cuboid B

Cuboid A can print _____ and _____ .
Cuboid B can print ☐ different rectangles.

❷ How many triangle faces are there?
How many square faces are there?

The ▼ has ☐ triangle faces and ☐ square face.
The ◣ has ☐ triangle faces and ☐ square faces.
The ◢ has ☐ triangle faces and ☐ square face.

178

PUPIL TEXTBOOK 1A PAGE 178

DEEPEN In question ❸, ask children what shapes the curved surfaces of a cylinder and a cone would print if rolled. Children can predict, justify their predictions and test what happens .

ASSESSMENT CHECKPOINT Question ❷ should determine whether children can count and describe all faces of the pyramids. Can children use their knowledge of 3D shapes to count hidden faces?

Refer to Dexter's statement. Question ❸ will expose any insecurities in children's knowledge that a flat face will print a 2D shape. Assess whether children can identify curved surfaces of 3D shapes.

ANSWERS

Question ❶: Cuboid A can print squares and rectangles. Cuboid B can print 3 different rectangles.

Question ❷:

The ▼ has 4 triangle faces and 1 square face.

The ◣ has 4 triangle faces and 0 square faces.

The ◢ has 4 triangle faces and 1 square face.

Question ❸: The cylinder, the cone and the hemisphere can all print a circle. The sphere cannot print a circle.

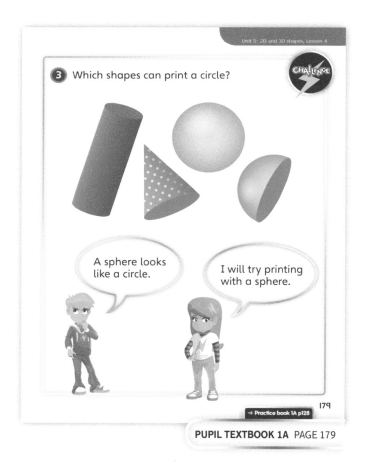

❸ Which shapes can print a circle?

CHALLENGE

A sphere looks like a circle.

I will try printing with a sphere.

→ Practice book 1A p128

179

PUPIL TEXTBOOK 1A PAGE 179

Practice

WAYS OF WORKING Pair work

IN FOCUS Question **4** requires children to identify individual 2D shapes from compound shapes before they identify which 3D shapes were used to produce the compound shapes. Question **4** is a two-step problem with more than one possible answer. For example, circles can be printed using a cone, a hemisphere or a cylinder.

STRENGTHEN Children could use concrete 3D shapes to create their own simpler version of the picture in question **5** and challenge their partner to identify the order in which the shapes were printed. Their partner could also identify the 3D shapes used to print each 2D shape by name.

DEEPEN In question **2**, the rectangle could be made by printing two overlapping squares. Ask children whether there is any way they could use the cube to print the rectangle. Children could try drawing around a cube.

Extend question **4** by asking children whether there is only one possible solution for each print or whether other shapes could be used.

ASSESSMENT CHECKPOINT Question **1** will help you decide whether children can identify 2D faces of 3D shapes.

Question **3** will help you assess whether children can apply their knowledge of 3D shapes to count faces that are not visible.

In question **4**, assess whether children are able to determine basic 2D shapes from composite shapes and identify 3D shapes with the corresponding 2D faces. In question **5**, check whether children can apply their knowledge of 2D shapes to identify partially obscured shapes.

ANSWERS Answers for the **Practice** part of the lesson appear in the separate **Practice and Reflect answer guide**.

Reflect

WAYS OF WORKING Pair work

IN FOCUS This **Reflect** part of the lesson requires children to distinguish between 2D and 3D shapes and match them to their corresponding names.

ASSESSMENT CHECKPOINT Assess whether children are secure in their understanding of which shapes are 2D and which shapes are 3D. Can children label 2D and 3D shapes correctly?

ANSWERS Answers for the **Reflect** part of the lesson appear in the separate **Practice and Reflect answer guide**.

After the lesson

- Were any children still using 2D names for 3D shapes or 2D names for 3D shapes?
- Did children have a good understanding of what faces are and the types of faces that different 3D shapes have?
- Were children aware that different 3D shapes may share common shaped faces?

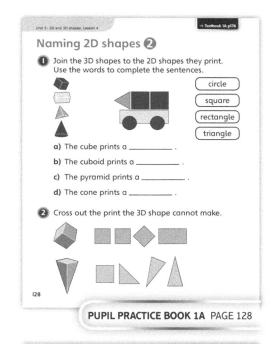

PUPIL PRACTICE BOOK 1A PAGE 128

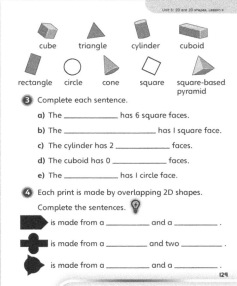

PUPIL PRACTICE BOOK 1A PAGE 129

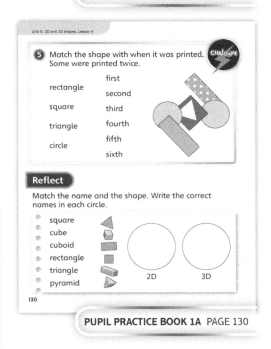

PUPIL PRACTICE BOOK 1A PAGE 130

Making patterns with shapes

Learning focus

In this lesson, children will apply their previous knowledge to identify 2D and 3D shapes within repeating patterns. Children will reason to describe the patterns and to help them identify missing shapes.

Small steps

→ Previous step: Naming 2D shapes (2)
→ **This step: Making patterns with shapes**
→ Next step: Counting and writing numbers to 20

NATIONAL CURRICULUM LINKS

Year 1 Geometry – Properties of Shape
- Recognise and name common 2D and 3D shapes, including: 2D shapes [for example, rectangles (including squares), circles and triangles]; 3D shapes [for example, cuboids (including cubes), pyramids and spheres].
- Recognise and create repeating patterns with objects and with shapes

ASSESSING MASTERY

Children can identify and describe the repeated part (the core) of a repeating pattern and reason about how to complete or continue repeating patterns. They can devise their own repeating patterns and summarise the cores of these patterns.

COMMON MISCONCEPTIONS

When trying to find the missing part of a pattern, children may focus only on the missing section and fail to look before or beyond to see how the pattern continues. This can mean that children do not gather enough information in order to complete the pattern. Ask:
- *How do you know what the missing shape is?*
- *Which parts of the pattern did you look at to help you?*

STRENGTHENING UNDERSTANDING

Give children concrete 2D and 3D shapes to print with or draw around. Ask children to replicate the patterns in the questions in this lesson and identify what shapes are being repeated.

GOING DEEPER

Encourage children to create their own repeating patterns and write descriptions to go with them. They can begin to make their patterns more complex by including longer cores and by making more than one line.

KEY LANGUAGE

In lesson: shape, under, rectangle, **pattern**, big, small, triangle, continue, hidden, **repeated**, square, circle, cube, cuboid, sphere

Other language to be used by the teacher: 3D, 2D, rotate, core

STRUCTURES AND REPRESENTATIONS

3D and 2D representations of cube, cuboid, sphere, cone, square, rectangle, triangle, circle

RESOURCES

Mandatory: concrete representations of 2D and 3D shapes: circles (big and small), rectangles, triangles (big and small), squares, cubes, spheres, cuboids, cones

Optional: paint and paper for printing

Teaching Tools In the eTextbook of this lesson, you will find interactive links to a selection of teaching tools.

Before you teach

- Are children secure naming 2D and 3D shapes?
- Are children able to recognise shapes in different orientations and understand that rotating the shape does not change the shape?

Discover

Unit 5: 2D and 3D shapes, Lesson 5

Making patterns with shapes

Discover

WAYS OF WORKING Pair work

ASK

- *Can you describe the patterns on the invite?*
- *How are the circles different?*
- *How do the rectangle and triangle change in the patterns on the invite?*
- *What shape would come before the first shape in each pattern on the invite? How do you know?*

IN FOCUS In question ① b), children identify the pattern and then reason about how many shapes are covered. Children must look beyond the covered shapes to determine the shapes that are covered, and then reason about how many rectangles or circles will fit under the pencil case or mug.

ANSWERS

Question ① a): There is 1 small circle under the 🍵 .

Question ① b): There are 8 rectangles on the invite.

Dear Sophie

You are invited to my party on Saturday 4th.

I hope you can come.

From Bilal

① a) What shape is under the 🍵 ?

b) How many rectangles are on the invite?

180

Share

WAYS OF WORKING Whole class teacher led

ASK

- Question ① a): *How did you know which shape was under the mug?*
- Question ① a): *What would be the next three shapes in the pattern?*
- Question ① b): *How did you work out that three rectangles were covered?*
- Question ① b): *Can you draw the part of the pattern that is covered?*

IN FOCUS The picture in question ① b) provides scaffolding for the reasoning behind solving the problem. Where did children start looking? Starting from the top of the pattern gives more information about the pattern up to the covered shapes. Encourage children to reason about how many rectangles from the pattern fit into the covered area.

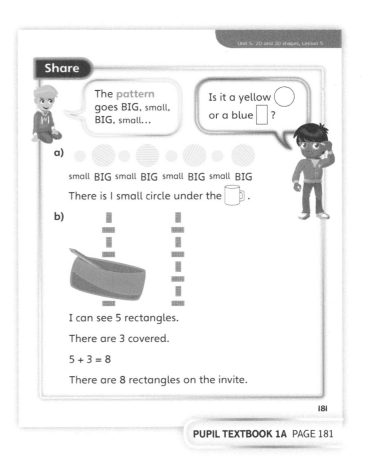

Unit 5: 2D and 3D shapes, Lesson 5

Share

The **pattern** goes BIG, small, BIG, small...

Is it a yellow ◯ or a blue ▯ ?

a)

small BIG small BIG small BIG small BIG

There is 1 small circle under the 🍵 .

b)

I can see 5 rectangles.

There are 3 covered.

5 + 3 = 8

There are 8 rectangles on the invite.

181

Think together

Whole class teacher led (I do, We do, You do)

ASK

- *How would you describe the patterns?*
- *Which shape would come before the first shape in each pattern?*
- *How many shapes are in the repeating part of each pattern?*
- *How did you work out which shapes were missing?*

IN FOCUS Question **3** introduces children to a pattern that has three shapes in its core, illustrating that patterns are not limited to two repeating elements. This means that children need to look at more of the pattern in order to determine the hidden shape.

STRENGTHEN Have concrete 2D and 3D shapes available so children can create each pattern and identify the core by separating it from the rest of the pattern. Cover one or more shapes and ask: *Which shape is covered?* Children could continue this with a partner.

DEEPEN Encourage children to apply their knowledge of each pattern beyond what is represented on the page. For example, in question **2** a), ask children to predict the seventh shape in the pattern and justify their choice.

ASSESSMENT CHECKPOINT In question **1**, assess whether children are able to identify which part of the pattern is being repeated.

In questions **2** and **3**, assess whether children can describe the patterns to their partner. Prompt children by referring them to the language used by Dexter, especially the words 'pattern', 'repeated' and '3D'.

ANSWERS

Question **1**: It is ▼▲ because the size of the triangles and the direction they face matches the pattern.

Question **2** a): ◆

Question **2** b): ⬛

Question **3**: ⬜ The pattern repeats cube, sphere, cuboid.

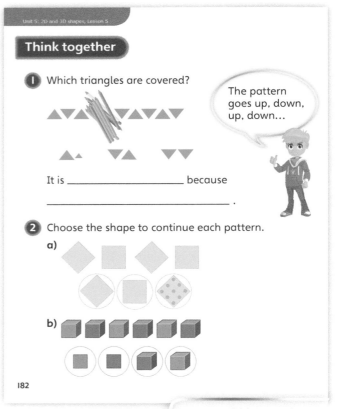

PUPIL TEXTBOOK 1A PAGE 182

PUPIL TEXTBOOK 1A PAGE 183

Practice

WAYS OF WORKING Pair work

IN FOCUS Question **3** b) uses a cone twice in the core, which means that identifying the core becomes more complex. Encourage children to look closely and to name the shapes as they go down the line.

Question **5** uses a pattern that is visually very different. Children need to calculate the missing number in the part-whole model, but the pattern is determined by its orientation. Discuss where the numbers need to go and how the shape has changed: has it been flipped or rotated?

STRENGTHEN Have concrete 2D and 3D shapes for children to use in order to replicate the patterns. Encourage them to point out and name each shape to their partner. Ask: *Can you hear the repeating part of the pattern?*

DEEPEN Ask children to predict the tenth, eleventh and twelfth shapes in each pattern. How do they know what these shapes will be?

ASSESSMENT CHECKPOINT In question **2**, determine whether children can apply their knowledge of a pattern to work out which shapes are missing. Do children look at enough of the pattern in order to identify the repeating part and the missing shapes?

Question **3** will expose whether children are able to identify and describe the core of the pattern. Are children looking at enough of the pattern in order to identify the core?

ANSWERS Answers for the **Practice** part of the lesson appear in the separate **Practice and Reflect answer guide**.

Reflect

WAYS OF WORKING Pair work

IN FOCUS The **Reflect** part of the lesson requires children to apply their knowledge of patterns to create their own repeating pattern. Encourage children to challenge their thinking by using one or more of the shapes more than once in their pattern's core.

ASSESSMENT CHECKPOINT Assess whether children can describe their pattern's core. Have they continued the pattern long enough so the core can be identified? The complexity of their patterns can help determine how secure children are in their understanding of repeating patterns.

ANSWERS Answers for the **Reflect** part of the lesson appear in the separate **Practice and Reflect answer guide**.

After the lesson ⏸

- Did children understand that a pattern needs to have a core?
- How confident were children identifying and describing the core of a pattern?
- Did children develop an understanding of and ability to use cores with three or more elements?

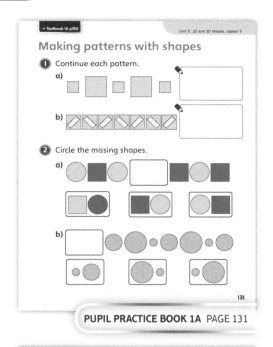

PUPIL PRACTICE BOOK 1A PAGE 131

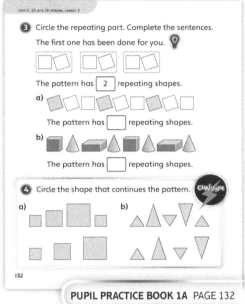

PUPIL PRACTICE BOOK 1A PAGE 132

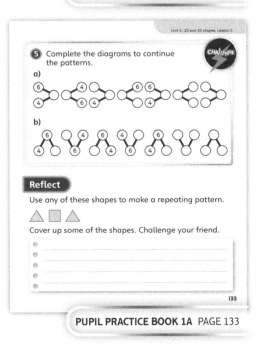

PUPIL PRACTICE BOOK 1A PAGE 133

End of unit check

Don't forget the End of unit check proforma (page 184)!

WAYS OF WORKING Group work – adult led

IN FOCUS

- Questions **1** and **2** assess children's recognition of 3D shapes, including when they are presented in different orientations.
- Question **3** assesses children's recognition of 2D shapes, in particular triangles, including when they are presented in different orientations.
- Question **4** assesses children's ability to recognise patterns using 2D shapes and their written names.
- Question **5** focuses on vocabulary and distinguishing between 2D and 3D shapes.

Think!

WAYS OF WORKING Pair work or small groups

IN FOCUS

- This question assesses children's ability to distinguish between 2D and 3D shapes.
- Draw children's attention to the words at the bottom of the My journal page. Which group(s) does each word describe?
- Encourage children to think through or discuss how the shapes in each group are the same before writing their answer in My journal. Can they match the 2D shapes to the 3D shapes?

ANSWERS AND COMMENTARY Children will be able to describe the differences between 2D and 3D shapes using the correct mathematical vocabulary. They will be able to name and describe the properties of a variety of 2D and 3D shapes.

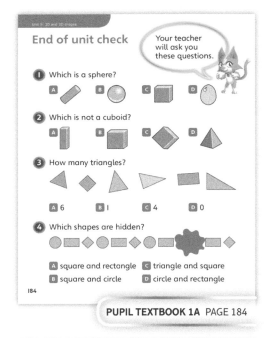

PUPIL TEXTBOOK 1A PAGE 184

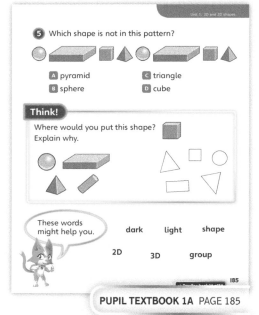

PUPIL TEXTBOOK 1A PAGE 185

Q	A	WRONG ANSWERS AND MISCONCEPTIONS	STRENGTHENING UNDERSTANDING
1	B	A or D suggests that the child has identified the curved face and associated this with what they know about a sphere.	Provide children with 2D and 3D shapes to manipulate and explore. Ask them to match the shapes with those in the problems. If they are still having difficulties correctly naming the shapes, provide labels and ask them to match them with the shapes, talking about their properties in the process. Ask children to sort the shapes and discuss the criteria that they have used. They could be prompted to sort them by their properties; for example, curved face / not curved face or 6 faces / not 6 faces.
2	D	A suggests that the child does not recognise a cuboid with 'unusual' dimensions, despite its familiar orientation.	
3	C	B suggests that the child only recognises regular triangles.	
4	B	A, C, or D suggest that the child could not identify the pattern core or that they do not understand the shape vocabulary.	
5	C	A suggests that the child has misidentified the pyramids pictured as triangles.	

My journal

WAYS OF WORKING Independent thinking

ANSWERS AND COMMENTARY

The cube belongs in the group of 3D shapes.

Possible explanations include:
- I put the shape there because it is a 3D shape like the rest in the group.
- I put the shape there because it has a dark face like the rest in the group.
- I put the shape there because it is shaded like the rest in the group.
- I put the shape there because the other group has 2D shapes.

If children are unable to correctly place the shape or justify their choice appropriately, they may need more time grouping and sorting 2D and 3D shapes practically. Ensure that you encourage children to give a running commentary, to promote mathematical language and clear articulation of their thinking.

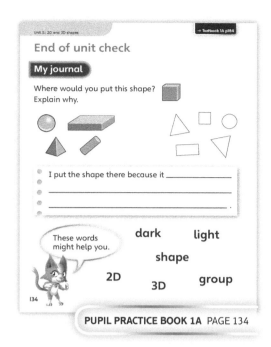

PUPIL PRACTICE BOOK 1A PAGE 134

Power check

WAYS OF WORKING Independent thinking

ASK

- *How do you feel about naming and describing 2D and 3D shapes?*
- *Were there any parts that you found challenging? Why?*

Power puzzle

WAYS OF WORKING Pair work or small groups

IN FOCUS Use this Power puzzle to see if children can use the names of 2D shapes when discussing the problem with a partner. Attempt the puzzle in front of the class and break the rules to see if they understand them and can identify where you went wrong; for example, use more than three colours or colour two adjacent shapes the same colour. When children are secure, ask them to take turns colouring while their partner gives advice about what to do. This will encourage children to be clear in their descriptions and use correct mathematical vocabulary.

ANSWERS AND COMMENTARY Children who complete the Power puzzle successfully, giving clear descriptions of the shapes as they do so, can identify shapes based on their properties and have a good understanding of pattern. If children cannot give their partner clear advice, or cannot follow their partner's advice, they may not be secure with identifying and naming 2D shapes.

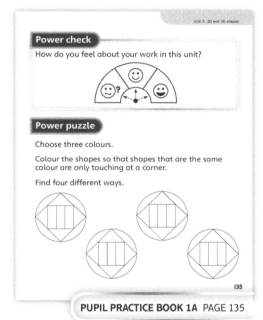

PUPIL PRACTICE BOOK 1A PAGE 135

After the unit ⏸

- How can you find opportunities to reinforce the learning of this unit by identifying shapes in everyday contexts?
- Can you make cross-curricular links, drawing on children's learning from this unit?

Strengthen and *Deepen* activities for this unit can be found in the Power Maths online subscription.

Unit 6
Numbers to 20

Mastery Expert tip! "When teaching this unit it is important to make links to prior content covered. Doing so helps children not only to consolidate their prior learning; helping secure it in long-term memory, but also to see maths as one big interconnected journey rather than different topics meaning different things."

Don't forget to watch the unit 6 video!

WHY THIS UNIT IS IMPORTANT

This unit lays the essential foundations of place value, as children begin to recognise the place value of each digit in a 2-digit number. This is an important skill that children will develop when they add and subtract and begin to work with larger numbers.

Children will count in tens and ones, learning that they can partition a 2-digit numbers into tens and ones. They will find the number that is one more or one less than a given number, noticing when the tens digit changes and when only the ones digit number changes.

As they become more fluent, they will begin to compare and order numbers to 20 using the < and > symbols.

WHERE THIS UNIT FITS

→ Unit 5: 2D and 3D shapes
→ **Unit 6: Numbers to 20**
→ Unit 7: Addition within 20

This unit builds on children's work on numbers to 10 in Units 1–2, extending their ability to count, compare and order numbers to 20. Unit 7 will focus on addition within 20.

Before they start this unit, it is expected that children:
- recognise numbers bonds within 10
- understand how to partition a number within 10
- can compare and order numbers within 10.

ASSESSING MASTERY

Children who have mastered this unit will be able to partition numbers above 10 into tens and ones. They will be able to work with many different concrete and pictorial representations of numbers, and use correct mathematical language to describe and compare numbers.

They will be able to count forwards or backwards to 20, beginning at 0 or 1, or from any given number. They will also be able to identify 'one more' and 'one less' than a given number.

COMMON MISCONCEPTIONS	STRENGTHENING UNDERSTANDING	GOING DEEPER
Children may miss out numbers, or say the wrong number, when counting (for example, saying 'thirty' instead of 'thirteen', or 'fiveteen' instead of 'fifteen').	Give children opportunities to say the words out loud together as a class and in discussion with each other.	Allow children to explore with different representations of number. Which one do they think represents the numbers most clearly?
Children may think that 2-digit numbers are made up of ones and ones rather than tens and ones (for example, thinking that 17 is made up of 1 and 7 rather than 10 and 7).	Discuss what representations numbers do not show as well as what they do show. For example, show children a ten frame with one counter and a ten frame with seven counters. *Why does this not show 17? What does it show?*	Give children problems that have more than one possible answer (for example, *Find all the ways of completing 18 >* ▢ . Encourage , children to be systematic in their approach.

WAYS OF WORKING

Introduce the unit using teacher-led discussion. Give children time to discuss each question in small groups or pairs and then discuss their ideas as a class.

STRUCTURES AND REPRESENTATIONS

Ten frame: Ten frames play a key role in helping children to recognise the structure of 2-digit numbers.

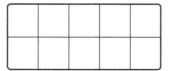

Number line: Number lines can be used to support children in counting on or back and in comparing numbers.

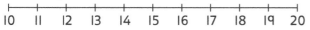

Bead string: Bead strings can be used to help children partition numbers into tens and ones, and to support them in finding one more or one less than a number.

Straws: Straws help children see the importance of ten: it is much easier to count in tens when counting large numbers and using straws emphasises this.

10

KEY LANGUAGE

There is some key language that children will need to know as part of the learning in this unit.

→ numbers 11–20

→ count, backwards, forwards

→ tens, ones

→ more, less

→ greatest, smallest, fewer, fewest, most, least

→ order, compare

→ equal to, more than, less than

PUPIL TEXTBOOK 1A PAGE 186

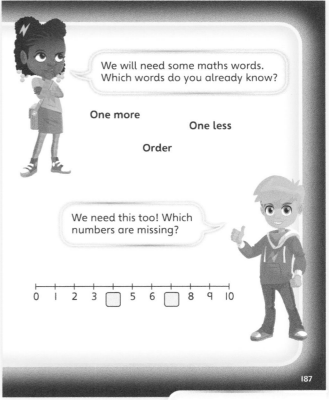

PUPIL TEXTBOOK 1A PAGE 187

Counting and writing numbers to 20

Learning focus

In this lesson, children will count numbers up to and including 20. They will write the numbers to 20 in numerals and words.

Small steps

→ Previous step: Making patterns with shapes
→ **This step: Counting and writing numbers to 20**
→ Next step: Tens and ones (1)

NATIONAL CURRICULUM LINKS

Year 1 Number – Number and Place Value
- Count to and across 100, forwards and backwards, beginning with 0 or 1, or from any given number.
- Identify and represent numbers using concrete objects and pictorial representations including the number line, and use the language of: equal to, more than, less than (fewer), most, least.

ASSESSING MASTERY

Children can confidently count aloud numbers to 20, forwards and backwards, and write them using words and digits.

COMMON MISCONCEPTIONS

When counting, children may miss out numbers or say the wrong number. For example, they may say 'thirty' instead of 'thirteen', or 'fiveteen' instead of 'fifteen'. Ask:
- *Which numbers are the most difficult to say? Let's practise those together.*

When counting pictures or objects, some children will always start at 1 rather than look for ways they could count more efficiently. To challenge this misconception, ask:
- *Did anyone count those objects differently? Let's see how many different ways you counted.*

STRENGTHENING UNDERSTANDING

To strengthen understanding, ensure children have lots of opportunities to say numbers out loud and focus on their pronunciation. Link this to prior learning to explore how some of the numbers above 10 link directly to the numbers within 10 when said out loud. For example, 9 and 19 directly link, whereas 1 and 11 do not. Children could group and sort numbers that link and numbers that do not.

GOING DEEPER

Use prior learning of numbers to 10 to explore ways children can count more efficiently. As an example, here we can see two ten frames.

 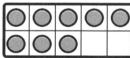

Some children will count each counter and others will recognise that one ten frame is full and the other has two spaces missing, so there must be 10 and 8, which makes 18. This is a great discussion point for the class.

KEY LANGUAGE

In lesson: numbers 11–20, how many, count, backwards, more, missing number

Other language to be used by the teacher: forwards

STRUCTURES AND REPRESENTATIONS

Ten frame, number line

RESOURCES

Mandatory: ten frame, number line, cubes and counters

Optional: stopwatch, selection of objects for counting such as toy cars, shapes, blocks, pencils

Teaching Tools In the eTextbook of this lesson, you will find interactive links to a selection of teaching tools.

Before you teach 🕚

- Are children secure with the idea of one-to-one correspondence used in numbers to ten?
- What resources will you provide for children who are still developing these ideas?

Discover

WAYS OF WORKING Pair work

ASK

- *How did you count the cars? Can you show me?*
- *How did your partner count the cars? Was it the same way you counted them?*
- *Which was the quickest way of counting the cars?*

IN FOCUS In this part of the lesson, encourage children to count the cars and discuss with a partner how they counted them. Children should then think about how other people might count the cars.

ANSWERS Question ❶: There are 13 cars.

Children could have counted them in many ways, for example: one by one; in twos; recognised 10, then added 3; recognised two lots of 5, then added 3.

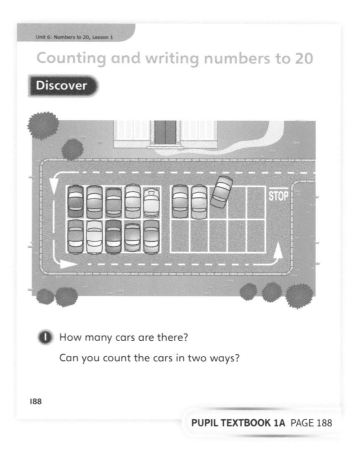

Counting and writing numbers to 20

Discover

❶ How many cars are there?

Can you count the cars in two ways?

188

PUPIL TEXTBOOK 1A PAGE 188

Share

WAYS OF WORKING Whole class teacher led

ASK

- Refer to what Astrid and Flo are saying. *How did you count the cars?*
- *How many ways have you found of counting the cars?*
- *How does the way they are set out help you to count them?*

IN FOCUS Children explore different ways of counting while practising how to say and write numbers to 20.

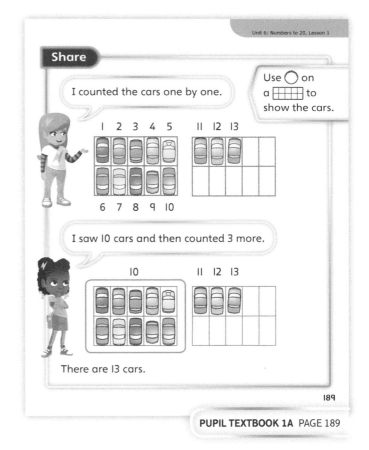

Share

I counted the cars one by one.

Use ⭕ on a ▦ to show the cars.

1 2 3 4 5   11 12 13

6 7 8 9 10

I saw 10 cars and then counted 3 more.

10   11 12 13

There are 13 cars.

189

PUPIL TEXTBOOK 1A PAGE 189

Think together

Whole class teacher led (I do, We do, You do)

ASK

- Question **1**: *Can you think how you could count backwards to find the answer?*
- Question **2**: *Do you need to count all the cars to work out this answer? How did you do it so quickly?*
- Question **3**: Refer to what Dexter is saying. *Can you count backwards in your pairs? Let's count backwards as a class. Can we count louder and more quickly?*

STRENGTHEN Children who continue to count one by one could spend some time with a ten frame practising counting. If needed, start with numbers within ten, such as seven, and ask children how they can see the number seven without counting from 1. For example, they may count 5, 6, 7 or 10, 9, 8, 7. Continue building up to larger numbers using two ten frames.

Practise counting backwards practically using toy cars or ten frames with the numbers written alongside.

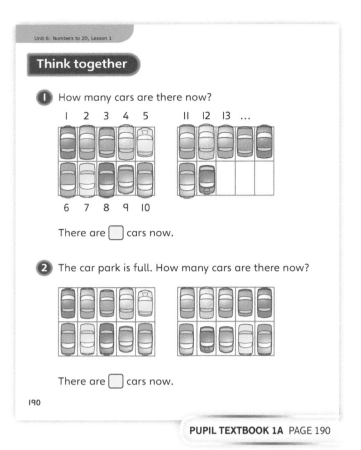

PUPIL TEXTBOOK 1A PAGE 190

DEEPEN Encourage children to explore lots of different ways of counting. Which is their preferred method? Why? How fast can they count backwards without making any mistakes and while still saying the words clearly? Give children access to a stopwatch so they can time each other.

ASSESSMENT CHECKPOINT Questions **1** and **2** should help you to see whether children have taken on board the earlier discussion about efficient counting. Encourage those that count one by one to look for links to make their counting quicker and more efficient.

Question **3** will help you to identify children who are struggling to count backwards.

ANSWERS

Question **1**: There are 17 cars now.

Question **2**: There are 20 cars now.

Question **3**: Children count backwards from 20 to 0.

PUPIL TEXTBOOK 1A PAGE 191

Practice

WAYS OF WORKING Independent thinking

IN FOCUS Questions in this section could be carried out practically using ten frames to represent each problem.

STRENGTHEN For questions **3**, **4** and **5** use ten frames to represent the number lines. Use different coloured counters or cubes to clearly represent the missing numbers.

DEEPEN Extend thinking in question **5** by encouraging children to make up some of their own missing number patterns. Ask children to work in pairs to fill in their partner's missing numbers.

ASSESSMENT CHECKPOINT Question **3** will help you check that children can write numbers in words.

Question **4** is the first question that checks counting backwards. At this point some children may benefit from practising practically with resources such as counters or cubes.

Question **6** reinforces a point made in the **Strengthening understanding** section of the lesson overview, where children were encouraged to say out loud the numbers above 10, up to 20. If children cannot spot the mistake in question **6**, go back to this activity.

ANSWERS Answers for the **Practice** part of the lesson appear in the separate **Practice and Reflect answer guide**.

Reflect

WAYS OF WORKING Independent thinking

IN FOCUS Children reflect on their counting to 20.

ASSESSMENT CHECKPOINT This section should help you pinpoint any specific areas that individual children need more support with. If necessary, prompt children to reflect on what they have learned with questions such as: *What did you find difficult? What was the trickiest part of the lesson? Can you spell all the numbers correctly?*

ANSWERS Answers for the **Reflect** part of the lesson appear in the separate **Practice and Reflect answer guide**.

After the lesson ⏸

- Did children find it harder to count backwards than forwards? Encourage daily practice using classroom resources, for example, counting the glue sticks backwards if they know there should be 20 in total.
- Did children tend to count in the same way or was there a lot of variety in how they counted? For instance, did most children begin the lesson by counting one by one?

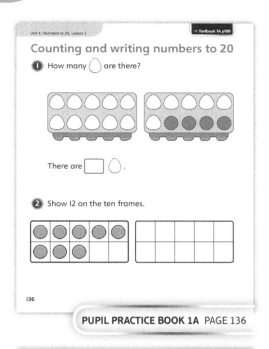

PUPIL PRACTICE BOOK 1A PAGE 136

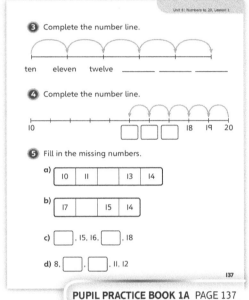

PUPIL PRACTICE BOOK 1A PAGE 137

PUPIL PRACTICE BOOK 1A PAGE 138

Tens and ones ❶

Learning focus

In this lesson, children will learn that the numbers 11–20 are made up of 1 ten and some more.

Small steps

→ Previous step: Counting and writing numbers to 20
→ **This step: Tens and ones (1)**
→ Next step: Tens and ones (2)

NATIONAL CURRICULUM LINKS

Year 1 Number – Number and Place Value
• Identify and represent numbers using objects and pictorial representations including the number line, and use the language of: equal to, more than, less than (fewer), most, least.
• Recognise the place value of each digit in a two-digit number (tens, ones) (year 2).

ASSESSING MASTERY

Children can express a number from 11 to 20 as tens and ones. For example, they will know that 16 is made up of 1 ten and 6 ones.

COMMON MISCONCEPTIONS

Children may think of the number 16, for example, as 1 and 6 rather than 10 and 6. To help address this, ask:
• *If you have 1 counter and 6 counters, how many counters do you have altogether?*
• *Why do you think you haven't got 16 counters?*

STRENGTHENING UNDERSTANDING

In this lesson straws could be used to represent the pens shown in the textbook so that children have something physical to handle. To represent the full pack of ten pens, ten straws can be bundled together. 16 straws would be represented as one bundle of ten straws and 6 separate straws. Bundling straws in this way will also reinforce learning from the previous lesson on counting to 20.

GOING DEEPER

Children could write full sentences explaining why 16 is made up of 1 ten and 6 ones rather than 7 ones.

Explore different ways of representing the numbers 11–20 using a variety of concrete and pictorial representations. Encourage children to explain which models show the idea of 1 ten and some ones best and why.

KEY LANGUAGE

In lesson: how many, one lot of ten, ten, ones, more

Other language to be used by the teacher: numbers 11–20

STRUCTURES AND REPRESENTATIONS

Ten frame, bead string

RESOURCES

Mandatory: ten frame, cubes, counters

Optional: straws, pens, sweets, toys or classroom objects for counting

Teaching Tools In the eTextbook of this lesson, you will find interactive links to a selection of teaching tools.

Before you teach ⓫

• Are all children secure with the idea of counting to 20?
• What resources will you provide for children who are still developing these ideas?

Discover

Unit 6: Numbers to 20, Lesson 2

WAYS OF WORKING Pair work

ASK

- *In your pairs, do you agree on the number of pens?*
- *Can you show me the number of pens using these straws?*
- *How could you arrange the straws to make them easier to count?*

IN FOCUS In this part of the lesson, children should practise their counting and start thinking about the idea of ten.

ANSWERS

Question 1 a): There are 15 🖊.

Question 1 b): 10 🖊 fit in a pack.

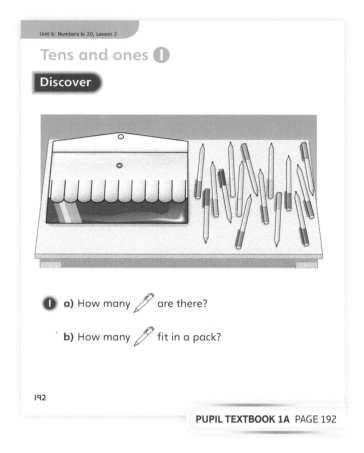

PUPIL TEXTBOOK 1A PAGE 192

Share

WAYS OF WORKING Whole class teacher led

ASK

- *Use these counters to represent the pens. Do they fit on a ten frame?*
- *How do you know there are more than ten?*
- *How does the way they are set out help you count?*

IN FOCUS Children are beginning to learn about partitioning numbers between 11 and 20. They are learning about the importance of ten and how this can help them count more efficiently.

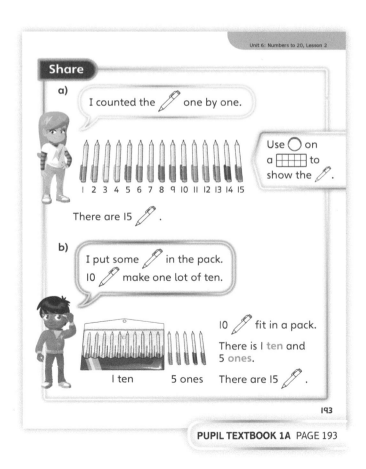

PUPIL TEXTBOOK 1A PAGE 193

Think together

WAYS OF WORKING Whole class teacher led (I do, We do, You do)

ASK

- Question **1**: *Explain how you knew there were 13 pens. How did you count?*
- Question **2**: *Did you have to count any pens here?*
- Question **2**: *How did you answer so quickly?*
- Question **3**: *Can you show me 16 with some of the equipment on your desk? You can choose which you want to use. How many different ways have people shown 16?*
- Question **3**: *If 16 has 1 ten and 6 ones, how many tens and ones do you think 17 has? Can you show me? What about 14?*

STRENGTHEN Children can spend some time with counters and a ten frame making sets of ten and some more and talking about what each represents.

DEEPEN In question **3**, children should understand that the pen pack needs to be full in order to be a ten. To extend and consolidate learning, give children some examples where a ten frame is not full and there are some single counters to the side. Ask:

- *How can you make this easier to count?*
- *Will you count one by one or will you move a counter onto the ten frame?*

ASSESSMENT CHECKPOINT Question **1** is a good opportunity to check children are confident with their counting. Ask children to count the pens one by one to prove there are 13.

Question **3** introduces the idea that the pack of pens or ten frame must be full to count to ten.

ANSWERS

Question **1**: There are 13 pens.

Question **2**: There are 20 pens in 2 packs.

Question **3**: There are 16 pens. There is 1 ten and 6 ones.

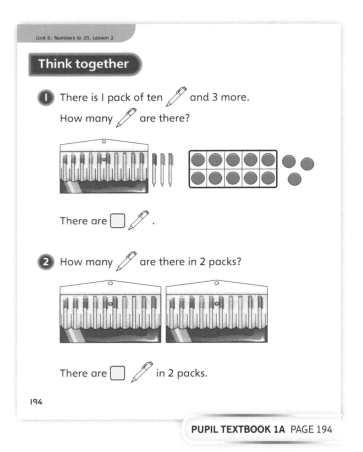

PUPIL TEXTBOOK 1A PAGE 194

PUPIL TEXTBOOK 1A PAGE 195

Practice

WAYS OF WORKING Independent thinking

IN FOCUS Through this activity children are learning that they can represent the numbers 11–20 in different ways, using different representations and writing number sentences in different ways. The questions reinforce the use of the = symbol by placing it in different places. Children can see that 1 ten and 6 ones = 16 is the same as 16 = 1 ten and 6 ones. This prepares them for tackling questions presented in a variety of ways.

STRENGTHEN Question ④ e) may confuse some children. This would be a good point to stop and discuss as a class. Ask children why this question is different: *Is it possible to show zero tens? Would both these answers be correct (07 and 7)?*

DEEPEN Children could show and write numbers in a variety of ways. Ask them to think about all they have learned on numbers so far and to show the numbers 11–20 in as many different ways as they can. For example, they could show 19 as:

- ✏️/ / / / / / / / /
- 1 ten and 9 ones = 19
- 19 = 1 ten and 9 ones
- Nineteen = one ten and nine ones
- One ten and nine ones = nineteen
- 19 ones = 19

ASSESSMENT CHECKPOINT For questions ①, ② and ③, check that children have understood the basics of the lesson. They could spend more time with practical equipment to consolidate these ideas before moving on to question ④.

Check how children tackle question ⑥. If children start counting from one because the ten frame is not full, they have not fully grasped the idea of using ten as a means to count larger numbers. Children who re-group to fill the ten frame show a deeper understanding.

ANSWERS Answers for the **Practice** part of the lesson appear in the separate **Practice and Reflect answer guide**.

Reflect

WAYS OF WORKING Independent thinking

IN FOCUS Children splitting a number into tens and ones will reinforce the idea that numbers 11–20 consist of 1 ten and some more (or two tens).

ASSESSMENT CHECKPOINT Go around the class asking for examples of children's reflection numbers. If nobody says 20, you could pick up on this example and ask the class how many tens and ones this number is made up of.

ANSWERS Answers for the **Reflect** part of the lesson appear in the separate **Practice and Reflect answer guide**.

After the lesson ⏸
- Did any children fall behind in this lesson?
- Have all children explored the misconception that 11 is not made up of one and one, but is made up of 10 and 1?

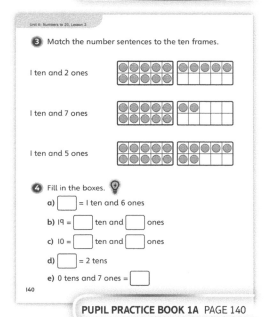

PUPIL PRACTICE BOOK 1A PAGE 139

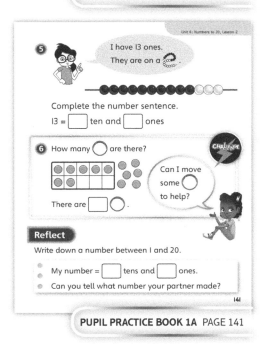

PUPIL PRACTICE BOOK 1A PAGE 140

PUPIL PRACTICE BOOK 1A PAGE 141

Tens and ones ②

Learning focus

In this lesson, children will continue to learn that the numbers 11–20 are made up of 1 ten and some more. They will also use the + and = symbols to express numbers 11–20.

Small steps

→ Previous step: Tens and ones (1)
→ **This step: Tens and ones (2)**
→ Next step: Counting one more, one less

NATIONAL CURRICULUM LINKS

Year 1 Number – Number and Place Value
- Identify and represent numbers using objects and pictorial representations including the number line, and use the language of: equal to, more than, less than (fewer), most, least.
- Recognise the place value of each digit in a two-digit number (tens, ones) (year 2).

ASSESSING MASTERY

Children can express a number from 11 to 20 as tens and ones and use the addition and equal to symbols. For example, children will know that 16 is made up of 1 ten and 6 ones, which can be written as $10 + 6 = 16$.

COMMON MISCONCEPTIONS

Children may think of the number 16 as 1 and 6 rather than 10 and 6. To expose this misconception, ask:
- *If you have 1 counter and 6 counters, how many counters do you have altogether?*
- *Why do you think you don't have 16 counters?*

STRENGTHENING UNDERSTANDING

Throughout this lesson, consider asking children to bundle the straws themselves as this will reinforce their learning on numbers within 10.

GOING DEEPER

Ask children to explain in full sentences how a number from 11 to 20 is made up of 1 ten and some ones. Give them words they must include, such as 'plus' and 'equal to', and ensure they write numbers out in words rather than using digits. Can they also represent the numbers in different ways using a variety of concrete materials? Encourage them to be creative: what could they use from around the classroom?

KEY LANGUAGE

In lesson: how many, more, count, group, same, tens, ones

Other language to be used by the teacher: numbers 11–20, different, one lot of ten, add, equal to, true, false, number sentence

STRUCTURES AND REPRESENTATIONS

Ten frame

RESOURCES

Mandatory: ten frame, cubes, counters, straws

Optional: milk cartons, smiley face stickers

Teaching Tools   In the eTextbook of this lesson, you will find interactive links to the following teaching tools: Ten frame

Before you teach

- Are all children secure with the idea of counting to 20 and knowing that a number from 11 to 20 is made up of 1 ten and some ones?
- What resources will you provide for children who are still developing these ideas? Have straws, ten frames and Base 10 available.

Discover

WAYS OF WORKING Pair work

ASK

• *How does the way the milk cartons are set out help you to count them?*
• *Can anyone use the + symbol to show the total number of milk cartons?*

IN FOCUS Children will recap the previous lesson and think about how a number from 11 to 20 is made up of 1 ten and some ones, or 2 tens if it is 20.

ANSWERS

Question ❶ a): There are 12 🥛.

Question ❶ b): There are 20 ⌐ .

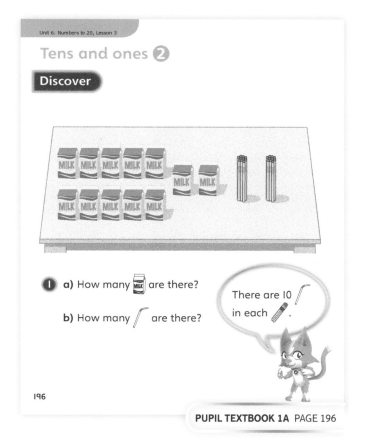

PUPIL TEXTBOOK 1A PAGE 196

Share

WAYS OF WORKING Whole class teacher led

ASK

• *Can you show the milk cartons on a ten frame?*
• *How do you know there are more than ten?*
• *Can you write a number sentence to show the total number of milk cartons? Can anyone write it using words instead of numerals?*

IN FOCUS Children consolidate their understanding of ten and explore different ways to write a sentence to show numbers greater than ten.

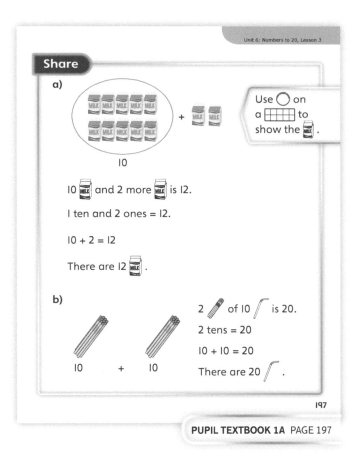

PUPIL TEXTBOOK 1A PAGE 197

Think together

Whole class teacher led (I do, We do, You do)

ASK

- Question ❶: *Did you need to count every single straw?*
- Question ❷: *Does the way the cartons are set out help you to count them?*
- Question ❸: *Which was the most difficult to count, the children, the straws or the milk? Why?*
- Question ❸: *Can you show each object on a ten frame? Use a different coloured counter or cube to represent the children, the straws and the milk.*

STRENGTHEN Strengthen understanding by asking children to solve these questions practically. They could start with familiar objects such as pencils or toys, then move on to more generic equipment such as the ten frame. Having the familiar equipment and ten frame side by side will help children to see the link. They are simply replacing the item with a counter or cube.

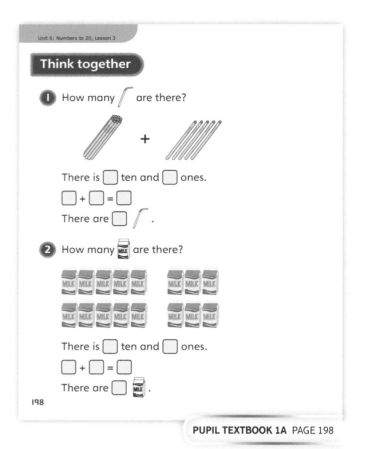

PUPIL TEXTBOOK 1A PAGE 198

DEEPEN In question ❸, when counting the children, encourage children to look for ten. Reinforce 'ten' by asking children to group ten faces. Ask: *How many tens are there? How many ones are there? How many are there in total?*

Question ❸ gives a good opportunity for depth. Ask children to describe how they counted and compare that with how others counted. *Which object was the easiest to count? Why was it easier?*

ASSESSMENT CHECKPOINT When answering the questions, look out for who is secure that a ten is a ten and who counts all the cartons, milk and children individually.

Question ❶ is a good opportunity to check if children are still counting one by one instead of using their knowledge of ten.

Question ❸ checks that children are flexible and can apply their knowledge to different scenarios.

ANSWERS

Question ❶: There is 1 ten and 5 ones. 10 + 5 = 15.
There are 15 /.

Question ❷: There is 1 ten and 6 ones. 10 + 6 = 16.
There are 16 🥛.

Question ❸: Yes, there are 16 children, 16 / and 16 🥛.

PUPIL TEXTBOOK 1A PAGE 199

Practice

WAYS OF WORKING Independent thinking

IN FOCUS This section gives children the opportunity to practise representing any number to 20 using the vocabulary, 'tens, and, ones'. In each question, they write number sentences using the + and − symbols to express numbers 11–20. Later, children can show their depth of understanding by reasoning whether a statement is true or false. Question **6** checks the misconception that 16 is made up of 1 and 6 rather than 1 ten and 6 ones.

STRENGTHEN Use a variety of concrete resources so that children can see the same problems in slightly different contexts. All activities can be completed practically to support children and scaffold learning.

DEEPEN Children could show and write numbers in a variety of ways. Ask them to think about all they have learned on numbers so far and to show the numbers 11–20 in as many different ways as they can. For example, they could show 15 as:

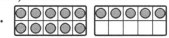

- 1 ten and 5 ones = 15
- 15 = 1 ten and 5 ones
- Fifteen = one ten and five ones
- One ten and five ones = fifteen
- 15 ones = 15
- 10 + 5 = 15
- 15 = 10 + 5

ASSESSMENT CHECKPOINT Questions **5** and **6** should help you assess whether children can think differently through less routine questions. This will enable you to see whether they have thoroughly grasped the concept of tens and ones.

ANSWERS Answers for the **Practice** part of the lesson appear in the separate **Practice and Reflect answer guide**.

Reflect

WAYS OF WORKING Independent thinking

IN FOCUS Children are able to think about the number 15 in a different way.

ASSESSMENT CHECKPOINT This is a good opportunity to discuss the different ways children have expressed 15. Tease out ways they may have missed. Use a worded sentence to reinforce key vocabulary, for example, fifteen is equal to one ten plus five ones.

ANSWERS Answers for the **Reflect** part of the lesson appear in the separate **Practice and Reflect answer guide**.

After the lesson ❚❚

- Have all children grasped that they can use the + symbol instead of the word 'and'?
- Are children flexible in how they can express a number from 11 to 20? For example, rather than simply write 1 ten + 6 ones = 16, can they write the number sentence the other way around and can they write the number sentence using words rather than digits?

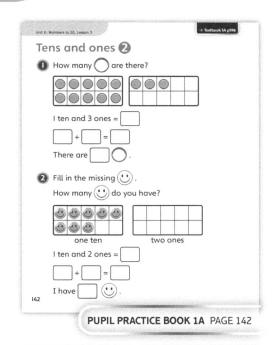

PUPIL PRACTICE BOOK 1A PAGE 142

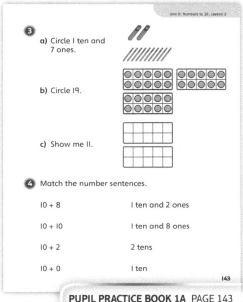

PUPIL PRACTICE BOOK 1A PAGE 143

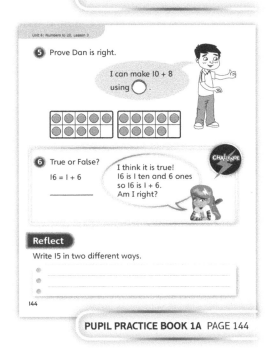

PUPIL PRACTICE BOOK 1A PAGE 144

Counting one more, one less

Learning focus

In this lesson, children learn that one more and one less is the same as adding one or subtracting one, or counting one forwards or one backwards.

Small steps

→ Previous step: Tens and ones (2)
→ **This step: Counting one more, one less**
→ Next step: Comparing numbers of objects

NATIONAL CURRICULUM LINKS

Year 1 Number – Number and Place Value
- Identify and represent numbers using objects and pictorial representations including the number line, and use the language of: equal to, more than, less than (fewer), most, least.
- Given a number, identify one more and one less.

ASSESSING MASTERY

Children can understand the language of one more and one less and link this with adding and subtracting and counting forwards and backwards, starting from any number to 20.

COMMON MISCONCEPTIONS

Children may misunderstand the meaning of 'one more' and 'one less' and may not consistently identify the number before or after a given number. Ask:
- *Will adding one more make the number bigger or smaller? you have to count forwards or backwards?*

STRENGTHENING UNDERSTANDING

A practical activity such as asking children to line up, then adding one more person or taking away a person (one less) will help children understand the language in this lesson. Children can take it in turns to count and a variety of questions can be asked during the activity, such as:
- *How many people are in the line now?*
- *How many will there be if I add one more person? How many will there be if there were one less person?*

GOING DEEPER

To deepen thinking about the strengthening understanding activity above, ask:
- *Does it matter if children leave the back of the line or the front of the line or the middle of the line? Does that change the answer?*

Children could also tackle problems that have more than one possible answer, such as 'One less than _ is one more than _ '.

There are multiple answers to this problem. One answer could be 'one less than 14 is one more than 12'. Children could look at how the numbers change if the sentence is written the other way around. For example, 'one more than 14 is one less than 16'.

KEY LANGUAGE

In lesson: how many, one more, one less, more than, less than

Other language to be used by the teacher: numbers 11–20, tens, ones, add, take away

STRUCTURES AND REPRESENTATIONS

Number line, cubes, ten frame, bead string

RESOURCES

Mandatory: bead string, number line

Optional: ten frame, objects for counting and taking away

 Teaching Tools In the eTextbook of this lesson, you will find interactive links to a selection of teaching tools.

Before you teach ⏸

- Are all children secure with the idea of counting to 20 and knowing that a number from 11 to 20 is made up of 1 ten and some ones?
- What resources will you provide for children who are still developing these ideas?

Discover

WAYS OF WORKING Pair work

ASK

- *When one more joins the line, does the number of children get bigger or smaller?*
- *When one child gets lunch, is the number in the line bigger or smaller?*

IN FOCUS Children learn about the vocabulary of one more and one less.

ANSWERS

Question ❶ a): There are 13 children waiting now.

Question ❶ b): There are 12 children waiting now.

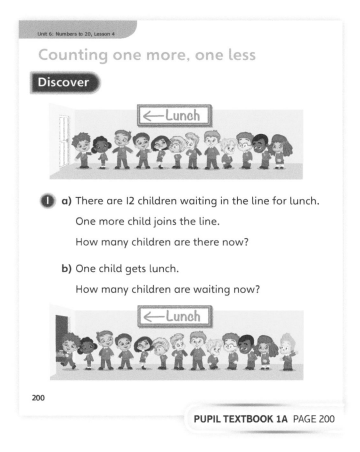

PUPIL TEXTBOOK 1A PAGE 200

Share

WAYS OF WORKING Whole class teacher led

ASK

- Refer children to what Ash is saying. *Can you represent the number of children in the line on your bead string?*
- *When one more child joins the line, do you have more beads or less beads? Is your number bigger or smaller?*
- *When one child gets lunch, do you count forwards or backwards to find the new number of children lined up?*

IN FOCUS Children learn about one more and one less in a slightly more abstract way; they also consolidate learning on tens and ones and counting forwards and backwards.

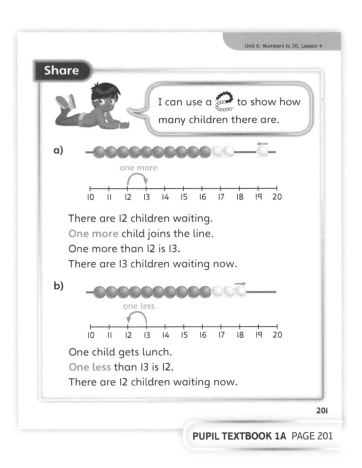

PUPIL TEXTBOOK 1A PAGE 201

Think together

WAYS OF WORKING Whole class teacher led (I do, We do, You do)

ASK

- Question ❶ : *Can you show me 11 on your bead string?*
- Question ❶ : *Show me one more than 11. Did you count forwards or backwards to find your answer?*
- Question ❷ : *What number is made up of 1 ten and 6 ones?*
- Question ❷ : *What number is one less than this? Did you count forwards or backwards to find your answer?*
- Question ❸ : Refer to what Ash is asking: *Did the ones change or the tens change?*

STRENGTHEN Children could line up teddy bears or toy cars to practise counting one more or one less. To further reinforce their learning, children could then represent these numbers using a bead string.

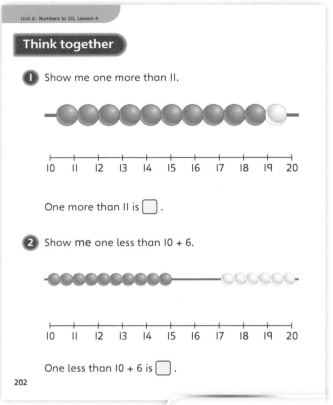

PUPIL TEXTBOOK 1A PAGE 202

DEEPEN In question ❸ , when finding one more or one less, children should notice that the ones column is changing, not the tens column. To find their answer, they either count forwards one or backwards one, not forwards or backwards ten.

Ask children for an example of when the tens change (19 to 20). Ask: *Does this mean that you have added ten?* Get them to show you using practical equipment, such as a ten frame, to prove that they have still only added one, not ten.

ASSESSMENT CHECKPOINT Questions ❶ and ❸ will help you decide if children understand the phrase 'more than'.

Question ❷ checks children's understanding of 'less' whilst also checking prior learning on tens and ones.

ANSWERS

Question ❶ : One more than 11 is 12.

Question ❷ : One less than 10 + 6 is 15.

Question ❸ : One more than 1 ten and 3 ones is 14.

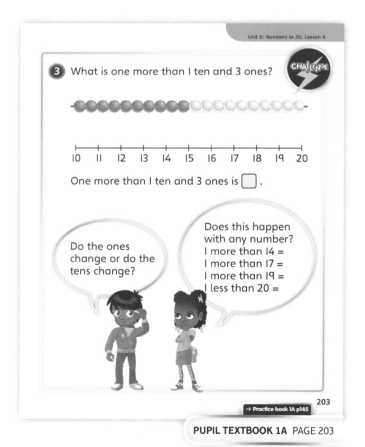

PUPIL TEXTBOOK 1A PAGE 203

Practice

WAYS OF WORKING Independent thinking

IN FOCUS Children find one more or one less than any number from 11 to 20. The questions in this section help children practise and reinforce their understanding that the ones are changing, not the tens, and that they either have to count forwards or backwards to find their answer.

Question ❸ is an opportunity for children to think more deeply about 'one more'. Children can experiment to see if it is always the ones column that changes. They could do this by simply listing numbers to check what happens.

STRENGTHEN In questions ❶ and ❷, encourage children to mark their starting number on the number line and then either jump one forwards or one backwards to find their answer. Children can use practical equipment to support them. A ten frame would be useful for question ❶, using counters or cubes to represent the cars.

DEEPEN In question ❻, encourage children to deepen and consolidate their learning by writing down their answers. For example, they could write: 'One more than thirteen is one less than 1 ten and five ones. Refer children to what Flo asks. How many different answers can they find?

ASSESSMENT CHECKPOINT Questions are asked in a variety of ways to help check that children have grasped prior learning as well as current learning. Throughout the activity, questions are asked using number sentences with words instead of digits or numbers written as tens and ones'. Questions 3 and 4 in particular build on prior learning. Children answering these questions well are showing a good grasp of the concepts covered so far.

ANSWERS Answers for the **Practice** part of the lesson appear in the separate **Practice and Reflect answer guide**.

Reflect

WAYS OF WORKING Independent thinking

IN FOCUS Children think about what equipment they can use to show one more or one less. For example, they could show one more and one less on a number line.

ASSESSMENT CHECKPOINT This is a good opportunity to discuss the different ways children can show one more or one less. For example, on a number line, using a bead string, using a ten frame, etc.

ANSWERS Answers for the **Reflect** part of the lesson appear in the separate **Practice and Reflect answer guide**.

After the lesson ⏸

- How could you consolidate one more, one less in everyday life?
- What percentage of the class were able to link prior learning to new learning on one more, one less?

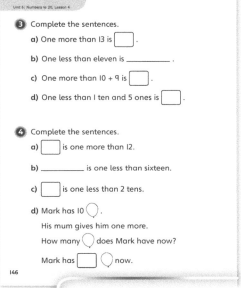

PUPIL PRACTICE BOOK 1A PAGE 145

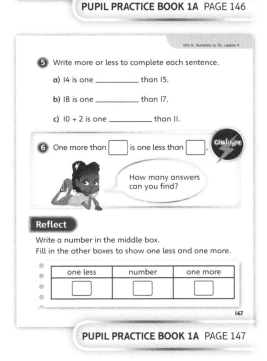

PUPIL PRACTICE BOOK 1A PAGE 146

PUPIL PRACTICE BOOK 1A PAGE 147

Comparing numbers of objects

Learning focus

In this lesson, children will use the <, > and = symbols to compare two groups of objects.

Small steps

→ Previous step: Counting one more, one less
→ **This step: Comparing numbers of objects**
→ Next step: Comparing numbers

NATIONAL CURRICULUM LINKS

Year 1 Number – Number and Place Value

Identify and represent numbers using objects and pictorial representations including the number line, and use the language of: equal to, more than, less than (fewer), most, least.

ASSESSING MASTERY

Children can compare numbers of objects using <, > and =. They will link the words that they used last lesson: 'equal', 'greater/more than' or 'less/fewer than' to the symbols =, < and >.

COMMON MISCONCEPTIONS

When using the symbols < and >, children may write them the wrong way around. They may need some more time using concrete materials to help them set up the correct symbol.

Children may think that a larger object means the number is worth more; for example, they may think that 11 footballs is greater than 12 tennis balls or they may think that if objects are spread out more they are larger in number than objects that are placed close together. Ask:
- *How can you set these objects out to help you see which you have most of?*
- *Can you use something else to represent the footballs and tennis balls to help you see which you have more of?*

STRENGTHENING UNDERSTANDING

Use cubes and straws or draw lines on a mini whiteboard to show the symbols <, > and =.

This helps children to understand the symbols and why we write them a certain way to reflect the actual size of numbers.

GOING DEEPER

Children may find lots of different ways to make a statement using < or > true. Going even deeper, they can work systematically to find all of the different ways. For example, find all the ways of filling in ___ < 17.

KEY LANGUAGE

In lesson: how many, more, fewer, fewest, tens, ones

Other language to be used by the teacher: equal to, more than, greater than, less than, fewer than, compare

STRUCTURES AND REPRESENTATIONS

Multilink cubes, ten frame

RESOURCES

Mandatory: cubes, counters

Optional: straws, marbles, variety of toys or classroom objects for counting and taking away

 In the eTextbook of this lesson, you will find interactive links to a selection of teaching tools.

Before you teach

- Are all children secure with the idea of counting to 20 and knowing that a number from 11 to 20 is made up of 1 ten and some ones?
- Do children need a recap of comparing fewer than ten objects using the symbols <, > and =?

Discover

WAYS OF WORKING Pair work

ASK

- *Who looks like they have more? Explain your reasons.*
- *How can we know for certain who has more?*
- *Can you use either < or > to show why Sam has more?*

IN FOCUS At first glance it looks as though Tom has more marbles than Sam, as ten of Sam's marbles are hidden inside a bag. This activity reinforces the fact that numbers from 11 to 20 are made up of 1 ten and some ones.

ANSWERS

Question ❶ : Sam has 14 ⬤ . Tom has 11 ⬤ .

Sam has more ⬤ than Tom because 14 > 11.

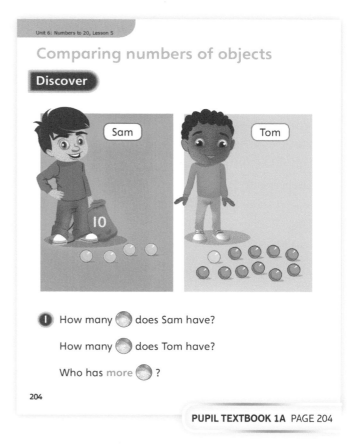

PUPIL TEXTBOOK 1A PAGE 204

Share

WAYS OF WORKING Whole class teacher led

ASK

- *Can you say a sentence using the words 'ten' and 'ones' to describe how many marbles Sam and Tom each have?*
- *How does lining up the marbles help us to compare them?*
- *Would imagining them as towers help us to decide which symbol to use?*

IN FOCUS Refer to what Astrid and Flo are saying. Encourage children to discuss the fact that Sam had 10 marbles hidden in a bag. Look at ways of representing the marbles in class and setting them out to compare them.

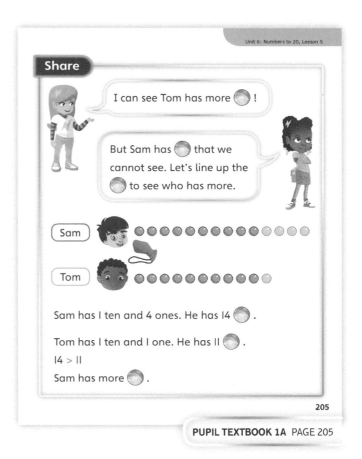

PUPIL TEXTBOOK 1A PAGE 205

Think together

WAYS OF WORKING Whole class teacher led (I do, We do, You do)

ASK

- Question **1**: *Why is it easy to see who has the fewest in this question?*
- Questions **2** and **3**: *Can you use cubes to show me who has more? How can you arrange them to make it clear?*
- Question **3**: *Can you tell me why a longer line doesn't always show more objects?*

IN FOCUS Question **3** highlights the potential misconception that objects that are more spaced out (and therefore the line of objects is longer), must be greater in number than objects closer together.

STRENGTHEN Children could represent the marbles and the cubes in this section with physical objects. They could then represent them as towers drawn on paper or a mini whiteboard to help them decide which way around the symbol goes. Ask:

- *Which tower is taller? How does this picture help you to draw the correct symbol?*

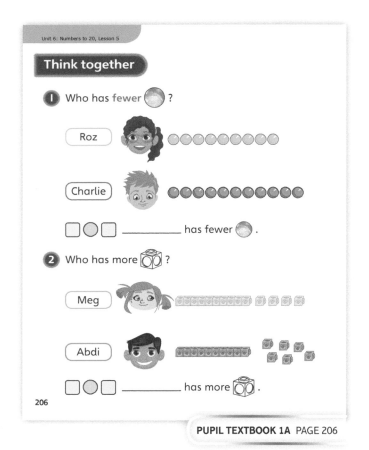

DEEPEN Question **3** is a good opportunity to deepen understanding. Can children prove whether Astrid's statement is sometimes, always or never true? Can they write a sentence using key words to explain their reasons? For example, 'Astrid's statement is only sometimes true because it depends how the objects are set out. If there is a lot of space between each object, it can make it look like more than it is. If the objects are very close together, it can look like there are fewer.'

ASSESSMENT CHECKPOINT Question **1** assesses understanding of the word 'fewer' and if children can write a number sentence using the < symbol.

Question **2** assesses if children can use the > symbol correctly. Are children able to read 4 > 3 as 'four is greater than three'?

ANSWERS

Question **1**: 9 < 11. Roz has fewer ⬤ .

Question **2**: 16 > 14. Abdi has more ⬤ .

Question **3**: 13 < 15. Mia has the fewest ⬤ .

Practice

WAYS OF WORKING Independent thinking

IN FOCUS Questions ❸ and ❹ focus on the words 'more' and 'less'. Use Ash's statement as a reasoning opportunity to expand thinking. Children can compare their answers and think about what the lowest possible answer is and what the highest possible answer is.

STRENGTHEN Encourage children to say number sentences out loud. This will especially help children to grasp the appropriate use of the word 'fewer' as they often replace this with the word 'less'. Ask children to make up their own sentences correctly using the key words from the lesson: fewer, fewest, more and less.

DEEPEN Questions ❹ and ❺ are good opportunities to extend learning as they encourage children to explore how many answers they can find. Ask: *Have you found all the answers? How do you know?* Can children record their answers in a clear way, such as in a table? Can they think of a different question that has exactly 10 possible answers?

ASSESSMENT CHECKPOINT This practice section will help you assess whether children have understood the key vocabulary: fewest, fewer, most, more and less.

ANSWERS Answers for the **Practice** part of the lesson appear in the separate **Practice and Reflect answer guide**.

Reflect

WAYS OF WORKING Independent thinking

IN FOCUS Children think about different ways they can compare objects. Options include: writing a sentence, using cubes or counters to represent objects and then lining them up or grouping them, or using the symbols <, > and =.

ASSESSMENT CHECKPOINT This is a good opportunity to check how thoroughly children have grasped the lesson. Check what children have written down. Have they managed to think of three ways to compare objects?

ANSWERS Answers for the **Reflect** part of the lesson appear in the separate **Practice and Reflect answer guide**.

After the lesson ⏸

- Are children confident with all of the language used in the lesson?
- Are they able to use the symbols <, > and = confidently or do they still need to draw a picture to help them decide which way around they go?

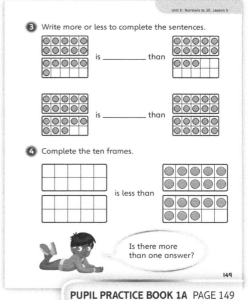

PUPIL PRACTICE BOOK 1A PAGE 148

PUPIL PRACTICE BOOK 1A PAGE 149

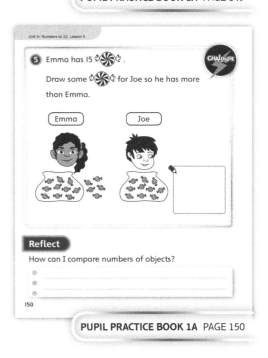

PUPIL PRACTICE BOOK 1A PAGE 150

Comparing numbers

Learning focus

In this lesson, children identify whether a number is more than, less than or equal to another when given two or more numbers within 20. They will use the less than (<), more than (>) or equal to (=) signs.

Small steps

→ Previous step: Comparing numbers of objects
→ **This step: Comparing numbers**
→ Next step: Ordering objects and numbers

NATIONAL CURRICULUM LINKS

Year 1 Number – Number and Place Value
- Identify and represent numbers using objects and pictorial representations including the number line, and use the language of: equal to, more than, less than (fewer), most, least.
- Compare and order numbers from 0 up to 100; use <, > and = signs (year 2).

ASSESSING MASTERY

Children can correctly compare numbers using <, > and =. They will link the words 'equal', 'greater/more than' or 'less/fewer than' to the symbols =, > and <.

COMMON MISCONCEPTIONS

Children may write the symbols < and > the wrong way around. Ask:
- *How could you draw a picture to help you decide which way to write the symbol?*

STRENGTHENING UNDERSTANDING

Model < , > and = to encourage children to understand the symbols.

This helps children understand the symbols and why we write them a certain way to reflect the actual size of numbers. Move on to drawing the cubes and lines rather than using the physical equipment. Eventually, children should be able to visualise this picture to help them remember which way around to write the symbols.

GOING DEEPER

Children may be able to explore questions where there is more than one answer. For example, 'find all the ways of filling in 18 > ___'.

Children could create their own questions. For example, they could write a number sentence comparing two numbers in two different ways, such as '19 < 20' and 'twenty is greater than nineteen'.

KEY LANGUAGE

In lesson: most, least

Other language to be used by the teacher: equal to, more than, greater than, less than, fewer than, tens, ones, compare

STRUCTURES AND REPRESENTATIONS

Cubes and number line

RESOURCES

Mandatory: cubes

Optional: straws, sweets, toys or other classroom objects that could be used for counting

Teaching Tools In the eTextbook of this lesson, you will find interactive links to a selection of teaching tools.

Before you teach ⏸

- Are children secure with the language used in previous lessons such as more, less, fewer, fewest?
- Are children confident comparing fewer than ten objects using the symbols <, > and =?

Discover

WAYS OF WORKING Pair work

ASK

- *Can you write a sentence describing what you have found? Who can write a different sentence?*
- *Can you use a symbol to show which film got the most votes?*
- *How many ways can you write the numbers 15 and 18?*

IN FOCUS Questions here ask children to use their acquired knowledge from previous lessons to compare two numbers. They are introduced to the vocabulary 'most'.

ANSWERS

Question ❶: Space Fun got the most votes because:
- 18 is greater than 15
- 15 is fewer than 18
- 18 > 15
- 15 < 18
- 10 + 8 > 10 + 5
- 1 ten and 5 ones < 1 ten and eight ones.

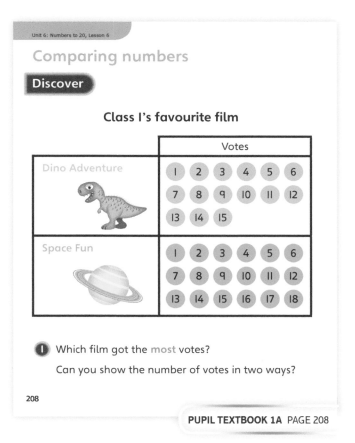

Share

WAYS OF WORKING Whole class teacher led

ASK

- *How do the towers help you to see which film got the most votes? What if the towers don't start at the same place? Is it still helpful?*
- *How many more votes did Space Fun get? How can you tell by just looking at the towers?*
- *How does the number line help you to decide which number is bigger?*

IN FOCUS Children decide which number is the biggest by looking at the heights of two towers.

Think together

WAYS OF WORKING Whole class teacher led (I do, We do, You do)

ASK

- Question ①: *Can you say a sentence to describe why the towers show which colour got the most/least votes?*
- Questions ① and ②: *Can you draw a picture to help you write the correct symbol between the numbers?*
- Question ③: *Can you draw a picture to show which symbol you should use now?*

IN FOCUS An example of each symbol is used in this section so that children can make the links between the word, the picture and the symbol.

STRENGTHEN Strengthen understanding of the < and > symbols by using a standard diagram that children can input various numbers into. For example, here they know that 18 is greater than 12, so they put 18 in the taller tower and 12 in the smaller tower:

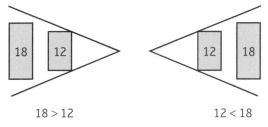

18 > 12   12 < 18

The same diagrams can be used for any combination of numbers (unless they are equal).

DEEPEN Question ③ gives children the opportunity to explore the equal to symbol in detail. Children can make the numbers with cubes to prove they are equal. Ask:
- *How do you know they are equal?*
- *Can you draw a picture to prove you should use the = symbol to compare these numbers?*

ASSESSMENT CHECKPOINT The questions focus on children understanding the vocabulary 'most' and 'least'. You should be checking that they are able to write the symbols the correct way around and link them to the correct word.

ANSWERS

Question ①: 12 > 9; orange got the most votes.

Question ②: 18 > 15; green got the least votes.

Question ③: 13 = 13; purple and yellow got an equal number of votes.

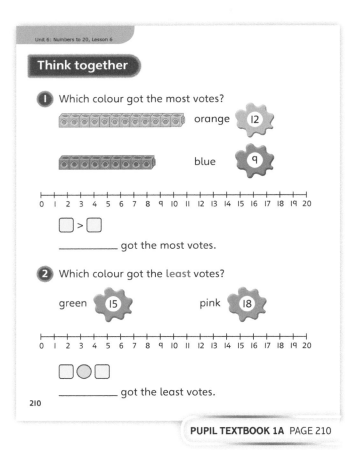

PUPIL TEXTBOOK 1A PAGE 210

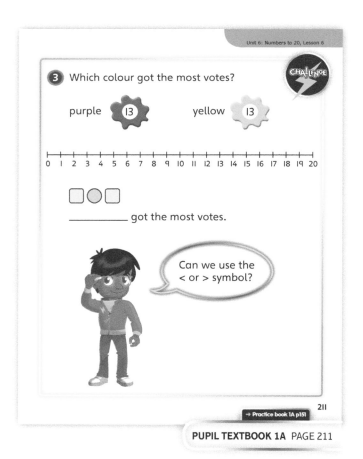

PUPIL TEXTBOOK 1A PAGE 211

238

Practice

WAYS OF WORKING Independent thinking

IN FOCUS The practice questions increase in complexity, consolidating prior learning and giving children the opportunity to reason and problem solve towards the end of the exercise. Questions ❶ and ❷ present information in different ways, for example, the number 15 is presented as 15, and as 10 + 5. Question ❹ provides an opportunity for children to find all the possible answers in a systematic way rather than randomly.

STRENGTHEN Children can use concrete manipulatives or pictorial representations to aid their understanding but ensure they are also writing the abstract number sentences. It is important that children gradually manage to use the < and > symbols through visualisation. Ask children to close their eyes and picture the towers that represent the numbers. This will help them choose the correct symbol without always having to build the towers or draw them.

DEEPEN Questions ❺ and ❻ require a deep understanding of learning on numbers 11–20. Ask children to write their numbers in a variety of ways, using both numerals and words. A complex sentence may be something like '10 + 3 is less than fifteen and < 2 tens'. This shows a thorough and deep understanding; the child can combine learning and be creative with their number sentences.

ASSESSMENT CHECKPOINT In question ❸, children are combining their learning of counting, tens and ones and comparing numbers. Check whether children have reverted back to counting from 1 rather than recognising 10, then counting on. Ask them to explain how they got their answer or simply watch and listen as they answer questions. If they are still counting from one, consider pairing them with a child who isn't so that they can discuss their different ways.

ANSWERS Answers for the **Practice** part of the lesson appear in the separate **Practice and Reflect answer guide**.

Reflect

WAYS OF WORKING Independent thinking

IN FOCUS Children think of numbers for themselves that make the statements correct. The lack of guidance will help you see if children have understood the lesson. They have to think of numbers for themselves, which is more difficult than when they are given numbers to use.

ASSESSMENT CHECKPOINT This is a good opportunity to check how thoroughly children have grasped the lesson. Check what they have written down. Have they understood the question?

ANSWERS Answers for the **Reflect** part of the lesson appear in the separate **Practice and Reflect answer guide**.

After the lesson ⏸

- Are children confident with all of the language used in the lesson?
- Are children able to use the symbols <, > and = confidently or do they still need to draw a picture to help them decide which way around they go?

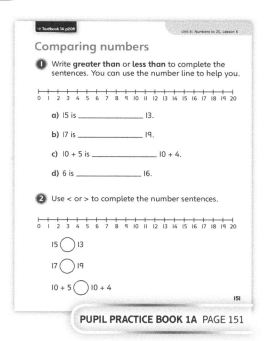

PUPIL PRACTICE BOOK 1A PAGE 151

PUPIL PRACTICE BOOK 1A PAGE 152

PUPIL PRACTICE BOOK 1A PAGE 153

Ordering objects and numbers

Learning focus

In this lesson, children order numbers and objects using vocabulary learned in previous lessons and the < and > symbols.

Small steps

→ Previous step: Comparing numbers
→ **This step: Ordering objects and numbers**
→ Next step: Add by counting on

NATIONAL CURRICULUM LINKS

Year 1 Number – Number and Place Value
- Identify and represent numbers using objects and pictorial representations including the number line, and use the language of: equal to, more than, less than (fewer), most, least.
- Compare and order numbers from 0 up to 100; use <, > and = signs (year 2).

ASSESSING MASTERY

Children can correctly compare and order numbers and objects using <, > and =, and use vocabulary learned in previous lessons, such as more, less, fewer, greater, etc.

COMMON MISCONCEPTIONS

When ordering numbers of objects, children may count them all rather than set them out in a way that makes them easy to compare.
- *Do you have to count all the objects to put them in order? How else could you order them?*

STRENGTHENING UNDERSTANDING

Use practical and familiar examples to reinforce the words 'least' and 'most'. For example, some children could come to the front holding some cubes or a number card. Children can work together to arrange themselves from the least to the most, then from the most to the least.

GOING DEEPER

Some children may be able to explore questions where there is more than one answer or children could create their own questions. For example, children could work systematically to find all of the different ways of filling in ___ < 10 + 2.

Children can link to prior learning. For example, they could write a number sentence such as 'one ten and nine ones is fewer than two tens but greater than one ten and six ones because 16 < 19 < 20'.

KEY LANGUAGE

In lesson: order, least, most, less than, greater than, smallest

Other language to be used by the teacher: more than, fewer than, tens, ones, compare, largest

STRUCTURES AND REPRESENTATIONS

Cubes, number line

RESOURCES

Mandatory: cubes

Optional: ten frame, sweets, other toys or classroom objects for counting

Teaching Tools In the eTextbook of this lesson, you will find interactive links to a selection of teaching tools.

Before you teach ▉

- Are children able to write numbers in different ways? For example, can they write 11 as eleven, 1 ten and 1 one, and 10 + 1?
- Are children confident comparing fewer than ten objects using the symbols <, > and =?

Discover

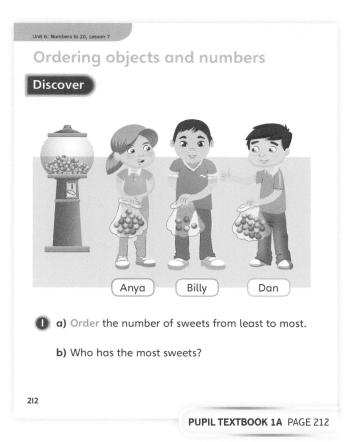

WAYS OF WORKING Pair work

ASK

• *Without counting, can you guess who has the least sweets? Can you guess who has the most sweets?*
• *Who do you think has fewer than 10 sweets?*
• *Who do you think has more than 10 sweets?*
• *Is it difficult to see who has the most between Anya and Dan?*

IN FOCUS Children order the number of sweets from least to most. This helps to reinforce the vocabulary as they can see and compare the size of groups of objects. Using familiar objects like sweets draws them into the problem and makes it more interesting. Which child would they rather be, Anya, Billy or Dan?

ANSWERS

Question ❶ a): 5, 15, 16

Question ❶ b): Dan has the most sweets.

Share

WAYS OF WORKING Whole class teacher led

ASK

• *Has anyone used a different colour to show ten? How does this help us see which tower is bigger?*
• *Can you think of a picture we could draw to help us get the symbols the correct way around?*
• *By how much is 16 bigger than 15?*

IN FOCUS Children use cubes and a number line to compare and order numbers. Children should try to use language they have learned so far to describe the situation in a variety of ways. For example:
• 5 is less than 15 and less than 16
• 5 sweets are fewer than 15 sweets
• Billy has the fewest sweets
• Dan has the greatest number of sweets.

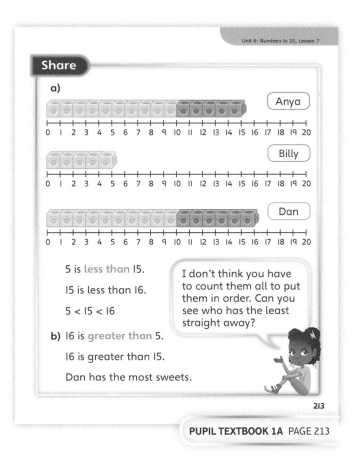

Think together

WAYS OF WORKING Whole class teacher led (I do, We do, You do)

ASK

- Question ❶: *Do you need to count from one?*
- Question ❶: *Can you write the answer in a different way?*
- Question ❷: *How does the number line help you see which number is smallest?*
- Question ❸: *How many different answers are there for each number sentence?*

IN FOCUS It is important that children make the link between the size of numbers and their place on a number line. Children can line cubes up on a number line and explain why this shows whether a number is bigger or smaller than another. For example, 16 cubes are greater than 15 cubes because they go further up the number line. The further up the number line, the bigger the number.

STRENGTHEN Children can draw pictures to help them decide which way around the symbols go and use different coloured cubes to emphasise that they can count from ten rather than start at one each time. For question ❷ encourage children to make each number to prove which order they go in. They should be able to talk about the height of each tower to justify their answer.

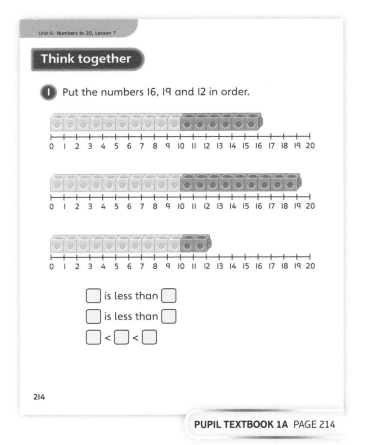

Think together

❶ Put the numbers 16, 19 and 12 in order.

☐ is less than ☐
☐ is less than ☐
☐ < ☐ < ☐

214

PUPIL TEXTBOOK 1A PAGE 214

DEEPEN Question ❸ provides a good opportunity to deepen understanding. There is more than one possible answer for each example given. Interestingly, two will have the same possible answers, whereas the third example looks the same but is different. Encourage children to write their number sentences in different ways, for example:

- 13 < 14 < 17
- Thirteen is less than 14, which is less than 17
- 1 ten and 3 ones < 1 ten and 4 ones < 1 ten and 7 ones

ASSESSMENT CHECKPOINT In question ❶ check whether children are still starting to count from one rather than starting at ten. Question ❷ checks that they understand how the placement on a number line tells them about the size of the numbers. Ask children to explain their answers either verbally or as a written sentence.

ANSWERS

Question ❶: 12 is less than 16; 16 is less than 19;
12 < 16 < 19

Question ❷: 13 < 14 < 16

Question ❸: 13 < (14 or 15 or 16) < 17;
17 > (16 or 15 or 14) > 13;
13 < 17 < (18 or 19 or 20)

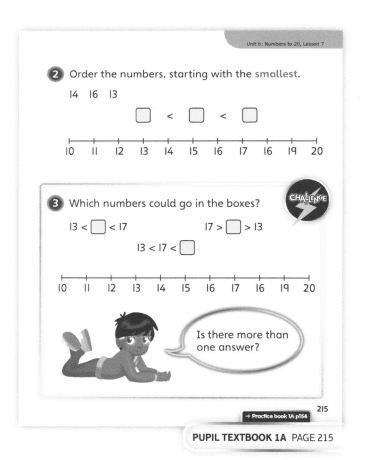

❷ Order the numbers, starting with the smallest.

14   16   13

☐ < ☐ < ☐

❸ Which numbers could go in the boxes?

13 < ☐ < 17   17 > ☐ > 13

13 < 17 < ☐

Is there more than one answer?

→ Practice book 1A p154

215

PUPIL TEXTBOOK 1A PAGE 215

Practice

WAYS OF WORKING Independent thinking

IN FOCUS Children order three numbers and numbers of objects from least to most or largest to smallest. It is important that children explore questions with more than one possible answer and look at questions in a variety of contexts. The questions use different objects and more abstract contexts such as questions with just numbers and symbols. Question **6** asks children to prove their answer. They should be encouraged to discuss the different ways they can do this so that they realise there is not always just one way to answer a question.

STRENGTHEN Ensure children are writing the abstract number sentence alongside their representation. It is important that children gradually manage to use the < and > signs through visualisation. Children should also be encouraged to say their number sentences out loud. This will help embed the key vocabulary in the lesson.

DEEPEN Questions **5** and **6** both require a deep understanding of numbers 11–20. To deepen even further, ask children to write their numbers in a variety of ways using both numerals and words.

ASSESSMENT CHECKPOINT Question **1** assesses that children understand the words most and least. They should be able to order these numbers without counting the cherries.

Question **3** checks whether children are ready to answer an ordering question abstractly.

Questions **5** and **6** are more complex, giving children opportunities to reason and problem solve.

ANSWERS Answers for the **Practice** part of the lesson appear in the separate **Practice and Reflect answer guide**.

PUPIL PRACTICE BOOK 1A PAGE 154

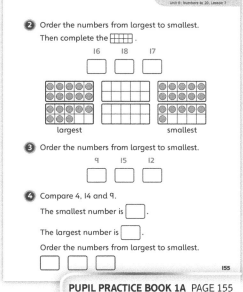

PUPIL PRACTICE BOOK 1A PAGE 155

Reflect

WAYS OF WORKING Independent thinking

IN FOCUS Children think about the different ways they can order a set of numbers.

ASSESSMENT CHECKPOINT Have children understood that they can order numbers from smallest to largest and largest to smallest?

ANSWERS Answers for the **Reflect** part of the lesson appear in the separate **Practice and Reflect answer guide**.

After the lesson ⏸

- Ideas for comparing numbers occur in many situations that happen throughout the day at school. For example, who has the most carrots on their plate?
- What opportunities can you identify to reinforce and apply this lesson's learning?

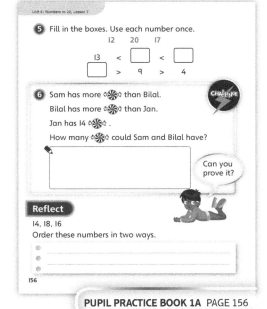

PUPIL PRACTICE BOOK 1A PAGE 156

243

End of unit check

> Don't forget the End of unit check proforma (page 216)!

WAYS OF WORKING Group work – adult led

IN FOCUS

- Question **2** is designed to assess children's understanding of the structure of 2-digit numbers.
- Questions **4** and **5** both require an understanding of the < and > symbols.

Think!

WAYS OF WORKING Pair work or small groups

IN FOCUS

- This question presents numbers using a variety of representations. Children need to interpret each representation to read the number, identify which is the odd one out and justify their decision with an explanation.
- Encourage children to use the vocabulary at the bottom of the **My journal** page. Can they describe each number using 'tens' and 'ones'?
- Encourage children to think through or discuss what is the same, and what is different, about the five numbers before writing their answer in **My journal**.

ANSWERS AND COMMENTARY Children who have mastered the concepts of this unit will be able to work confidently with numbers within 20. They will be able to count forwards and backwards from any number and count one more and one less. They will know that a number between 10 and 20 is made up of ten and some ones and use this knowledge to order and compare numbers within 20.

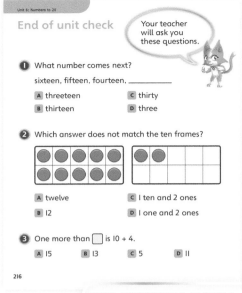

PUPIL TEXTBOOK 1A PAGE 216

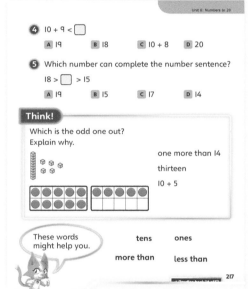

PUPIL TEXTBOOK 1A PAGE 217

Q	A	WRONG ANSWERS AND MISCONCEPTIONS	STRENGTHENING UNDERSTANDING
1	B	Any wrong answer indicates that children are not confident with the number names, spoken or written.	Allow children to use cubes to check and prove their answers as they work.
2	D	Any wrong answer suggests that children do not have a secure understanding of the structure of 2-digit numbers. They may think that the '1' in 12 stands for one not ten.	
3	B	A suggests that children have not carefully read and understood the question. C or D indicates that children have only looked at part of the number sentence; they may not fully understand the concept of partitioning numbers.	
4	D	A or B suggests that children do not understand the < sign. C suggests that children think the answer needs to be written in the same format as the question.	
5	C	Any wrong answer suggests that children do not have a thorough understanding of the < and > symbols.	

My journal

WAYS OF WORKING Independent thinking

ANSWERS AND COMMENTARY

The odd one out is thirteen because all the other representations show 15.

Children are likely to give a simple explanation for their choice. Encourage them to expand upon it, using some of the key words. For example: 'The odd one out is thirteen because it is made up of 1 ten and 3 ones and the others are made up of 1 ten and 5 ones. Thirteen is less than 15.'

Observe how children identify the numbers represented by the Base 10 equipment and on the ten frame. Did children count from one or ten? If not, they may need further support in partitioning numbers into tens and ones before moving on to addition within 20 in the next unit.

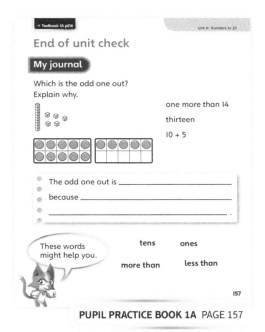

PUPIL PRACTICE BOOK 1A PAGE 157

Power check

WAYS OF WORKING Independent thinking

ASK

• *What part of the unit did you find the most challenging?*
• *What helped you understand this part the most?*

Power puzzle

WAYS OF WORKING Pair work or small groups

IN FOCUS Use this Power puzzle to see if children can find one more or one less than a number and identify numbers between two given numbers. They could either complete the puzzle together, or work individually and then compare their answers. It is unlikely that they will all complete it in the same way so this activity will promote a lot of discussion. Incorrect answers are most likely to be the result of using the same number twice, or approaching the puzzle from top row to bottom row. It is more efficient to fill in the boxes that cannot change (the 'one more' and 'one less' columns) first, and then address the middle column.

ANSWERS AND COMMENTARY Here is a possible solution.

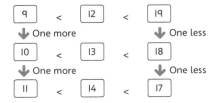

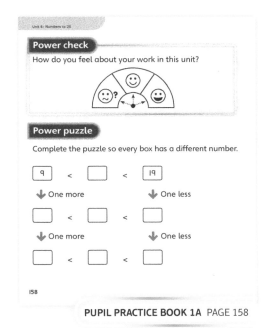

PUPIL PRACTICE BOOK 1A PAGE 158

After the unit ⏸

• How confident are children using the greater than and less than symbols to compare numbers? What strategies could you give those who are not confident?
• Are children willing to approach unfamiliar problems like the Power puzzle?

Strengthen and *Deepen* activities for this unit can be found in the Power Maths online subscription.

Published by Pearson Education Limited, 80 Strand, London, WC2R 0RL.

www.pearsonschools.co.uk

Text © Pearson Education Limited 2017
Edited by Pearson, Little Grey Cells Publishing Services and Haremi Ltd
Designed and typeset by Kamae Design
Original illustrations © Pearson Education Limited 2017
Illustrated by Nadene Naude, Kamae, Daniel Limon, Adam Linley, Laura Arias, Jim Peacock, Eric Smith, Nigel Dobbyn and Phil Corbett at Beehive Illustration
Cover design by Pearson Education Ltd
Back cover illustration © Will Overton at Advocate Art and Nadene Naude at Beehive Illustration.

Series Editor: Tony Staneff
Consultant: Professor Jian Liu

The rights of Tony Staneff, David Board, Natasha Dolling, Caroline Hamilton, Julia Hayes and Timothy Weal to be identified as authors of this work have been asserted by them in accordance with the Copyright, Designs and Patents Act 1988.

First published 2017

20 19
10 9 8 7 6 5 4 3

British Library Cataloguing in Publication Data
A catalogue record for this book is available from the British Library

ISBN 978 0 435 18983 9

Printed in the UK by Ashford Colour Press

www.activelearnprimary.co.uk

Note from the publisher
Pearson has robust editorial processes, including answer and fact checks, to ensure the accuracy of the content in this publication, and every effort is made to ensure this publication is free of errors. We are, however, only human, and occasionally errors do occur. Pearson is not liable for any misunderstandings that arise as a result of errors in this publication, but it is our priority to ensure that the content is accurate. If you spot an error, please do contact us at resourcescorrections@ pearson.com so we can make sure it is corrected.